Artificial

Intelligence

Techniques

in Prolog

Artificial

Intelligence

Techniques

in Prolog

Yoav Shoham

Morgan Kaufmann Publishers, Inc.
San Francisco, California

Sponsoring Editor: Michael B. Morgan
Production Manager: Yonie Overton
Assistant Editor: Douglas Sery
Copyeditor: Fran Taylor
Proofreader: Judy Bess
Cover Design: Studio Silicon
Printer: R.R. Donnelley & Sons

Editorial Offices:
Morgan Kaufmann Publishers, Inc.
340 Pine Street, Sixth Floor
San Francisco, CA 94104

Library of Congress Cataloging-in-Publication Data

Shoham, Yoav.
     Artificial intelligence techniques in Prolog / Yoav Shoham.
         p.   cm.
     Includes bibliographical references and index.
     ISBN 1-55860-319-0 (cloth)
     ISBN 1-55860-167-8 (paper)
     1. Artificial intelligence—Data processing. 2. Prolog (Computer
program language) I. Title
Q336.S543 1994
006.3—dc20   92-42117
                                  CIP

To Orit and Maia

Contents

Preface

The field of artificial intelligence (AI for short) spans a bewildering array of topics. Although usually thought of as part of computer science, AI overlaps with disciplines as diverse as philosophy, linguistics, psychology, electrical engineering, mechanical engineering, and neuroscience. It is also quite young as scientific fields go. One result of this breadth and youth is an atmosphere of creative excitement and pioneering. Indeed, given AI's relatively short history, the number of innovations that have emerged from within AI, and their effects on neighboring disciplines, are striking.

Another outcome of this diversity and dynamism has been a lack of uniformity of research issues and scientific methodology. Although in general this outcome has both positive and negative ramifications, its effect on AI *teaching* has been largely negative; all too often the effect has been to sacrifice either breadth or depth of coverage. Teachers are hardly at fault here; simply too much happens under the umbrella called AI for teachers to adequately cover it all in a one-semester (let alone one-quarter) course. Thus some courses emphasize the cognitive-science component of AI, some concentrate on knowledge representation, some on knowledge-based systems, some on reasoning techniques, and so on. By necessity, the broader the material covered in an introductory course, the shallower the coverage. The best balance for an introductory AI course is still a topic for debate.

This book is not a broad introduction to AI; the book's primary aim is to provide a crisp introduction to the well-established algorithmic techniques in the field. As a result, it is not particularly gentle, but instead plunges rather directly into the details of each technique. Most importantly, the book gives short shrift to conceptual issues, mentioning them briefly only by way of positioning the material within the AI landscape. Questions such as

"What is the nature of intelligence?"; "What does the Turing Test actually measure?"; and "Is symbol manipulation the best framework within which to model natural intelligence or to create an artificial one?" will remain fascinating and outside the scope of this book.

The techniques included in the book cover general areas such as search, rule-based systems, truth maintenance, constraint satisfaction, and uncertainty management, and specific application domains such as temporal reasoning, machine learning, and natural language. These areas are sufficiently diverse that I have had to omit much material. I hope that the following is nonetheless true of the selection:

- The material is self-contained in two ways. First, I include coverage of basic techniques, even those with which many readers are likely to be familiar (this is true especially of the search chapter). Second, I include (brief) summaries of required background material.

- The techniques discussed are completely demystified. Although I deliberately try to keep the presentation informal, the techniques are explained clearly; sufficient details are supplied to remove ambiguity, and details that are not essential to understanding the techniques are omitted. When desirable and possible, I present the techniques in stages, adding functionality or improving efficiency incrementally.

- The material is up-to-date and balanced. Since the material includes basic techniques as well as some more advanced ones, and, since the areas covered are quite diverse, the coverage of all areas is necessarily partial. Nonetheless, the most influential recent techniques in each area are included.

References for further reading, whether to achieve deeper theoretical understanding or to further explore the techniques discussed, are mentioned at the end of each chapter and appear in the bibliography at the end of the book. In addition, many of the exercises at the end of each chapter have been designed to explore issues which are not treated in the text.

Some readers might wonder why I insist on presenting programs, rather than simply explaining the algorithms in language-neutral terms. Indeed, in many places the programs are preceded by high-level pseudo code. However, it is not without reason that AI practitioners have developed a healthy skepticism of unimplemented ideas. Many of the techniques we will discuss are quite intricate and messy, and, in the past, many reasonable-looking procedures turned out, upon being put to use, to have swept under the rug some of the most important details. Interpreters and compilers help keep one honest; if nothing else, our programs will expose the limitations of the procedures they implement.

In selecting Prolog as the implementation language, I also hope to dispel some misconceptions about the language. Prolog is a fun language, and students take a quick liking to it. This makes it a good choice for pedagogical reasons. For historical reasons, there are those in AI, especially in the United States, who have claimed that Prolog is unsuited for implementation of all but a narrow slice of AI techniques. As we shall see, this claim is quite false.

Prolog grew out of research in logic, and is the best-known representative of *logic programming* languages. I will nevertheless say little about logic in this book. This is particularly ironic, as much of my own research has been concerned with the application of logic in AI. However, perhaps precisely for this reason, I have too much respect for both Prolog and logic to be glib about the complex relationship between them. In this book I use Prolog as a flexible, efficient, and, yes, procedural language. Furthermore, in various places in the book, efficiency and purity were sacrificed for the sake of clarity. I believe that the utility and beauty of Prolog show nonetheless.

I have not included an introduction to Prolog. Excellent textbooks, such as Clocksin and Mellish's *Programming in Prolog* [7] and Sterling and Shapiro's *The Art of Prolog* [77], already exist for this purpose. A rough criterion for the requisite Prolog knowledge is familiarity with the material in Clocksin and Mellish's book. Chapter 1 elaborates on the required Prolog knowledge and introduces additional Prolog material that will be used in the book.

This book grew out of the course notes for a class I have been teaching at Stanford University, titled "AI techniques in Prolog." I have always started the class with a crash course in Prolog; I have found six 75-minute lectures quite adequate, although students are offered an additional laboratory section as an option. The balance of the course covers material in this book. No single course is likely to cover the entire corpus included here; the topics chosen will depend on the background and interests of the audience. I have tended to divide the time roughly as follows: search (2 lectures), meta-interpreters (1–2), forward chaining and production systems (1–2), truth maintenance (2), uncertainty (1), planning and temporal reasoning (2), learning (2), and natural language (1). This selection is appropriate for students who have had one course in AI, or for those who have had none but are willing to compensate by studying on their own. If less is assumed on the part of the students, some of the advanced material must be omitted. Conversely, students with more experience may need to spend less time on some of the earlier chapters, for example those on search and forward chaining.

Acknowledgements

This book has been written over about four years, long enough a period to benefit from the feedback of a large number of people. I know that after the book is published it will dawn on me that I neglected to acknowledge the invaluable help of some dear friend; I apologize in advance.

Four research assistants helped tremendously. First and foremost, I thank Dominique Snyers. Dominique helped design the book outline, researched the strengths and weaknesses of existing books covering related material, and helped write some of the code. In particular, the natural language chapter would not have been written without Dominique.

The subsequent research assistants were (in chronological order) Anuchit Anuchitanukul, Avrami Tzur, and Robert Kennedy. They each provided crucial help in designing new algorithms or improving existing ones, implementing them, and debugging. For example, Anuchit came up with the meta-interpreter to handle 'cut,' Avrami wrote the first known implementation of Nilsson's RSTRIPS in the western world, and Robert simplified Allen's temporal constraint-satisfaction procedure. They each did much more, and have my deepest admiration and gratitude.

The following colleagues were very generous with their time, either filling in gaps in my knowledge or commenting on early drafts, or both: Eugene Charniak, Keith Clark, Tom Dean, Rina Dechter, Mark Drummond, Markus Fromherz, Herve Gallaire, Robert Goldman, Maria Gini, Steve Hanks, Pentii Hietala, Pekka Ketola, Apostolos Lerios, Jalal Maleki, David McAllester, Judea Pearl, and Udi Shapiro.

I'd be remiss if I did not single out Richard O'Keefe for special thanks. Richard has sent me what must amount to fifty pages of comments on earlier drafts. Most of his pointed suggestions were too good to ignore, and the result is a better if later book. Chapters 1-3 particularly benefitted from

Richard's comments. For example, in Chapter 1 some of the utility predicates (such as `call / n`) were supplied directly by Richard, and in Chapter 2 the minimax implementation is based on his suggestion.

I am indebted to a number of colleagues at Stanford. The Robotics Laboratory, where I have worked for the past five years, is a stimulating environment. In particular, this book has benefitted from continuous interaction with Jean-Claude Latombe and Nils Nilsson.

I have a lot for which to thank Mike Morgan from Morgan Kaufmann, who was engaged in this project from an early stage; his intelligent advice has been invaluable, and his informal style a real pleasure. I also thank Yonie Overton for a very friendly and astute production management.

Members of my research group, *knowbotics,* have been my primary source of intellectual challenge and satisfaction. Over the past few years they have included Ronen Brafman, Sylvie Cazalens, Kave Eshghi, Nita Goyal, Ronny Kohavi, James Kittock, Phillipe Lamarre, Fangzhen Lin, Eyal Mozes, Andrea Schaerf, Anton Schwartz, Grisha Schwarz, Moshe Tennenholtz, Becky Thomas, Mark Torrance, and Alvaro del Val; thank you all.

Software Availability

This book contains a substantial amount of Prolog code. The software is obtainable in one of the following ways:

- It may be retrieved through *anonymous FTP*.

- It may be ordered from the publisher.

The first service is free of charge; the second entails a charge to cover the publisher's costs. The sections below provide additional details about each option.

I regret that neither I nor the publisher will be able to provide software support, whether with regard to installing the software or to running it. However, I do welcome comments on the code and suggestions for improvements. Such comments should be sent only through electronic mail, addressed to `aitp@cs.stanford.edu`.

A word about quality control. All the code has been debugged and tested, but not at the level of commercial software. Accordingly, while every attempt has been made to provide correct code, no warranty is implied. Similarly, I have tried to make sure that the software being distributed matches the code given in the book, but some discrepancies are inevitable.

Using anonymous FTP

The *File Transfer Protocol (FTP)* is a standard protocol for transferring files over the Internet. In order to use it, you must be logged into a computer that is hooked into the net. If you do not have access to the net, then this method will be of no use to you. If you do have access to the Internet but have never used FTP, get help from someone who has.

The code is available for anonymous FTP from the computer `unix.sri.com`. It resides in the directory `pub/shoham`; the file `README` in that directory explains more about the various other files, and gives advice on what to copy.

A sample FTP session initiated by a user named `smith` at the Internet site `dept.univ.edu` might look as follows (user input in *slanted font*):

```
% ftp unix.sri.com (or ftp 128.18.10.3)
Name (unix.sri.com:smith): anonymous
331 Guest login ok, send indent as password
```

```
Password:   dept.univ.edu
230 Guest login ok, access restrictions apply
ftp> cd pub/shoham
250 CWD command successful.
ftp> ls
... (list of files)
ftp> prompt
Interactive mode off
ftp> mget*
...
ftp> bye
%
```

Anonymous FTP is a privilege, not a right. The site administrators at `unix.sri.com` have made the system available out of the spirit of sharing, but there are real costs associated with network connections, storage, and processing, all of which are needed to make this sharing possible. To avoid overloading the system, do not FTP between 7:00 a.m. and 6:00 p.m. local (pacific) time. If you are using this book for a class, do not FTP the code yourself; have the professor FTP it once and distribute code to the class. In general, use common sense and be considerate: none of us want to see sites close down because a few are abusing their privileges.

Ordering from the publisher

If you do not have access to the Internet, you may obtain the code for a modest fee from the publisher. You may contact the publisher either by mail or by phone:

Morgan Kaufmann Publishers, Inc.
340 Pine Street, Sixth Floor
San Francisco, CA 94104
415.392.2665
800.745.7323

When you do so, specify which of the following formats you desire:

Macintosh diskette
DOS 5.25 diskette
DOS 3.5 diskette
Unix TAR tape

Chapter 1

On Prolog

As explained in the preface, this book includes little material on Prolog itself. The present chapter is an exception; its purpose is threefold:

- to explain the required Prolog background;

- to provide a little additional Prolog material; and

- to define a small library of routine predicates that will be used later in the book.

There exist good introductory Prolog texts, including Clocksin and Mellish's tried-and-true *Programming in Prolog* [7], and Sterling and Shapiro's more advanced *The Art of Prolog* [77]. Among the truly advanced texts, O'Keefe's *The Craft of Prolog* [61] stands out. The material in this book presupposes a working knowledge of standard 'Edinburgh' Prolog. A rough criterion of the required background is familiarity with the material in Clocksin and Mellish's book. To further help the reader gauge his/her[1] preparedness, the next section provides a checklist of concepts and built-in predicates that the reader is expected to know.

The section following that introduces some additional Prolog material that a reader might have missed in previous exposure to Prolog. Some of the material, such as that on lists and all-solutions predicates, is likely to

---

[1]From here on I will use the generic masculine form, intending no bias.

be familiar. Other material, such as that on indexing, difference lists, and
bit vectors, may be less so. Some of these topics are crucial to much of the
material in the book, and some play only a minor role. The section indicates
which topics are crucial; you should understand these well before proceeding.

There is no need to read the last section right now. This section defines
a number of mundane predicates that will be used later in the book. Since
this book presents complete programs, these predicates must be included;
however, it would be a shame to clutter the book with repeated definitions of
the append/3 predicate and such. Therefore, the last section of this chapter
will serve as a routine library, and predicates defined there will be used
later in the book without further definition (however, when the less obvious
predicates are used, the reader will be alerted to their definition here).

1.1   A checklist

The reader is expected to be familiar with Prolog terms, Prolog rules (and
Prolog facts as special cases), unification, the *and-or* computation tree induced by a Prolog program and a query, the depth-first, left-to-right traversal
of that tree by the standard Prolog interpreter, and the following built-in
predicates:

Unification and equality: =, ==, \==
Comparators: >, <, =<, >=, =\= (and their @-versions)
Term classification: atom, integer, float, number, atomic, var
Arithmetic: is, +, −, *, /, //, mod
Term dissection: functor, arg, =.. ('univ')
Database inspection and modification:
    assert, asserta, assertz, retract, retractall, clause, consult, reconsult
IO: seeing, see, seen, telling, tell, told, write, writeq, read, put, get, get0, nl, tab
Control: ! ('cut'), -> ('if then'), ; ('or'), \+ ('negation as failure')
All-solutions predicates (also discussed below): setof, bagof, findall
Other: true, fail, name, call, the op declaration

1.2   Additional Prolog material

The first four subsections among the following – on lists, all-solutions predicates, indexing, and last-call optimization – are important, and it is a good idea to make sure you understand them before delving too deeply into the rest of the book. The remaining sections are relevant only to limited parts of the book; you may skip them now and refer back as the need arises.

1.2.1   Standard lists and 'and' lists

Prolog contains two similar-looking list-like notations, a state of affairs that may be confusing at first. A typical standard list is [1,2,3], which is shorthand for '.'(1,'.'(2,'.'(3,[ ]))); '.' is the standard list constructor, and [ ] is a special atom called the 'empty list.' A typical 'and' list is (1,2,3), which is shorthand for ','(1,','(2,3)); ',' is the 'and' list constructor. Note that there is no analogue to the empty list in 'and' lists; a and (a) are identical terms.

It is therefore somewhat misleading to think of 'and' lists as lists at all, but the notion of 'remainder' reinforces the analogy between the two notions. Standard lists allow for a 'remainder' notation: The unification [a,b,c,d] = [X,Y|Z] will succeed with X = a, Y = b, Z = [c,d]; the unification [a,b] = [X,Y|Z] will succeed with X=a, Y=b, Z=[ ]; the unification [a] = [X,Y|Z] will fail. In general, [X|Y] will unify with any list containing at least one element.

Because the ',' operator associates to the right, 'and' lists will behave in a very similar fashion: The unification (a,b,c,d) = (X,Y,Z) will succeed with X = a, Y = b, Z = (c,d); the unification (a,b) = (X,Y,Z) will fail. In general, (X,Y) will unify with any 'and' list containing at least two elements.

1.2.2   'All-solutions' predicates

The general form of an all-solutions goal is *op(pattern, goal, ans)*, where *op* is a built-in all-solutions predicate, *pattern* is a term, *goal* is any Prolog query, and *ans* is the output parameter, which will be instantiated to a list consisting of instantiations of *pattern,* one instantiation for each successful computation of *goal.* For example, one of the all-solutions operators is setof, and the goal setof(X,(member(X,[1,2,3]),X<3),L) will succeed with L = [1,2]. This will be true also if setof is replaced by one of the other two main all-solutions operators, bagof and findall.

It is important to note the following facts about all-solutions operators.

- In all three, the first argument may be an arbitrary term. For example,
  setof(found(X),(member(X,[1,2,3]),X<3),L) will succeed with
  L = [found(1),found(2)].

- The difference between setof and bagof is that in the former the answer
  is sorted, and duplicates are removed. For example, the goal
  bagof(X, member(X, [2,3,1,3,2]), L) will succeed with L = [2,3,1,3,2], whereas
  setof(X, member(X, [2,3,1,3,2]), L) will succeed with L = [1,2,3].

- Unlike findall, neither bagof nor setof returns the empty list; if no solutions exist they fail. For example, findall(X,(member(X,[1,2,3]),X<0),L) will
  succeed with L=[ ], while setof(X,(member(X,[1,2,3]),X<0),L) and
  bagof(X,(member(X,[1,2,3]),X<0),L) will both fail. We will find use for the
  following extension of setof:

  setof0(A, B, C) :- setof (A, B, C).
  setof0(A, B, [ ]) :- not(setof (A, B, _)).

- In contrast to findall, both setof and bagof have the property that
  variables appearing in *goal* but not in *pattern* cannot be instantiated
  differently in different solutions. For example, the goal
  findall(X,member((X,Y),[(1,1),(2,2)]),L) will succeed only once, with
  L = [1,2]. On the other hand, the goal setof(X,member((X,Y),[(1,1),(2,2)]),L)
  will first succeed with L = [1], and, upon failure, will succeed once more
  with L = [2] (the same is true of bagof). The reason for this is that in the
  two answers, the free variable Y is instantiated differently. However,
  variables may be existentially quantified, using the ˆ operator, in which
  case they may receive different values among solutions. For example,
  the goal setof(X,Yˆmember((X,Y),[(1,1),(2,2)]),L) will succeed only once, with
  L=[1,2].

1.2.3   Indexing

In writing efficient programs it is important to understand the speed with
which Prolog retrieves clauses from the database. In general, that speed
depends on the particular Prolog implementation. However, a feature common in Prolog implementations that are in the 'Edinburgh tradition'[2] is to

---

[2] These include, among others, Dec-10/20 Prolog, CProlog and Quintus^{TM} Prolog.

employ a hash table, through which clauses are efficiently accessed. In these implementations, the hashing function is based on the structure of the head of the clause; more specifically, it is based on the main functor of the head, as well as the main functor of the first argument. For example, in these implementations the clauses whose heads are father(john,bill) and father(john,X) will fall in the same bucket (that is, will have the same hash value), but father(john,bill), father(X,bill), and father(john,bill,adoption) would be expected to fall in different buckets.

1.2.4   Last-call optimization

During execution, Prolog maintains a stack of goals. Roughly speaking, when a clause is found for the goal at the top of the stack, the body of the clause is added to the stack; when a goal is solved it is popped off the stack. The stack can grow to be quite large, especially in the presence of recursive programs. For example, given the program

```
a(X) :- X<10000, Y is X+1, a(Y).
a(10000).
```

and the goal ?- a(1), a naive Prolog implementation would succeed after creating a stack 10,000 blocks deep (if one were lucky enough to have sufficient memory). The idea behind last-call optimization is to replace the top of the stack, rather than add to it. In the above example, when the subgoal a(2) is reached, there is no need to keep the goal a(1) around, since a(2) is the only remaining relevant goal (all preceding goals are deterministic; there are no later goals, nor alternative matching clauses). Indeed, all respectable Prolog implementations recognize this and do not grow the stack in such situations.

Although this feature is one of the Prolog implementation rather than of the Prolog language, it calls for care in writing programs; small changes may lead to dramatic differences in memory consumption. Here is another example, taken from *The Craft of Prolog* [61], showing how 'accumulators' can change a non-tail-recursive program to a tail-recursive one. Here are two programs to compute the length of a given list:

```
len1( [ ], 0 ).
len1( [_ | Tail], N ) :- len1( Tail, N1 ), N is N1+1.
```

```
len2( List, Length ) :- len2( List, 0, Length ).
len2( [ ], N, N ).
len2( [_ | Tail], N1, N) :- N2 is N1+1, len2( Tail, N2, N ).
```

It is not hard to see that len1 will grow an unbounded stack, but, in the presence of last-call optimization, len2 will retain a constant stack size.

1.2.5   Difference lists and 'holes'

Data structures can contain variables that become instantiated during computation. The variables can be instantiated completely, or only partially; that is, they can be bound to terms that contain variables themselves. For example, the term f(X) may become partially instantiated to f(f(Y)) and then f(f(f(Z))). It may eventually become completely instantiated, but it also may continue to contain a 'hole,' or a variable that can be further instantiated.

This property of Prolog terms is very useful; its most common usage is in so-called *difference lists*. Consider the operation of adding an element to the end of a standard list; its time complexity is proportional to the length of the list. But what if the list contained a variable tail? In that case we could simply unify that tail with the new element. For example, rather than have a list [1,2,3], we would have a list [1,2,3 | T]; to add the number 4 to its end, we could simply unify T with [4]. Of course, if we do that, we lose the ability to augment the list further. So instead we unify T with [4 | NewT], and NewT becomes the tail of the new list.

This is exactly the idea behind difference lists. A difference list is a pair (*front, back*), where *front* is a list ending with a variable, and *back* is that variable. For example, a difference-list representation of [1,2,3] is ([1,2,3 | T], T). Now we can define various list operations, such as adding an element to the end of the list or appending two lists to one another. Here is one difference-list version of the append program:

```
dl_append( (A,B), (B,C), (A,C) ).
```

It is surprising at first that there is nothing more to it. It is perhaps a bit less surprising if the program is written as follows:

```
dl_append( (Af,Ab), (Bf,Bb), (Cf,Cb) ) :- Ab = Bf, Af = Cf, Bb = Cb.
```

The following picture may help even more:

```
| a b c d | e f g h | i j . . .
|Af        |Ab
          |Bf        |Bb
|Cf                  |Cb
```

If this is clear, then the next step is to realize that there is no need to group the *front* and *back* into a compound term called a difference list; we may instead simply use two arguments. For example, the append program can be written as a six-argument predicate:

dl_append(A, B, B, C, A, C).

and called accordingly, as in dl_append([1,2|X], X, [3,4|Y], Y, Z, Ztail).

1.2.6 Static and dynamic predicates

Predicates with side effects such as assert and retract can lead to ambiguities. Consider the conjunctive goal

?- assert(p), retract(p), asserta(p), fail.

Clearly this goal cannot succeed, but should it terminate? While the intuitive answer is probably that it should, in fact in some Prolog implementations it will not; in those, upon each failure, the retract clause discovers a 'new' clause for p to be retracted, namely the one asserted after the previous retract.

This feature is controversial, and by and large avoided. In any event, interspersing Prolog execution with database modification is tricky, and a number of implementations provide default precautions. Quintus^{TM} Prolog partitions predicates into 'static' and 'dynamic' ones. The static ones cannot be accessed by assert, retract, and clause, but the dynamic ones can. By default, all predicates in a consulted file are static, unless preceded by a

:- dynamic *predicate* / *arity*.

or, in some implementations,

:- dynamic(*predicate* / *arity*).

directive. All predicates asserted during execution are dynamic.

1.2.7   Bitwise operations

'Edinburgh style' Prolog implementations provide bitwise operations. These operations include:

Shift right: The goal X is 4>>1 succeeds with X = 2.
Shift left: The goal X is 4<<1 succeeds with X = 8.
Bitwise union: The goal X is 2\/1 succeeds with X = 3.
Bitwise intersection: The goal X is 2/\1 succeeds with X = 0.
Bitwise complementation: The goal X is \(1) succeeds with X = –2.

The arguments to all the bitwise operations must be integers, or an error occurs.

1.2.8   Database references

Every clause in the database has a unique internal reference, called its *database reference,* or *dbref* for short. Ordinarily these IDs are only used internally by Prolog, but in fact they are accessible to the programmer via the predicates assert / 2, asserta / 2, assertz / 2 and clause / 3 (that is, versions of the familiar predicates with one additional argument), and the predicate erase / 1. These predicates are explained via the following example:

| ?- asserta(p,R).

R = '$ref'(8679312,1)

| ?- assert(q,R).

R = '$ref'(8679408,2)

| ?- clause(p,Body,R).

Body = true,
R = '$ref'(8679312,1)

| ?- erase('$ref'(8679312,1)).

yes

| ?- clause(p,B).

no
| ?-

1.3 Utility predicates

We conclude the chapter with a number of simple predicates that we will
assume later in the book. Most of these predicates are well known; some
even appear as built-in in some Prolog implementations. Certainly these
predicates, or ones just like them, appear in a number of widely available
Prolog libraries. However, to make this book self-contained, we repeat them
here.

List operations

```
member( X, [X|_] ).
member( X, [_|Y] ) :- member( X, Y ).

append( [ ], X, X ).
append( [X|Y], Z, [X|W] ) :- append( Y, Z, W ).

remove( X, [X|Y], Y ).
remove( X, [Y|Z], [Y|W] ) :- remove( X, Z, W ).

reverse( L1, L2 ) :- reverse1( L1, [ ], L2 ).
reverse1( [A | B], C, D ) :- !, reverse1( B, [A | C], D).
reverse1( [ ], A, A ).

union( [ ], X, X).
union( [X|More], Y, Z ) :- member( X, Y ), !, union( More, Y, Z ).
union( [X|More], Y, [X|Z] ) :- union( More, Y, Z ).

intersection( [ ], X, [ ]).
intersection( [X|More], Y, [X|Z] ) :- member( X, Y ), !, intersection( More, Y, Z ).
```

intersection([X|More], Y, Z) :- intersection(More, Y, Z).

subtract([ ], X, X). subtract([X|More], Y, Z) :- remove(X, Y, W), !, subtract(More, W, Z).
subtract([X|More], Y, Z) :- subtract(More, Y, Z).

% membership in an 'and' list:
amember(X, (A, B)) :- !, (X = A ; amember(X, B)).
amember(A, A).

% membership in a difference list:
dlmember(X, Head, Tail) :- Head == Tail, !, fail.
dlmember(X, [X|_], _).
dlmember(X, [_|Y], Tail) :- member(X, Y, Tail).

% appending an 'and' list to a regular list:
mixed_append((X,Y), Z, T) :- !, mixed_append(Y, Z, W), T = [X | W].
mixed_append(X, Y, [X | Y]).

list_to_and([Head | Tail], And) :- list_to_and_1(Tail, And, Head).
list_to_and_1([ ], Item, Item).
list_to_and_1([Head | Tail], (Item, And), Item) :- list_to_and_1(Tail, And, Head).

Input-Output

writel([ ]).
writel([X|Y]) :- write(X), writel(Y).

Arithmetic

max(X, Y, Z) :- X=<Y, !, Y=Z.
max(X, _, X).

min(X, Y, Z) :- X>=Y, !, Y=Z.
min(X, _, X).

Miscellaneous

% not / 1 is of course not true logical negation

```
not( X ) :- call( X ), !, fail ; true.


once( X ) :- call(X), !.


doall( X ) :- call(X), fail ; true.
```

% term_copy / 2 *accepts a term, and returns the same term with all variables*
% *(if any) replaced by newly generated ones. In many Prologs this is built-in.*
% *In most, the following easy implementation will work*
```
term_copy( X, Y ) :- asserta(termcopydummy(X)), retract(termcopydummy(X)).
```

% *the following are arity-2 and -3 versions of the standard* call / 1 *command:*
```
call( Atom, Arg ) :- % call / 2
    atom( Atom ), !,
    Goal =.. [Atom ,Arg],
    call( Goal ).
call( Closure, Arg ) :-
    Closure =.. FrozenFormals,
    append( FrozenFormals, [Arg], List ),
    Goal =.. List,
    call( Goal ).


call( Atom, Arg1, Arg2 ) :- % call / 3
    atom( Atom ), !,
    Goal =.. [Atom, Arg1, Arg2],
    call( Goal ).
call( Closure, Arg1, Arg2 ) :-
    Closure =.. FrozenFormals,
    append( FrozenFormals, [Arg1, Arg2], List ),
    Goal =.. List,
    call( Goal ).


retractall( X ) :- doall(( retract(X), retract( (X :- _) ) )).


setof0( A, B, C ) :- setof ( A, B, C ).
setof0( A, B, [ ] ) :- not( setof ( A, B, _ ) ).
```

Chapter 2

Search

At one time it was claimed that all AI problems reduce to that of *search*. Indeed, graph search is a framework sufficiently general to include many AI problems within its definition. We will review the mathematical definitions below, but, loosely speaking, a graph consists of a collection of 'nodes,' some pairs of which are connected by 'arcs.' The *search problem* is to find whether a 'path' exists in the graph between two given nodes, meaning that one can get from the first node to the second by traversing arcs. This abstract characterization allows many applications. Nodes may represent sets of facts, locations of objects in a room, partial parses of natural-language statements, and so on. Correspondingly, arcs may represent valid inference steps, robot motions, applications of parsing rules, and so on.

An example commonly given in AI is that of the *8-puzzle,* the game in which a 3×3 board contains 8 squares, each bearing a different number between 1 and 8. A typical configuration might be:

The goal is to rearrange the puzzle by sliding the squares one at a time to some prespecified final configuration, say:

The graph nodes therefore represent puzzle configurations, and the arcs represent legal transitions between them. A typical arc would be:

The view of AI problems as search problems motivated Newell and Simon to create the well-known General Problem Solver (GPS), the ideas in which remain influential to this day. Nowadays, most AI practitioners agree that this claim about search is probably too strong, in that the particular nature of specific applications dominates the uniform search aspect. Nevertheless, there is no disagreement that search remains a key ingredient in AI.

Of course, graph search is not an AI invention. A rich literature on graph algorithms exists in discrete mathematics, and AI has built on that work. However, AI search problems are characterized by uncertainty and open-endedness, and these properties have given rise to search techniques that have a more speculative flavor than traditional graph algorithms. This more speculative search has been termed *heuristic* search.

This chapter is organized as follows. We first review basic graph-theoretic terminology and discuss the representation of graphs as Prolog terms. Then, after we briefly review the basic search techniques, we discuss the implementation of several major search procedures in Prolog.

2.1   Review of basic graph-theoretic terminology

We begin by recalling basic definitions of graph theory. The reader who finds this reminder too brief should consult one of the texts mentioned at the end

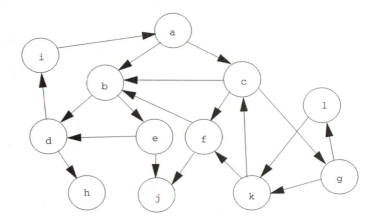

Figure 2.1: Example of a directed graph

of the chapter for a full discussion.

A *directed graph* G is defined by a set of *nodes* (or *vertices*) V, and a set of *arcs* (or *edges*) E, where an arc is an ordered pair of nodes from V. If $(v_1, v_2) \in E$ then we say that there is an arc from v_1 to v_2 in G, or that v_2 is a neighbor of v_1, or that v_2 is a successor of v_1, and that v_1 and v_2 are, respectively, the beginning and end points of that arc. The pictorial representation of directed graphs depicts nodes as objects such as circles, and arcs as arrows between them. Figure 2.1 shows a typical directed graph.

An *undirected graph* is similar, except that in it arcs are *unordered* pairs of nodes. For the purposes of search problems we will transform each undirected graph to a directed one, in which every undirected arc is replaced by two directed arcs, one in each direction. From here on we will use the term graph to mean a directed graph, unless explicitly stated otherwise.

A *path* in a graph is a sequence of arcs, such that the end point of any one arc in the sequence is the beginning point of the following arc. A *cycle* is a finite path such that the beginning point of the first arc and the end point of the last arc coincide.

A *directed acyclic graph (DAG)* is a graph containing no cycles. A *rooted tree* (or simply a *tree*) is a graph containing a node (the root) from which there is a unique path to every other node. It is easy to see that a tree is a DAG. By convention, graphical representation of trees always places a node above its descendents, and thus the arrows may be omitted. Figure 2.2 shows a typical tree.

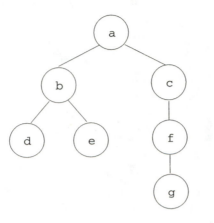

Figure 2.2: Example of a tree

A *bipartite* graph is a graph whose nodes are partitioned into two types, and whose arcs only connect nodes of different types. We will restrict our attention to the special case of bipartite trees. In fact, the term 'bipartite' is uncommon in AI, and is usually replaced by more specific terms that reflect the application. The most common terms are *and-or* trees and *game trees.* In the first case the two types of node are *or* nodes and *and* nodes, and by convention the root is an *or* node. In the second case the two types are *max* and *min,* and by convention the root is a *max* node. Figure 2.3 shows a typical *and-or* tree.

The terms *and* and *or* reflect a certain interpretation of these trees. Successors of *and* nodes represent tasks to be done (such as theorems to be proved or states of the world the robot is to achieve), and an *and* node is said to be 'solved' when all the tasks associated with its successors have been successfully solved. Successors of *or* nodes represent alternative ways of getting the task done, and an *or* node is said to be solved when one of its successor nodes is solved. We will see that an ordinary tree can be viewed as a redundant kind of *and-or* tree, in which each *and* node has exactly one (*or*-node) successor.

A Prolog program and a query together form an *and-or* computation tree; the *and* node successors are conjunctive goals to be proven, and the *or* node successors are different clauses that may be used to reduce goals to subgoals. Search of these *and-or* trees will lie at the heart of our discussion of *meta-interpreters* in Chapter 3.

In this chapter we focus on game trees, which reflect a different interpre-

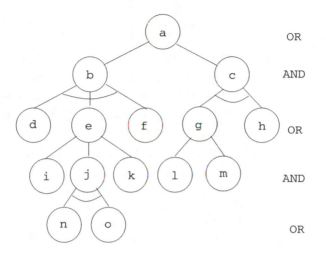

Figure 2.3: Example of an *and-or* tree

tation. These are viewed as representing adversarial situations such as exist in game playing, where the two kinds of node represent the choices available to each of the two adversaries. The reason for the terms *min* and *max* are discussed later in the chapter.

2.2 Representing graphs in Prolog

Having recalled the basic mathematical definitions, we now turn to the Prolog representation of graphs. It should be mentioned, however, that, since graphs are so important, there exist substantial Prolog libraries that implement them efficiently. The reader with access to one of these will do well to use it.

2.2.1 Representing graphs

If the nodes of a (directed) graph are $a_1 \dots a_n$, then the graph can be represented as a boolean *adjacency matrix* A in which the element A_{ij} is 1 if the vertex a_i is connected to the vertex a_j, and 0 otherwise. This representation has advantages for some applications, such as computing transitive closure of graphs. However, from the point of view of search algorithms, adjacency matrices have significant disadvantages. In particular, adjacency

matrices are typically sparse, that is, made up mostly of zeros. Besides
wasting storage space, this representation makes it difficult to write efficient
search algorithms, which tend to rely on being able to find successive neighbors
of a node in constant time. Specifically, we will want a predicate arc / 2
such that the query ?- arc(a,X) will, in constant time (or close to it), bind
X to the first neighbor of a, and will, in constant time per neighbor upon
backtracking, bind X to successive neighbors of a.

For this reason a preferred graph representation is that which stores for
each vertex its *adjacency list,* sometimes also called its *incidence list.* An
adjacency list for a given vertex is the list of vertices to which it is connected.
For the graph shown in Figure 2.1 we get:

$$a : b, c$$
$$b : d, e$$
$$c : b, f, g$$
$$d : h, i$$
$$\vdots$$
$$l : k$$

The Prolog implementation of adjacency lists depends on whether the
graph is to be a term that is passed around as an argument or a construct
residing in the database. In the former case, a natural representation is a
mere repunctuation of the abstract representation; for example, the above
graph might be represented by:

$$
\begin{array}{ll}
[& a - [b,c], \\
& b - [d,e], \\
& c - [b,f,g], \\
& d - [h,i], \\
& \vdots \\
& l - [k] \qquad]
\end{array}
$$

For any graph G, the arc / 2 predicate can be defined by

arc(X, Y) :- member(X–L, G), member(Y, L).

Of course, in this representation the time to retrieve the adjacency list
of a given node is not constant, but rather linear in the number of nodes.

If the graph is to be stored in the database, a natural Prolog representation is as a collection of Prolog facts, each representing a different adjacency list:

$$incid(a,[b,c]).$$
$$incid(b,[d,e]).$$
$$incid(c,[b,d,f]).$$
$$incid(d,[h,i]).$$
$$\vdots$$
$$incid(l,[k]).$$

This representation allows the following definition of arc / 2:

$$arc(X, Y) :- incid(X, L), member(Y, L).$$

This representation yields constant-time access to adjacency lists. In fact, often an even simpler representation is possible. As discussed in Chapter 1, all reasonable implementations of Prolog include some indexing mechanism for efficient retrieval of clauses, and it is common to index clauses by the main functor and first argument. In these cases one may simply represent each arc as a separate fact using arc / 2, and attain the same efficiency. For example, the graph discussed above can be rewritten as follows:

$$arc(a,b).$$
$$arc(a,c).$$
$$arc(b,d).$$
$$arc(b,e).$$
$$arc(c,b).$$
$$\vdots$$
$$arc(l,k).$$

Now, for example, the goal arc(a,A) will return A = b, and upon backtracking the indexing mechanism will guarantee that the next answer, A = c, will be found essentially in constant time.

The advantage of the first database implementation is that the database is accessed only once. The advantage of the second is modularity: An edge can be added or deleted without having to modify the rest of the graph. A disadvantage of the second choice is that if node names are not atomic, the indexing will not provide immediate retrieval. For example, one representation of nodes in the 8-puzzle is eight_node(L), where L is some permutation of the numbers 1-8. In this case the indexing mechanism will not help. However, if we use the representation eight_node_name(a), eight_node_content(a,L), we will again be able to capitalize on the indexing. Thus, the choice of implementation is largely a matter of taste, and efficiency will depend on the exact application. In this book we will simply use the arc / 2 predicate, and let the reader decide on a favorite representation.

2.2.2   Representing trees

Since trees are graphs, the discussion in Section 2.2.1 applies to trees as well. For example, the tree shown in Figure 2.2 can be represented by the following adjacency lists:

$$a : b, c$$
$$b : d, e$$
$$c : f$$
$$d :$$
$$e :$$
$$f : g$$
$$g :$$

These adjacency lists can be implemented in several ways, including the ones discussed in Section 2.2.1. However, the special property of trees permits a more compact representation. Since there is a single path from the root to each node, we can essentially replace each element in the adjacency list by its own adjacency list. Specifically, we may represent a tree in the form

tree(*node, children*)

where *node* is any node label, and *children* is a (possibly empty) list of (recursively defined) trees. We may further optimize and abbreviate tree(*node,* [ ]) by node. For example, the tree of Figure 2.2 is represented by the term

tree(a, [tree(b, [d, e]), tree(c, [tree(f, [g])])])

2.2.3   Representing and-or trees

Other than the labels of its nodes, an *and-or* tree is an ordinary tree and can be represented as such. Furthermore, since the root is by convention always an *or* node, and since arcs only connect nodes of different types, the labels of the nodes in such a tree (*and* and *or*) can be deduced from the same representation. In principle, therefore, we need not require a separate representation for *and-or* trees. Indeed, some implementations are simplified under this uniform representation. Still, sometimes it is convenient to be able to tell the type of node without having to reconstruct it from the nesting structure. We may therefore adopt the following representation: Use the notation or(*node,children*) for *or* nodes, and and(*node,children*) for *and* nodes. For example, under this scheme the *and-or* tree from Figure 2.3 will be represented as

```
or( a, [ and( b, [ d,
             or( e, [ i,
                  and( j, [ n,
                         o ] ) ],
                 k ) ,
             f ] ) ,
        and( c, [ or( g, [ l,
                  m ] ),
             h ] ) ] )
```

In the case of game trees, we will replace the or by max and the and by min.

2.3   Review of graph search techniques

We briefly review the basic notions involved in graph search, before discussing their Prolog implementation.

Given a graph G, a node $s \in G$ (the 'start' node), and a predicate *Goal* (defining the goal nodes), the simplest kind of search problem is to determine whether there is a path from s to a node t in G such that $Goal(t)$ holds. Most search algorithms employ two lists: The list OPEN contains nodes encountered but not yet explored, and the list CLOSED contains the nodes encountered and explored. The algorithms tend to have the following basic structure:

PROCEDURE SEARCH(*graph*:graph, *startnode*:node,
                         Goal:(procedure,unary))
OPEN ← {*startnode*} , *CLOSED* ← { }
found ← false
while *OPEN* is not empty and *found* is false do
    transfer a node *N* from *OPEN* to *CLOSED*
    if *goal(N)* then *found* ← true
    else find all the neighbors of *N* in the graph that are
        neither in *OPEN* nor in *CLOSED*, and add them to *OPEN*
    end if
end while
if *found* is true then return *N*; else fail

In addition, it is often required that, upon successful search, the algorithm return the path itself. We will assume this requirement here; only a slight modification need be made to the above general procedure.

The three basic algorithms that we will discuss differ on which node is selected among the OPEN nodes, that is, on the first line of the 'while' loop. These three are *depth-first search, breadth-first search,* and *best-first search,* and we discuss them in the following three sections.[1] We conclude the chapter with the topic of game-tree search.

2.4   Depth-first search

Depth-first search picks among the list of OPEN nodes the one added latest to the list. The resulting search can be thought of as extending paths deep into the graph until they cannot be extended further; the search then backtracks to the last point on the path from which there is an unexplored arc (this is called *chronological backtracking*) and proceeds to extend that path.

In the case of trees, the search is rather straightforward. Figure 2.4 depicts a depth-first search of a typical tree (the numbers by the nodes indicate the order of exploration). Note that in this case the search proceeded 'from left to right'; depth-first search may proceed from 'right to left,' or in no particular order among sibling nodes. Indeed, the process as described is

---

[1]This is a slight idealization; as we shall see, the most general form of best-first search departs somewhat from the basic template.

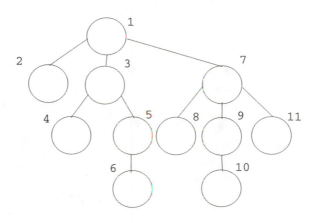

Figure 2.4: Depth-first search of a tree

indifferent to the order in which the neighbors of a given node are explored. If, however, the neighbors are ordered in some natural way, we can define *ordered depth-first search,* in which the order of neighbor exploration is defined by the procedure. In AI, search almost always means ordered search, and ordered trees are the most common case. This order is represented graphically by ordering the descendents of a node from left to right. (*And-or* trees can also be viewed as ordered, and searched in various ways. We return to this topic in connection with meta-interpeters in Chapter 3.)

Search of general graphs is slightly complicated by the need to avoid repeated exploration of the same node. Figure 2.5 depicts a depth-first search of the graph from Figure 2.1. Again, the numbers by the nodes indicate the order of exploration.

Depth-first search can be implemented very efficiently. The time complexity of the search can be kept linear in the total number of arcs in the graph, and the space complexity linear in the length of the longest path in the graph. The efficient implementation uses a *stack,* or a last-in first-out data structure: The program keeps a stack of the path uncovered so far, and extends it by pushing new elements onto it. If a path cannot be extended, elements are popped off until a previous node that can be extended in a new way is uncovered. We will use the adjacency-list representation, and, as explained in Section 2.2, assume the arc / 2 predicate.

The algorithm requires that we not explore any node more than once; the complexity of the implementation will depend on how we ensure this condition. The straightforward implementation, which we present here, maintains

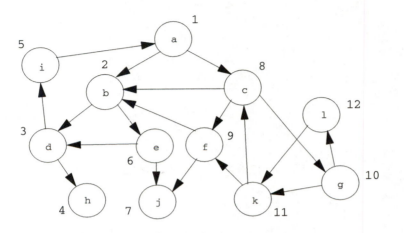

Figure 2.5: Depth-first search of a general graph

OPEN and CLOSED as simple lists, and checks new candidate nodes for nonmembership in either list. This results in quadratic time complexity; for a more efficient implementation, see Exercise 2.1.

Actually, the OPEN list will contain not only the nodes but also the path leading to each one. The paths will be stored in reverse order. For example, if the stack contains the two lists [p,q,r,s] and [t,r,s], then this will mean that there are two current nodes, p and t, that the path leading to p from the start node s is s-r-q-p, and that the path to t is s-r-t. Here is the depth-first search program.

```
% _____
% Depth-first search
% Arguments: arc function (+), start node (+), goal predicate (+),
% solution (i.e., path from start node to a node satisfying the goal predicate) (−)
% _____

depth_first_search(Arc, Start, GoalPred, Sol ) :- dfs( Arc, [ [ Start ] ], [ ], GoalPred, Sol ).
```

```
% _____
% The second argument to dfs is the OPEN stack,
% the third argument is the CLOSED list
% _____

dfs( _, [ [ Node | Path ] | _ ], _, GoalPred, [ Node | Path ] ) :-
    call( GoalPred, Node ). % see Chapter 1 for call / n
dfs( Arc, [ [ Node | Path ] | MoreOPEN ], CLOSED, GoalPred, Sol ) :-
    % find the new neighbors of the first OPEN node
    % and add the current path to each of them:
    findall( [ Next, Node | Path ],
            ( call( Arc, Node, Next ),
              not( member( [ Next | _ ], [ [ Node | Path ] | MoreOPEN ] ) ),
              not( member( Next, CLOSED ) ) ),
            NewPaths ),
    % place the new paths on top of the stack:
    append( NewPaths, MoreOPEN, NewOPEN ),
    dfs( Arc, NewOPEN, [ Node | CLOSED ], GoalPred, Sol ).
```

The quadratic complexity is the result of the not(member(...)) tests. Each call to the test requires time proportional to the lengths of the OPEN and CLOSED lists, which may be as great as the number of nodes in the graph. The test is performed once for every edge traversed by the algorithm, and in the worst case all graph edges will be traversed. Thus the worst-case time complexity of this implementation is $O(mn)$, where m is the number of edges and n the number of nodes. It is possible to do better, by maintaining the OPEN and CLOSED sets other than as lists. Also note that the space complexity of this implementation is quadratic in the number of nodes, as all paths are stored explicitly; this complexity too can be reduced. Exercise 2.1 explores this topic further.

Note also that although the above program allows multiple solutions, it does *not* find multiple paths to any given node. This is true of all search procedures belonging to the general class of search algorithms defined in Section 2.3.

2.5   Breadth-first search

Consider again the general search scheme of Section 2.3. We saw that depth-
first search specializes it by selecting for exploration the latest node encountered. Breadth-first search, in contrast, explores the *earliest* node encountered. The result is that the graph is searched in 'layers': The algorithm first
adds all the nodes adjacent to the start node, then all the new ones adjacent
to those, and so on. Thus it can be thought of as searching all paths from the
start node in parallel, at each stage augmenting each path a step farther. Of
course, a sequential algorithm replaces the 'parallel' addition of a new layer
by adding the nodes in the layer one by one. Searching the graph in this way,
i.e., layer by layer, not only avoids the danger of pursuing an infinite branch
while a solution lies on another branch, but it also guarantees finding the
shortest path to a goal node. Figure 2.6 shows an example of breadth-first
search (the numbers by the nodes denote the order of discovery) and the
induced layers. The graph searched is the same graph of Figure 2.1; don't
be misled by the different layout.

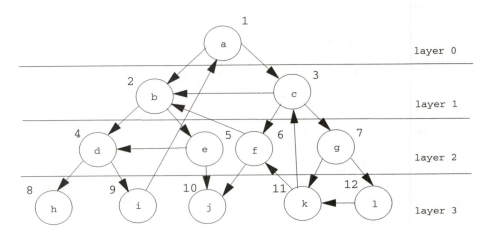

Figure 2.6: Example of breadth-first search

Breadth-first search can also be implemented to run in time that is linear
in the total number of arcs; however, unlike that of depth-first search, the
space complexity of its optimum implementation is also linear in the total
number of arcs in the graph, rather than in the length of the longest path.
The way to achieve the breadth-first order is simply to replace the stack of

depth-first search by a *queue,* or a first-in first-out data structure. Consider the graph depicted in Figure 2.6 as an example. The first few phases in the evolution of the queue during the breadth-first search will be as follows:

phase 1 :   a
phase 2 :   b   c
phase 3 :   c   d   e
phase 4 :   d   e   f   g
phase 5 :   e   f   g   h   i
phase 6 :   f   g   h   i   j

The following is a correct but inefficient implementation of breadth-first search. It is identical to the depth-first search program, except that the OPEN stack is replaced by a queue; this is achieved simply by reversing the arguments in the call to append. (In this program, as well as in subsequent ones, paths are once again stored in reverse order; the first node in the list is the farthest from the start node.)

% _____
% *Inefficient breadth-first search (nearly identical to* depth_first_search)
% _____

```
breadth_first_search_slow( Arc, Start, GoalPred, Sol ) :-
   bfs_slow( Arc, [ [ Start ] ], [ ], GoalPred, Sol ).


bfs_slow( _, [ [ Node | Path ] | _ ], _, GoalPred, [ Node | Path ] ) :-
   call( GoalPred, Node ).
bfs_slow( Arc, [ [ Node | Path ] | MoreOPEN ], CLOSED, GoalPred, Sol ) :-
   findall( [ Next, Node | Path ],
           ( call( Arc, Node, Next ),
             not( member( [ Next | _ ], [ [ Node | Path ] | MoreOPEN ] ) ),
             not( member( Next, CLOSED ) ),
           NewPaths ),
   % place the new paths at the bottom of the queue:
   append( MoreOPEN, NewPaths, NewOPEN ),
   bfs_slow( Arc, NewOPEN, [ Node | CLOSED ], GoalPred, Sol ).
```

In addition to those inefficiencies discussed in connection with the depth-first search program, this program contains a further inefficiency. Ordinary lists are a slow way to implement a queue: Whereas adding a new element to the stack in depth-first search was a constant-time operation, this breadth-first implementation requires time proportional to the length of the queue to add a new element to the end of the queue. The contribution of this step to the time complexity is once again quadratic in the number of nodes. As discussed in Chapter 1, the standard and elegant Prolog solution is to use difference lists. The following is a correct and more efficient breadth-first search program.

```
% _____
% More efficient breadth-first search
% _____


breadth_first_search( Arc, Start, GoalPred, Sol ) :-
  bfs( Arc, [ [ Start ] | Qtail ], Qtail, [ ], GoalPred, Sol ).

% if the queue is empty, fail
bfs( _, OPEN, Qtail, _, _, _ ) :- OPEN == Qtail, !, fail.
% otherwise, as in the previous implementation:
bfs( _, [ [ Node | Path ] | _ ], _, _, GoalPred, [Node | Path ] ) :-
  call( GoalPred, Node ).
bfs( Arc, [ [ Node | Path ] | MoreOPEN ], Qtail, CLOSED, GoalPred, Sol ) :-
  findall( [ Next, Node | Path ],
         ( call( Arc, Node, Next ),
            % dlmember / 3 determines membership in a difference list
            % (see Chapter 1)
            not( dlmember( [ Next | _ ], [ [ Node | Path ] | MoreOPEN ], Qtail ) ),
            not( member( Next, CLOSED ) ) ),
         NewPaths ),
  % and here is where the difference list pays off:
  append( NewPaths, NewQtail, Qtail ),
  bfs( Arc, MoreOPEN, NewQtail, [ Node | CLOSED ], GoalPred, Sol ).
```

As in the depth-first case, neither implementation finds multiple paths to any goal, although both find some path to every goal. And again, because of the not(member(...)) tests, the time complexity of this program is not linear even in the size of the graph.

2.6   Iterative deepening

Although breadth-first search has the advantage of systematicity, its space
requirements render it useless for all but the smallest problems. The iterative
deepening method attempts to have the best of all worlds, combining the
space economy of depth-first search with the exhaustiveness of breadth-first
search. Iterative deepening is a simple modification of depth-first search.
It sets a limit on the length of the paths being searched, and exhaustively
searches all paths whose length is within that limit. If no solution is found,
the limit on path length is increased, and the process is repeated. Although
this process might seem wasteful, since the search to level d repeats the
search just performed at level d-1, it can be shown that the waste is in fact
minimal.

Iterative deepening is too important a technique to go without mention. Its implementation, however, is a simple modification of the depth-first
search procedure and is left to the reader as Exercise 2.3.

2.7   Best-first search

Both depth-first search and breadth-first search fall into the category of
blind search, since the order of search in both is determined uniquely by
the structure of the graph. Sometimes there is additional information to
aid the search process, however. Best-first search is designed to use that
information and thus search the graph in a more insightful fashion. The
search estimates the 'goodness' of any given path already explored, and
extends the 'best' path. This measure of goodness is called the *heuristic
value* of the path; we will take these values to be numerical, with lower
numbers considered more promising than higher ones (a choice that will be
convenient for the implementation). Often the heuristic value of a path is
computed as a function of only the last node on the path. For example,
in the context of the 8-puzzle, we may consider the heuristic value of a
configuration to be the number of misplaced tiles; see Exercise 2.2. In these
cases all paths to a node have the same heuristic value, and we might as
well speak of the heuristic value of nodes rather than of paths. Figure 2.7
shows the same graph of Figure 2.1, with each node assigned a heuristic
value. Figure 2.8 shows the initial evolution of the ordered list of OPEN

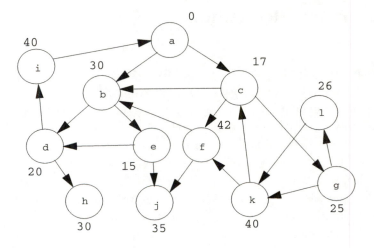

Figure 2.7: Heuristic values to nodes

nodes under best-first search of this graph.

2.7.1   The general best-first algorithm

We first present a general best-first search program, in which the heuristic function is one of the arguments. We then present the A^* search algorithm, a best-first search in which a specific heuristic function is assumed.

The idea behind the implementation of best-first search is to replace the stack of depth-first search or the queue of breadth-first search by an ordered

```
a
c   b
g   b   f
l   b   k   f
b   k   f
e   d   k   f
d   j   k   f
h   j   k   i   f
```

Figure 2.8: Evolution of the OPEN queue in a best-first search

list in which the paths are ordered by their heuristic values. Each element in the list will therefore be a pair Value-Path.

There is, however, a new complication. In the case of blind search we could safely ignore multiple paths to the same node. Now, however, a new path to a previously encountered node may yield a lower value than the previous path. The general scheme of Section 2.3 would not allow us to reconsider the path to that node, because it automatically disregards all neighbors that already exist in either the OPEN or CLOSED list. Since in the case of best-first search we are always interested in pursuing the most promising node, we should reconsider nodes already encountered. Suppose we have just found a path to a node N. If the OPEN list contains a path to N with a higher (worse) value, the new path should replace the old one. If the CLOSED list contains the node N, and the previous path to N was of higher value (before it was moved from OPEN to CLOSED), N should be removed from CLOSED and the new path added to OPEN (the reason is that, although the neighbors of N have already been explored and their paths added to OPEN, now better paths have been found to those neighbors). This last operation may lead to quite a lengthy execution, and there are special cases that avoid it.

We begin with the implementation of the general case; we will then discuss the special (and easier) cases. The following program is quite inefficient, and we will remark on this below. The program is also somewhat long, as a result of examining the various conditions explained above. Following this program we will present shorter programs, which are sufficient (and much more efficient) under certain conditions.

```
% _____
% General best-first search, unoptimized
% _____


best_first_search( Arc, Start, Hfun, GoalPred, Sol ) :-
   bstfs( Arc, [ 0 - [ Start ] ], [ ], Hfun, GoalPred, Sol ).


bstfs( _, [ _ - [ Node | Path ] | _ ], _, _, GoalPred, [ Node | Path ] ) :-
   call( GoalPred, Node ).
bstfs( Arc, [ Val - [ Node | Path] | MoreOPEN ], CLOSED, Hfun, GoalPred, Sol ) :-
   % first, extend the path to Node to all its neighbors:
   findall( Val1 - [ Next, Node | Path ],
         ( call( Arc, Node, Next ),
           call( Hfun, [ Next, Node | Path ], Val1 ) ),
         Neighbors ),
   % next, find among them the new neighbors:
   findall( Val1 - [ Node1 | Path1 ],
         ( member( Val1 - [ Node1 | Path1 ], Neighbors ),
           not( member( _- [ Node1 | _ ], [Val - [ Node | Path] | MoreOPEN] ) ),
           not( member( _- Node1, CLOSED) ) ),
         TmpOPEN1 ),
   % now, among the other neighbors, find those to which
   % a worse path exists in OPEN, and replace that path:
   improve_open( Neighbors, MoreOPEN, TmpOPEN2 ),
   append( TmpOPEN1, TmpOPEN2, TmpOPEN3 ),
   % finally, among the remaining neighbors (they must be CLOSED), find those
   % to whom the path found previously is worse than the current one; remove
   % them from the CLOSED list, and add the new path to the OPEN list:
   improve_closed( Neighbors, TmpOPEN3, CLOSED, TmpOPEN4, NewCLOSED ),
   move_smallest_to_top( TmpOPEN4, NewOPEN ),
   bstfs( Arc, NewOPEN, [ Val - Node | NewCLOSED ], Hfun, GoalPred, Sol ).


improve_open( [ ], OPEN, OPEN ).
improve_open( [ Path | More ], OPEN, NewOPEN ) :-
   scan_open( Path, OPEN, TmpOPEN ),
   improve_open( More, TmpOPEN, NewOPEN ).
```

```
scan_open( _, [ ], [ ] ).
scan_open( Val - [ Node | Path ], [ Val1 - [ Node1 | _ ] | More ], NewOPEN ) :-
    Node = Node1, Val < Val1, !, NewOPEN = [ Val - [ Node | Path ] | More ].
scan_open( _- [ Node | _ ], [ Val1 - [ Node1 | Path1 ] | More ], NewOPEN ) :-
    Node = Node1, !, NewOPEN = [ Val1 - [ Node1 | Path1 ] | More ].
scan_open( Path, [ Path1 | More ], [ Path1 | More1 ] ) :-
    scan_open( Path, More, More1 ).


improve_closed( [ ], OPEN, CLOSED, OPEN, CLOSED ).
improve_closed( [ Path | More ], OPEN, CLOSED, NewOPEN, NewCLOSED ) :-
    scan_closed( Path, OPEN, CLOSED, TmpOPEN, TmpCLOSED ),
    improve_closed( More, TmpOPEN, TmpCLOSED, NewOPEN, NewCLOSED ).


scan_closed( _, OPEN, [ ], OPEN, [ ] ).
scan_closed( Val - [ Node | Path ], OPEN, [ Val1 - Node1 | MoreCLOSED ],
                    NewOPEN, NewCLOSED ) :-
    Node = Node1, Val < Val1, !,
    NewOPEN = [ Val - [ Node | Path ] | OPEN ],
    NewCLOSED = MoreCLOSED.
scan_closed( _- [ Node | _ ], OPEN, [ Val1 - Node1 | MoreCLOSED ],
                    NewOPEN, NewCLOSED ) :-
    Node = Node1, !,
    NewOPEN = OPEN,
    NewCLOSED = [ Val1 - Node1 | MoreCLOSED ].
scan_closed( Path, OPEN, [ Node | More ], NewOPEN, [ Node | More1 ] ) :-
    scan_closed( Path, OPEN, More, NewOPEN, More1 ).


move_smallest_to_top( [ ], [ ] ).
move_smallest_to_top( [ Val - X | L ], [ S | R ] ) :- find_smallest( L, Val - X, S, R ).
find_smallest( [ ], T, T, [ ] ).
find_smallest( [ Val1 - X | L ], Val - T, S, [ Val - T | R ] ) :-
   Val1 < Val, !, find_smallest( L, Val1 - X, S, R ).
find_smallest( [ Val1 - X | L ], Val - T, S, [ Val1 - X | R ] ) :-
   find_smallest( L, Val - T, S, R ).
```

To get a feel for the program, the reader might try it on the graph of
Figure 2.7, ignoring the heuristic values listed beside each node; instead,
consider the following three heuristic functions:

hf1 The value of a path is the value of the last node in the path:
h([a | _], 20), h([b | _], 30), and so on.

hf2 The value of a path is the average value of nodes on that path.

hf3 The value of a path is minimum between the value of the node and the average value of nodes on the path leading to it.

Here is a sample run with the last heuristic, with appropriate print commands added to the program:

| ?- best_first_search(arc,a,hf3,goal,L).

New OPEN is: [0.0-[b,a],0.0-[c,a]]
New CLOSED is: [0-a]

New OPEN is: [0.0-[c,a],20.0-[d,b,a],15-[e,b,a]]
New CLOSED is: [0.0-b,0-a]

New OPEN is: [8.5-[f,c,a],8.5-[g,c,a],20.0-[d,b,a],15-[e,b,a]]
New CLOSED is: [0.0-c,0.0-b,0-a]

New OPEN is: [8.5-[g,c,a],19.6667-[j,f,c,a],20.0-[d,b,a],15-[e,b,a]]
New CLOSED is: [8.5-f,0.0-c,0.0-b,0-a]

New OPEN is: [14.0-[k,g,c,a],14.0-[l,g,c,a],19.6667-[j,f,c,a],20.0-[d,b,a],15-[e,b,a]]
New CLOSED is: [8.5-g,8.5-f,0.0-c,0.0-b,0-a]

New OPEN is: [14.0-[l,g,c,a],19.6667-[j,f,c,a],20.0-[d,b,a],15-[e,b,a]]
New CLOSED is: [14.0-k,8.5-g,8.5-f,0.0-c,0.0-b,0-a]

New OPEN is: [15-[e,b,a],20.0-[d,b,a],19.6667-[j,f,c,a]]
New CLOSED is: [14.0-l,14.0-k,8.5-g,8.5-f,0.0-c,0.0-b,0-a]

New OPEN is: [18.3333-[d,e,b,a],18.3333-[j,e,b,a]]
New CLOSED is: [15-e,14.0-l,14.0-k,8.5-g,8.5-f,0.0-c,0.0-b,0-a]

New OPEN is: [18.3333-[j,e,b,a],18.75-[i,d,e,b,a],18.75-[h,d,e,b,a]]
New CLOSED is: [18.3333-d,15-e,14.0-l,14.0-k,8.5-g,8.5-f,0.0-c,0.0-b,0-a]

```
L = [j,e,b,a]
| ?-
```

This program can be optimized in several ways; Exercise 2.4 suggests a few. However, even after optimization the program might run a long time, as nodes may be moved from the CLOSED list back into the OPEN list more than once. Fortunately, there are cases in which we can avoid this. Notice that in the sample run above, nodes were never removed from the CLOSED list; that is, whenever a node was placed in CLOSED, an optimal path to it had already been found. In general, a heuristic algorithm is called *admissible* if it finds not only a path to a goal node an optimal path, that is, a path of minimal heuristic value. Let us further define an algorithm to be *everywhere admissible* if, whenever it extends a path from a node x to its neighbors, it has already found an optimal path to x. (Clearly if an algorithm is everywhere admissible it is also admissible.) The terms 'admissible' and 'everywhere admissible' are also used to describe the heuristic function used by the algorithm.

'Everywhere admissibility' is quite a strong property, but it is not uncommon. For example, it holds for all heuristic functions that evaluate a path on the basis of only the last node in the path. Since nodes are never removed from the CLOSED list, everywhere-admissible algorithms may be simplified. Here is the resulting simplified program.

```
%
% Best-first search assuming 'everywhere' admissibility
%
```

```
best_first_search_ad( Arc, Start, Hfun, GoalPred, Sol ) :-
    bstfs_ad( [ 0 - [ Start ] ], [ ], Hfun, GoalPred, Sol ).
```

```
bstfs_ad( _, [ _ - [ Node | Path ] | _ ], _, _, GoalPred, [ Node | Path ] ) :-
    call(GoalPred,Node).
bstfs_ad( Arc, [ Val - [ Node | Path ] | MoreOPEN ], CLOSED, Hfun, GoalPred, Sol ) :-
    % (as before) extend the path to Node to all its neighbors:
    findall( Val1 - [ Next, Node | Path ],
             ( call( Arc, Node, Next ),
               call( Hfun, [ Next, Node | Path ], Val1 ) ),
             Neighbors ),
    % (as before) find among them the new neighbors:
    findall( Val1 - [ Node1 | Path1 ],
             ( member( Val1 - [ Node1 | Path1 ], Neighbors ),
               not( member( _ - [ Node1 | _ ], [Val - [ Node | Path] | MoreOPEN] ) ),
               not( member( _ - Node1, CLOSED ) ) ),
             TmpOPEN1 ),
    % (as before) update the paths to previous OPEN nodes:
    improve_open( Neighbors, MoreOPEN, TmpOPEN2 ),
    append( TmpOPEN1, TmpOPEN2, TmpOPEN3 ),
    move_smallest_to_top( TmpOPEN3, NewOPEN ),
    bstfs_ad( Arc, NewOPEN, [ Val - Node | CLOSED ], Hfun, GoalPred, Sol ).
```

% improve_open / 3 *as before; no need for* improve_closed / 5.

Many everywhere-admissible algorithms have an even stronger property: The very first path found to any node, even before it has been expanded and put in the CLOSED list, is also the best path to that node. Again, this is true for example whenever the heuristic function is based on only the last node in the path. Let us call an algorithm that has this property *strongly admissible*. Strongly admissible algorithms need not even examine the OPEN list, and we end up with the following further simplified program.

```
%
% Best-first search assuming 'strong' admissibility
%

best_first_search_st_ad( Arc, Start, Hfun, GoalPred, Sol ) :-
   bstfs_st_ad( Arc, [ 0 - [ Start ] ], [ ], Hfun, GoalPred, Sol ).


bstfs_st_ad( _, [ _ - [ Node | Path ] | _ ], _, _, GoalPred, [ Node | Path ] ) :-
   call(GoalPred,Node).
bstfs_st_ad( Arc, [ Val - [ Node | Path ] | MoreOPEN ], CLOSED, Hfun, GoalPred, Sol ) :-
   findall( Val1 - [ Next, Node | Path ],
            ( call( Arc, Node, Next ),
              call( Hfun, [ Next, Node | Path ], Val1 ) ),
            Neighbors),
   findall( Val1 - [ Node1 | Path1 ],
            ( member( Val1 - [ Node1 | Path1 ], Neighbors ),
              not( member( _ - [ Node1 | _ ], [Val - [ Node | Path] | MoreOPEN] ) ) ),
              not( member( _ - Node1, CLOSED) ) ),
            TmpOPEN1 ),
   % note difference:
   append( TmpOPEN1, MoreOPEN, TmpOPEN2 ),
   move_smallest_to_top( TmpOPEN2,NewOPEN ),
   bstfs_st_ad( Arc, NewOPEN, [ Val - Node | CLOSED], Hfun, GoalPred, Sol ).
```

Finally, if the graph searched is a tree, then we know that the first path to a node is not only the best one, but also the only one. In this case we need not even check that the neighbors do not already exist in either the OPEN or CLOSED list.

% _____

% *Best-first search of trees*

% _____

```
best_first_search_tree( Arc, Start, Hfun, GoalPred, Sol ) :-
    bstfs_tree( Arc, [ 0 - [ Start ] ], [ ], Hfun, GoalPred, Sol ).

bstfs_tree( _, [ _ - [ Node | Path ] | _ ], _, _, GoalPred, [ Node | Path ] ) :-
    call( GoalPred, Node ).
bstfs_tree( Arc, [ Val - [ Node | Path ] | MoreOPEN ], CLOSED, Hfun, GoalPred, Sol ) :-
    findall( Val1 - [ Next, Node | Path ],
            ( call( Arc, Node, Next ),
              call( Hfun, [ Next, Node | Path ], Val1 ) ),
            Neighbors ),
    append( Neighbors, MoreOPEN, TmpOPEN ),
    move_smallest_to_top( TmpOPEN, NewOPEN ),
    bstfs_tree( Arc, NewOPEN, [ Val - Node | CLOSED ], Hfun, GoalPred, Sol ).
```

2.7.2   The A* algorithm

The A^* algorithm is a special case of the general best-first search algorithm. It embodies a heuristic function that estimates the length of the path to the closest goal node, sums it with the distance from the start node *to* the current node, and selects the node with a minimal sum. Specifically, in the A^* algorithm the heuristic function is composed of two terms:

$$f(n) = g(n) + h(n)$$

where

1. $g(n)$ is the length of the path used to reach node n

2. $h(n)$ is a function estimating the length of the path from the node n to the goal node

This is illustrated in Figure 2.9.

For example, in a route-finding application, the metric distance between the current location and the destination might serve as a reasonable estimation function (even though in fact we might have to make detours to avoid obstacles). Since A^* is a special case of best-first search, its implementation

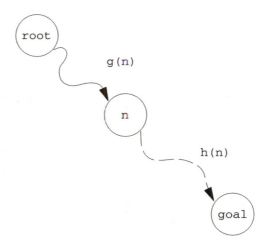

Figure 2.9: Length of the path

is straightforward. The following program assumes an application-dependent predicate h(Node, Hval).

% A* search

astar(Start, GoalPred, Sol) :- best_first_search(Start, astar_fun, GoalPred, Sol).

astar_fun([Node | Path], Fval) :-
    length(Path, Gval), h(Node, Hval), Fval is Gval+Hval.

Here we have used the most general best-first search procedure, but naturally the most concise and efficient version appropriate in the circumstances should be used. If we are guaranteed admissibility, we should use the second version. In general it is hard to determine admissibility, but the following is a well-known property of A^*. Let h^* be the function computing the actual distance to a closest goal node, and h the estimation function of A^* satisfying $h^* \geq h$ (that is, h never overestimates the distance); in this case A^* is everywhere admissible. But how do we know that $h^* \geq h$ holds? Fortunately, there is an additional known fact. h is called *monotone* if it satisfies the triangle inequality: if $p \rightarrow q$ is an arc, then $h(p) + 1 > h(q)$. As it turns out, if h is monotone then A^* is everywhere admissible; in this case, of course, the second version should be used. Similarly, if we are guaranteed strong admissibility then we should use the third version, and if the graph is a tree then we should use the fourth, most concise version.

2.8   Game-tree search

Section 2.1 mentioned that adversarial situations, such as in game playing, can often be represented as game trees. Nodes in the tree represent the situation (for example, a board position in chess), and arcs represent possible actions of each player. Arcs emanating from *max*-nodes correspond to choices available to one player, and arcs emanating from *min*-nodes correspond to choices available to the second player. Each path, therefore, represents the sequence of choices made alternately by the two opponents.

The definition of the search problem for game trees is different from its definition in the case of ordinary graphs. Whereas in the latter one is interested in a path, in the case of game trees one is interested in a *winning strategy*. Some leaves in the game tree are labeled as winning states for the first player (and therefore losing states for the second player). A winning strategy is one that guarantees that the first player (whose possible moves are represented by arcs starting at *max*-nodes) reaches a state in which he wins, no matter what choices are made by the second player (whose possible moves are represented by the arcs starting at *min*-nodes). This amounts to pruning the game tree by selecting at each *max*-node only one successor (which of course is a *min*-node) and eliminating all the other successors and the subtrees hanging off them, so that in the resulting pruned tree all leaves are winning states for the first player.[2]

Figure 2.10 depicts a game tree; Figure 2.11 presents a winning strategy for that tree.

In practice, entire game trees are huge and therefore impossible to generate. Instead, some partial tree is generated, starting at the root. In this subtree we lack the information to label leaves definitively as winning or losing; instead, each is assigned a *heuristic value*. The notion of a winning strategy is now generalized to that of an *optimal strategy*. The optimal strategy is one that guarantees the first player will reach a node with the highest possible value, assuming that the second player moves so as to minimize that value. The win/lose situation can be viewed as a special case in which the leaf values are boolean: win = 1, lose = 0.

---

[2]Observe that ordinary graph search can be viewed as a redundant case in which each *min*-node has exactly one *max*-node as a successor. That is, the "opponent" never has any alternatives (and therefore really it makes no sense to think of an opponent), and the pruned "tree" is actually a single path.

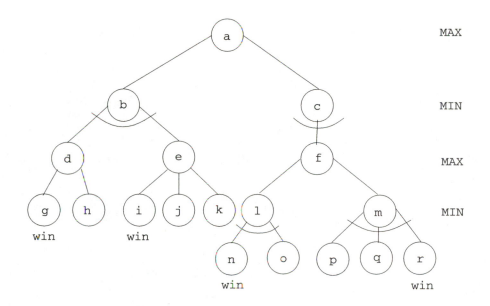

Figure 2.10: Two-level game tree

We will discuss the implementation of two procedures for finding an optimal strategy: first the straightforward *minimax* procedure, and then its optimization, α-β search. The exercises mention a few others. For clarity, the procedures we discuss do not return the actual pruned tree, but only the value guaranteed to the first player. Adding the other information to the output is not hard; this is the topic of Exercise 2.5.

2.8.1   Minimax search

The minimax search procedure is derived directly from the definition of the problem. In this section we will assume that the entire tree is generated (but see Exercise 2.7). The search starts with the leaf nodes and propagates values back to the internal nodes. Each *min*-node is assigned the minimum among the values of its successors (reflecting the assumption that the second player will choose the move that is the worst for the first player), and each *max*-node is assigned the maximum among the values of its successors (hence the names for the two node types). As a result, each node is assigned the highest value guaranteed to the first player at the state represented by that node. The value assigned to the root is thus the value guaranteed to the player at the outset. Figure 2.12 shows the propagation of leaf values in a

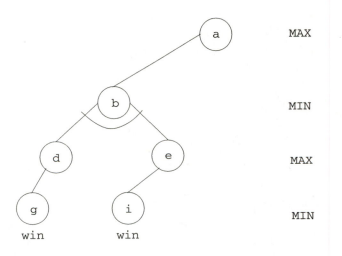

Figure 2.11: A winning strategy

two-level game.

The following is an implementation of this simple procedure. It assumes the representation discussed in Section 2.2.3. It also assumes a function leaf_value / 2 that given a leaf returns its value. The terms lowlimit and highlimit represent symbols less than and greater than any integer, respectively.

```
% _____
% minimax / 2 returns the Value of the Tree.
% Arguments: Tree (+), Value (−)
% _____

minimax( leaf( Label ), Value ) :-
    leaf_value( Label, Value ).
minimax( max( _, Children ), Value ) :-
    max_children( Children, lowlimit, Value ).
minimax( min( _, Children ), Value ) :-
    min_children( Children, highlimit, Value ).

max_children( [ ], Max, Max ).
max_children( [ Child | Children ], Max0, Max ) :-
    minimax( Child, Value ),
    max( Value, Max0, Max1 ),
    max_children( Children, Max1, Max ).
```

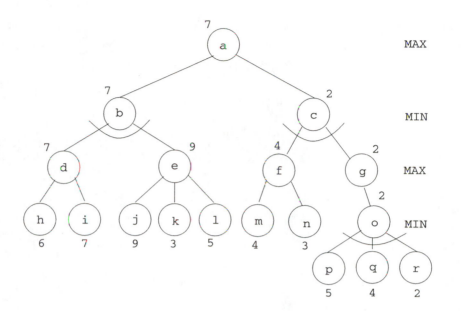

Figure 2.12: Minimax leaf value propagation

```
min_children( [ ], Min, Min ).
min_children( [ Child | Children ], Min0, Min ) :-
    minimax( Child, Value ),
    min( Value, Min0, Min1 ),
    min_children( Children, Min1, Min ).

ab_max( X, Y, Z ) :- greater( Y, X ), !, Z = Y.
ab_max( X, _, X ).

ab_min( X, Y, Z ) :- greater( X, Y ), !, Z = Y.
ab_min( X, _, X ).

greater( _, lowlimit ).
greater( highlimit, _ ).
greater( lowlimit, _ ) :- !, fail.
greater( _, highlimit ) :- !, fail.
greater( A, B ) :- A > B.
```

The following is a sample run of the program on the game tree in Figure 2.12. Printing commands were added to show the order in which node values were determined, as well as the values themselves. The database contains the facts leaf_value(r,2), leaf_value(q,4), and so on for all leaves.

```
| ?- minimax(max(a, [min(b, [max(d, [leaf(h), leaf(i)]),
                              max(e, [leaf(j), leaf(k), leaf(l)])]),
                       min(c, [max(f, [leaf(m), leaf(n)]),
                              max(g, [min(o, [leaf(p), leaf(q), leaf(r)])])])]),
             Val).
```

Node: h Val: 6 Type: leaf
Node: i Val: 7 Type: leaf
Node: d Val: 7 Type: max
Node: j Val: 9 Type: leaf
Node: k Val: 3 Type: leaf
Node: l Val: 5 Type: leaf
Node: e Val: 9 Type: max
Node: b Val: 7 Type: min
Node: m Val: 4 Type: leaf
Node: n Val: 3 Type: leaf
Node: f Val: 4 Type: max
Node: p Val: 5 Type: leaf
Node: q Val: 4 Type: leaf
Node: r Val: 2 Type: leaf
Node: o Val: 2 Type: min
Node: g Val: 2 Type: max
Node: c Val: 2 Type: min
Node: a Val: 7 Type: max
Val = 7

| ?-

Several modifications of this procedure are possible. The most modest one is based on the symmetric nature of the min and max operations; it simply maximizes the values at each node but inverts values at *min*-nodes. This so-called **negamax** procedure is the subject of Exercise 2.6. This modification affects neither the input-output relation nor the efficiency of the program.

A second modification does affect the input form. The above program accepts the entire game tree as input. However, in all interesting applications the game tree is very large and its exhaustive creation prior to the search is not feasible. An alternative is for the program itself to create as much of the game tree as computational resources allow, and to search that portion of the tree. This alternative is the subject of Exercise 2.7.

A third modification, which is aimed at speeding up the execution of the minimax search, is discussed in the next section.

2.8.2 α-β search

The minimax search visits all nodes of the game tree. This exhaustiveness is often unnecessary, and certain nodes may safely be ignored. Specifically, certain subtrees may be pruned without affecting the result. Consider again the tree in Figure 2.12. As soon as the algorithm discovers that the value of node j is 9, it may safely ignore nodes k and l, for the following reason. Since node b is a *min*-node, its value will be the least between 7 (the value of node d) and the value of node e. Since node e is a *max*-node, its value will be at least that of node j, namely 9. Therefore the value of node b will be 7, regardless of the values of nodes k and l. In a similar fashion it can be shown that the values of nodes g, o, p, q and r need not be computed. Figure 2.13 illustrates the pruned search tree.

This pruning is achieved by the α-β search algorithm. The name 'α-β' refers to numbers that are assigned to each node during the search. These numbers on the one hand affect the search by helping to prune certain subtrees, and on the other hand are themselves updated as a result of the search. More specifically, when the values of the successor nodes of some node N are computed sequentially, the precise role of α and β in determining the value V of N is as follows.

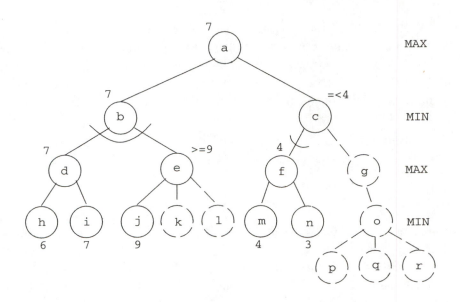

Figure 2.13: Pruning a game tree

min-nodes:

> As soon as one successor's value is less than α all remaining successors are ignored, and the value V of the *min*-node is set to α;
>
> until then, for each successor, β is set to min(β, W), where W is this successor's value, and if this is the last successor, the value V of the *min*-node is set to the minimum among the successors' values.

max-nodes:

> As soon as one successor's value is greater than β all remaining successors are ignored, and the value V of the *max*-node is set to β;
>
> until then, for each successor, α is set to max(α, W), where W is this successor's value, and if this is the last successor, the value V of the *max*-node is set to be the maximum among the successors' values.

Thus at *min*-nodes the search is affected by α and affects β, and at *max*-nodes the search is affected by β and affects α.

The following Prolog program is a modification of the minimax program embodying these principles. Arguments have been added for α and β; both the update and the pruning are indicated in comments.

```
% _____
% Alpha-Beta game-tree evaluation
% _____

alpha_beta( Tree, Value ) :-
  ab_minimax( Tree, lowlimit, highlimit, Value ).


ab_minimax( leaf( Label ), _, _, Value ) :-
  leaf_value( Label, Value ).                    % leaf value determined
ab_minimax( max( L, Children ), Alpha, Beta, Value ) :-
  ab_max_children( Children, Alpha, Beta, lowlimit, Value ).
ab_minimax( min( L, Children ), Alpha, Beta, Value ) :-
  ab_min_children( Children, Alpha, Beta, highlimit, Value ).


ab_max_children( [ ], _, _, Max, Max ).
ab_max_children( [ Child | Children ], Alpha, Beta, Max0, Max ) :-
  ab_minimax( Child, Alpha, Beta, Value ),
  ( greater( Value, Beta ) -> Max = Beta      % Beta pruning
  ; ab_max( Value, Alpha, Alpha0 ),           % Alpha update
    ab_max( Value, Max0, Max1 ),
    ab_max_children( Children, Alpha0, Beta, Max1, Max ) ).


ab_min_children( [ ], _, _, Min, Min ).
ab_min_children( [ Child | Children ], Alpha, Beta, Min0, Min ) :-
  ab_minimax( Child, Alpha, Beta, Value ),
  ( greater( Alpha, Value ) -> Min = Alpha    % Alpha pruning
  ; ab_min( Value, Beta, Beta0 ),             % Beta update
    ab_min( Value, Min0, Min1 ),
    ab_min_children( Children, Alpha, Beta0, Min1, Min ) ).
```

The following is a sample run of the program on the game tree in Figure 2.12. Again, printing commands were added to show the order in which node values were determined, the values themselves, the updates of α and β, and the pruning.[3]

---

[3]Printing commands need to be added at seven points in the program: The three points

| ?- alpha_beta(max(a, [min(b, [max(d, [leaf(h), leaf(i)]),
                               max(e, [leaf(j), leaf(k), leaf(l)])]),
                       min(c, [max(f, [leaf(m), leaf(n)]),
                               max(g, [min(o, [leaf(p), leaf(q), leaf(r)])])])]),
          Val).

Node: h Val: 6 Type: leaf
Alpha of node d changed from lowlimit to 6
Node: i Val: 7 Type: leaf
Node: d Val: 7 Type: max
Beta of node b changed from highlimit to 7
Node: j Val: 9 Type: leaf
Beta pruning; trees pruned: k, l
Node: b Val: 7 Type: min
Alpha of node a changed from lowlimit to 7
Node: m Val: 4 Type: leaf
Node: n Val: 3 Type: leaf
Node: f Val: 4 Type: max
Alpha pruning; trees pruned: [g,[o,p,q,r]]
Node: a Val: 7 Type: max
Val = 7

| ?-

2.9   Further reading

Introductions to graph algorithms in general can be found in many books; two recommended sources are Cormen et al.'s [8] and Even's [20] books. A detailed discussion of heuristic search in AI appears in Pearl's [62]; Korf provides a review of more recent developments in [37].

---

at which a node value is determined (one each for *max-*, *min-* and leaf nodes), the point at which the α-value of a node is updated, the point at which α pruning occurs, and the other two points at which β update and pruning take place. It is left to the reader to reconstruct the exact program.

2.10   Exercises

Exercise 2.1 The depth-first search implementation in Section 2.4 is of higher complexity than required; the complexity of the abstract algorithm is linear in both time and space.

(a) Modify the implementation so that the time complexity is reduced to $O(m \log n)$, where m is the number of arcs in the graph and n is the number of nodes in it. *Hint:* Include in CLOSED nodes also the nodes appearing in the OPEN list, and maintain CLOSED as a balanced-tree or a heap, rather than as a simple list.

(b) Further modify the implementation so that the space complexity is $O(m + n)$, rather than $O(n^2)$ as in the given implementation. *Hint:* Do not maintain all paths explicitly, but maintain enough information to reconstruct the path when a goal node is reached.

Exercise 2.2 Write programs to solve the 8-puzzle, described at the beginning of the chapter, using

(a) Depth-first search

(b) Breadth-first search

(c) Best-first search, using as a heuristic function

(i) The number of misplaced tiles
(ii) The sum of Manhattan distances from each tile to its final destination (the Manhattan distance is the length of the shortest path to the target, going only along rows or columns).

Compare the number of nodes generated in each implementation, and the total runtime in each case.

Exercise 2.3 The advantage of depth-first search is its focused nature, and low space complexity. The advantage of breadth-first search is its completeness: It will not miss a solution, even if the graph is infinite. *Iterative deepening* is a procedure that attempts to benefit from both worlds. It performs depth-first search to a bounded depth in the graph, and if that fails it increases the depth bound and repeats (the increment in bound can be 1 or more). Implement iterative deepening.

Exercise 2.4 It was mentioned in the text that the given implementation of the general version of the best-first search procedure, best_first_search / 4, can be greatly optimized. Optimize the program the best you can. *Hint*: As in Exercise 2.1, the CLOSED nodes may be maintained other than as a simple list. Also, the current implementation performs some redundant scanning. Is there an advantage, in the general case of best-first search, to keeping a completely sorted OPEN list?

Exercise 2.5 Implementations of both the minimax and α-β algorithms given in the text return only the value of the root. Modify them so that they return also the optimal strategy, that is, the pruned tree in which each *max*-node has only one successor.

Exercise 2.6 The minimax program alternates between maximizing and minimizing values at successive layers. It is possible to maximize values in *all* layers, and simply complement the numbers of *min*-nodes (that is, replace n by $-n$); this is called *negamax* search. The resulting program is more compact, though not more efficient. Implement negamax.

Exercise 2.7 Implementations of both the minimax and α-β algorithms given in the text assume that the tree can be searched exhaustively. This is an unrealistic assumption in all but the most trivial applications. Rewrite the programs so that they dynamically decide for each node whether to expand it, or instead to apply a given heuristic function to it and not expand the search further along that path. Examples of criteria for not expanding a node: (a) it is deeper than some given threshold, (b) its heuristic value is extremely high or low.

Exercise 2.8 The implementation of α-β search given in the text scans the tree from left to right. Other search orders are possible, sometimes yielding greater pruning. Write a heuristic version of the program that accepts as input, and uses, heuristic information about search order most likely to yield much pruning.

Chapter 3

Backward-Chaining Methods

Recall that a Prolog program and a query induce an *and-or* computation tree, the *or* nodes corresponding to different clauses and the *and* nodes to conjunctive goals in the body of a clause. The Prolog interpreter searches this tree from the root goal back to the leaf premises. Such search from goals back to premises is called *backward chaining*. Backward chaining is a basic AI problem-solving technique, and it is the topic of this chapter. Specifically, we will explore the Prolog implementation of backward chaining on *and-or* trees. Since Prolog itself employs backward chaining, we will end up writing *meta-interpreters*, or interpreters for Prolog programs written in Prolog. (The process of writing meta-interpreters is called meta-programming.)

This may seem at first unmotivated; if one already has an interpreter, why bother writing a meta-interpreter? Meta-interpreters typically add a layer of indirection and a corresponding slowdown in execution (although, as we shall see, in the case of Prolog the overhead is minimal), which is hardly a reason for introducing them. The answer is that once we explicate the mechanism of the interpreter, we can easily modify it to suit our needs. Meta-interpreters can search the *and-or* tree in different orders from the standard Prolog interpreter. In addition, they may augment the search with other features, resembling those commonly included in *expert systems*. It turns out that all this can be achieved very concisely in Prolog. Indeed, we will see that Prolog meta-interpreters are a powerful programming paradigm that can embody important AI techniques.

51

Several different meta-interpreters are presented in this chapter. The next section introduces a basic meta-interpreter emulating the standard left-to-right depth-first search in 'pure' Prolog. In the second section we augment the meta-interpreter to handle negation, all-solutions operations, and 'cut' (or !). In the third section we present a modest modification of the depth-first meta-interpreter, implementing a right-to-left search. In the fourth section we augment the interpreter with two features commonly included in expert-system shells: an 'explanation' facility and a 'query' mechanism. In the fifth section we show how a slight modification of the meta-interpreter results in *partial evaluation,* another important technique. The sixth and seventh sections are of a slightly different flavor; they replace the depth-first strategy by breadth-first and best-first ones, respectively.

3.1   The basic meta-interpreter

In this section, a Prolog program is developed that simulates the standard Prolog interpreter in Prolog. Of course, one such program is rather easy to write:

meta_trivial(A) :- A.

It is also a very unilluminating meta-interpreter. As we said, we write meta-interpreters in order to be able to modify them. Therefore our program will be useful only if it reflects in more detail the operations of the Prolog interpreter.

Recall that a Prolog program consists of clauses, and each clause consists of a head and a body. The body is either a single goal or a conjunction of goals. In the case of facts, the body is the goal true. This structure of programs motivates the structure of the standard meta-interpreter, which contains three main components:

- The first one executes a conjunction of goals in a left-to-right order.

- The second identifies built-in system predicates and executes them.

- The third finds clauses whose heads match the goal, again in a left-to-right order, and executes the body.

We start with a meta-interpreter for 'pure' Prolog, i.e., Prolog without 'cut' or other extended language features. Actually, we will allow most built-in predicates, but not all. Specifically, we disallow all-solutions operations, negation, disjunction (;) or 'cut' (!). The following program assumes the predicate system / 1, which is to succeed exactly when its argument is one of the built-in predicates mentioned in Chapter 1.[1] The following is a correct meta-interpreter, when applied to programs that do not contain all-solutions operators (bagof, etc.), 'cut' (!), the disjunction operator (;), or not.[2]

```
meta_basic( ( A, B ) ) :- !, meta_basic( A ), meta_basic( B ).
meta_basic( A ) :- system( A ), !, A.
meta_basic( A ) :- clause( A, B ), meta_basic( B ).
```

3.2 A full standard meta-interpreter

We will explore the above meta-interpreter further in the following sections, but first let us consider its extension to handle other Prolog features. This is really a Prolog issue rather than an AI technique, so this section is something of a digression, though hopefully an interesting one.

The addition of all-solutions operations is easy (the following implementation does not handle existentially quantified variables; this easy addition is left to the reader):

```
% _____
% standard meta-interpreter for 'pure' Prolog
% _____
meta_basic( ( A, B ) ) :- !, meta_basic( A ), meta_basic( B ).
meta_basic( bagof( H, Goal, Sol ) ) :- !, bagof( H, meta_basic( Goal ), Sol ).
meta_basic( setof( H, Goal, Sol ) ) :- !, setof( H, meta_basic( Goal ), Sol ).
meta_basic( findall( H, Goal, Sol ) ) :- !, findall( H, meta_basic( Goal ), Sol ).
meta_basic( A ) :- system( A ), !, A.
meta_basic( A ) :- clause( A, B ), meta_basic( B ).
```

---

[1]This can be implemented by a collection of facts: **system(true)**, **system(write(_))**, etc. Alternatively, certain built-in commands can be used in particular systems. For example, in Quintus Prolog the built-in **predicate_property** / 2 may be used.

[2]The second ! in the given program is necessary since a number of Prologs produce an error when **clause** / 2 is applied to a built-in predicate; the first ! is not strictly necessary.

Meta-interpreters are called *meta-circular* when they can be applied to themselves. Note that the basic meta-interpreter is not meta-circular, since it contains !, but cannot be applied to programs with !. We will now extend the meta-interpreter to handle ! (and thus derived operators such as ->, or if-then), but doing this will require a little subtlety. A naive implementation would use a clause such as the following:

meta(!) :- !.

It is important to see why this clause does not simulate ! correctly. Consider for example the following program for computing the absolute value of a number:

abs(N, M) :- N < 0, !, M is −N.
abs(N, N).

The query abs(−3, −3) will fail because of the commitment to the first clause due to the 'cut.' However, the naive 'cut' implementation will succeed on the goal meta(abs(−3, −3)). The reason for this is that the call meta(abs(−3, −3)) will invoke the conjunction meta(−3 < 0), meta(!), meta(−3 is −(−3)), and, although this conjunction will fail, backtracking will not be truncated by meta(!). Hence, the second clause for abs / 1 will be found, and (since the body of that clause is true) the goal will succeed.

The problem in the naive implementation is that the 'cut' is placed at the wrong level. One way to handle 'cut' is by adding another argument to meta. We call the new binary predicate meta_cut. The following program executes in a regular fashion, except that it does not prevent backtracking through 'cut'. It is the job of the additional argument to record the fact that illegal backtracking occurred; for legal computations this argument remains uninstantiated, but when backtracking through 'cut' it is instantiated to the atom bktrk.

```
% _____
% A meta-interpreter handling !
% _____
meta( A ) :- meta_cut( A, R ), ( R == bktrk, !, fail ; true ).

meta_cut( !, R ) :- !, ( true; R = bktrk ). % 'cut'
meta_cut( ( A ; B ), R ) :- !, ( meta_cut( A, R ) ; meta_cut( B, R ) ). % disjunction
meta_cut( ( A, B ), R ) :- !,
    meta_cut( A, R ), ( R == bktrk, ! ; meta_cut( B, R ) ). % conjunction
meta_cut( A, _ ) :- system( A ), !, A. % built-in
meta_cut( A, _ ) :-
    clause( A, B ), meta_cut( B, R ), ( R == bktrk, !, fail ; true ). % User defined
```

The following is a sample run of the above meta-circular interpreter on two queries. The database contains the above definition of abs / 2, as well as the facts system(true), system(fail), system(_ < _), system(_ is _), system(clause(_,_)), system(call(_)), system(_ == _) and system(_ = _).[3]

```
| ?- meta(abs(-3,L)).
L = 3 ;
no
| ?- meta(meta(meta(abs(-3,L)))).
L = 3 ;
no
| ?-
```

3.3   A modified depth-first meta-interpreter

So far we have merely reproduced the behavior of the Prolog interpreter in the meta-interpreter. We now begin to reap the fruits of our efforts, by modifying the design of the interpreter. From now on we will consider modifications of the basic meta-interpreter of Section 3.1 and will not consider special Prolog features such as all-solutions operations or !. We start with

---

[3]In addition, in Prologs that distinguish between dynamic and static predicates, the predicates abs / 2, meta / 1, meta_cut / 2 and system / 1 must be declared dynamic.

a modified interpreter that is little more than an exercise, in order to illustrate the ease of designing new meta-interpreters. In this first modified meta-interpreter we simply replace the left-to-right search of the *and* nodes by a right-to-left order, retaining the left-to-right search of the *or* nodes (where we still exclude the ';' operator, but refer to clause-level *or*).

```
% _____
% A right-to-left meta-interpreter
% _____
meta_rev( ( A, B ) ) :- !, meta_rev( B ), meta_rev( A ).
meta_rev( A ) :- system( A ), !, A.
meta_rev( A ) :- clause( A, B ), meta_rev( B ).
```

Note that this meta-interpreter is obtained from the standard one by simply permuting the two conjuncts in the body of the first clause. Now, although this interpreter is not particularly important, it does have an interesting property. Consider any sorting program, say the following one implementing the insertion sort algorithm (this one is taken from [77]):

```
isort( [ X | Xs ], Ys ) :- isort( Xs, Zs ), insert( X, Zs, Ys ).
isort( [ ], [ ] ).
insert( X, [ ], [ X ] ).
insert( X, [Y | Ys], [ Y | Zs ] ) :- X > Y, insert( X, Ys, Zs ).
insert( X, [ Y | Ys ], [X, Y | Ys ] ) :- X =< Y.
```

What happens to the goal isort(L, [1, 2, 3])? The declarative reading of Prolog suggests that the L will be bound successively to all permutations of [1, 2, 3]. In fact the program will enter into an infinite loop. This behavior is not particular to this implementation or to the insertion sort algorithm; similar horrors will occur with other sorting algorithms. The modified meta-interpreter, however, will behave rather nicely; here is a sample run (after system / 1 has been properly defined):

```
| ?- meta_rev(isort(L,[1,2,3])).
L = [3,2,1] ;
L = [3,1,2] ;
L = [2,3,1] ;
L = [2,1,3] ;
L = [1,3,2] ;
```

L = [1,2,3] ;
no
| ?-

Thus, at least in some cases, the modified meta-interpreter reverses the input-output direction of programs. Exercises 3.1 and 3.2 explore this meta-interpreter a little further.

3.4   Toward an expert-system shell

Since we have explored two depth-first meta-interpreters, it would be natural to explore next breadth- and best-first interpreters. We will indeed consider these later in the chapter, but first let us consider further modifications of the depth-first meta-interpreter. The additions we consider in this chapter are largely inspired by features found in *expert-system shells,* those programs that provide a framework in which to encode and manipulate rich knowledge about particular domains. We will consider two features common in such shells: explanations by the system, and queries to the user by the system. It should be emphasized, however, that these are austere programs as compared to modern expert-system shells, which contain many additional features.

3.4.1   An explanatory meta-interpreter

Often it is useful to get not only an answer to a query, but also an explanation as to why the answer is correct. This explanation can be useful for a number of purposes. For example, if we are unhappy with the answer, the explanation will help locate the problematic premise (or the bug in the query-answering program). In fact, in Chapter 10 we will discuss a learning technique called *explanation-based learning* that follows from this idea. Even if the answer is correct, we may have little experience with the program and hence little confidence in its answers (this is a well-known obstacle in the deployment of expert systems); by tracing the reasoning of the program we can develop this confidence.

The explanation, of course, depends on the reasoning mechanism. In this section we add an explanation facility to the standard Prolog interpreter. An explanation will consist of the proof tree, represented in the embedded-list format. Consider, for example, the following program:

Figure 3.1: Proof trees

wellpaid(X) :- department(X,Y), vital(Y).
department(john,research).
vital(research).

wellpaid(X) :- senior(X).
senior(X) :- manager(X).
manager(mary).

The proof trees corresponding to the queries **wellpaid(john)** and
wellpaid(mary) are given in Figure 3.1. If we adopt the list-structure representation of trees, the augmented meta-interpreter is as follows.

```
% _____
% An explanatory meta-interpreter
% _____

meta_exp( ( A, B ), Proof ) :- !,
    meta_exp( A, AProof ), meta_exp( B, BProof ),
    append_proofs( AProof, BProof, Proof ).
meta_exp( A, A ) :- clause( A, B ), system( B ), B.
meta_exp(A,tree(A,Proof)) :-
    clause(A,B), meta_exp(B,BProof),
    attach_proof(BProof,Proof).
```

```
append_proofs( AProof, [BProof | More], Proof ) :- !, Proof = [AProof, BProof | More].
append_proofs( AProof, BProof, [AProof, BProof] ).
attach_proof( [BProof | More], Proof ) :- !, Proof = [BProof | More].
attach_proof( BProof, [BProof] ).
```

The meta-interpreter will handle the queries about John and Mary thus:

```
| ?- meta_exp(wellpaid(john),Exp).
Exp = tree(wellpaid(john),[department(john,research), vital(research)])
| ?- meta_exp(wellpaid(mary),Exp).
Exp = tree(wellpaid(mary),[tree(senior(mary),[manager(mary)])])
| ?-
```

3.4.2 An interpreter with a query mechanism

We can often benefit from writing programs before we have either a complete algorithm or the full data needed to solve our problem. Our partial program will nonetheless be useful, provided the user can fill in the gaps by interactively providing the program with the missing information. Consider the example from the previous section, which identified well-paid individuals. Suppose the user is the company's marketing analyst, who has much more information about people's salaries, their positions, and other matters that have not yet been encoded in the form of Prolog facts and rules. However, the marketing analyst wishes to use the program, even before the overworked company programmer has had a chance to rewrite the program. Recognizing the incomplete stage of the program, the analyst is willing to aid the program by supplying it with the information it lacks. How might we modify the interpreter to allow the user to participate in the problem solving?

One way is simply to query the user, when all else fails. The following program implements this principle, albeit not in a particularly user-friendly fashion (but see Exercise 3.3). The user is queried about every failing goal, except for ground goals that are facts in the database; it is assumed that those are to succeed only once. (Recall that writel / 1, which appears in the following program and which was defined in Chapter 1, accepts a list and writes all the elements in it.)

```
%
% A querying meta-interpreter
%
meta_query( ( A, B ) ) :- !, meta_query( A ), meta_query( B ).
meta_query( A ) :- system( A ), !, A.
meta_query( A ) :- clause( A, B ), meta_query( B ).
meta_query( A ) :-
   not( clause( A, _ ) ), ground( A ),
   nl, writel( [ 'Should the goal ', A, ' succeed? ']),
   read( yes ).
meta_query( A ) :-
   not( ground( A ) ),
   ( nl, writel( [ 'Should the goal ', A, ' succeed ? ' ] ),
    ( read( yes ) -> true ; !, fail ),
    nl, writel( [ 'Which instantiation of ', A, ' should succeed? ' ] ),
    read( A )
    ;
    repeat,
    nl,writel( [ 'Should the goal ', A, ' succeed again? ' ]),
    ( read( yes ) ; !, fail ),
    nl, writel( [ 'Which other instantiation of ', A, ' should succeed? ' ] ),
    read( A ) ).
```

The following is a sample run of the meta-interpreter, assuming the well-paid / 1 program defined earlier.

```
| ?- meta_query(wellpaid(X)).
X = john ;
Should the goal department(_3077,_3215) succeed ? no.
X = mary ;
Should the goal manager(_3077) succeed ? yes.
Which instantiation of manager(_3077) should succeed? manager(joe).
X = joe ;
Should the goal manager(_3077) succeed again? no.
Should the goal senior(_3077) succeed ? yes.
Which instantiation of senior(_3077) should succeed? senior(nancy).
X = nancy ;
Should the goal senior(_3077) succeed again? no.
Should the goal wellpaid(_3077) succeed ? yes.
Which instantiation of wellpaid(_3077) should succeed? wellpaid(george).
```

X = george ;
Should the goal wellpaid(_3077) succeed again? no.
no
| ?-

3.5   Partial evaluation

In the previous section we discussed how to use a partially developed program by allowing the user to supply the missing information interactively. We will now discuss a related technique, called *partial evaluation.* As is the material in section 3.2, the material here is usually considered more closely related to Prolog and programming techniques in general than to AI. We discuss it here for two reasons: It is too important a technique to go without mention, and it is in fact related to techniques in machine learning that are discussed later in the book.

The idea behind partial evaluation is to evaluate the goal to the extent possible, and then to output those subgoals for which there is not yet sufficient information to proceed. Partial evaluation therefore functions as a transformer of programs: Given a goal and a general program, it produces a specialized version of the general program that is appropriate to the particular goal. The intention is that when eventually the program is subsequently run on the remaining data, the specialized program will behave more efficiently.

For which goals does the partial evaluator assume that there exists sufficient information? In general this is a difficult question, but here we adopt a simplified view, common in the Prolog community. In this view a goal is evaluated if either (a) it is a system goal with no side effects, whose arguments are sufficiently instantiated (such as X is 3+2), or (b) there is at least one user-defined clause whose head unifies with the goal. The philosophy behind this convention allows the user to completely omit the definition of some predicates, but if any clause for a predicate exists then it is assumed that the predicate is completely defined.

The following program performs partial evaluation, but is restricted to input programs whose computation trees are finite; see Exercise 3.6 for extensions.

```
% _____
% A simple partial evaluator
% _____

p_eval( X ) :- doall( ( premises( X, [ X ], P ),
                        listtoand( P, AP ),
                        write( ( X :- AP ) ), write( '.' ), nl ) ).
% Recall that doall / 1 is defined in Chapter 1.


% The meaning of arguments to premise / 3:
% Current input goals (+), Previously computed output goals (+),
% New output goals (−)
premises( ( X, Y ), Old, P ) :- !,
   premises( X, Old, P1 ), append( P1, Old, New ),
   premises( Y, New, P2 ), append( P1, P2, P ).
premises( X, _, P ) :-
   system( X ), !,
   ( executable( X ) -> call( X ), P = [ ]
                   ;    P = [ X ] ).
premises( X, Z, P ) :- clause( X, Y ), premises( Y, Z, P ).
premises( X, Z, [ X ] ) :- not(clause( X, _ )), not( member( X, Z ) ).
premises( X, Z, [ ] ) :- not(clause( X, _ )), member( X, Z ).
% listtoand / 2 converts regular lists to 'and' lists; see Chapter 1.
```

It remains to determine the system goals that are executable at the time of partial evaluation. We will define only the two that are needed in the following example:

```
executable(_ is B) :- ground(B).
executable(A > B) :- ground(A > B).
```

We now illustrate the operation of the partial evaluator through an example. Consider the following program, meant to determine whether a given employee's performance is satisfactory:

```
satisfactory(X) :- average_productivity(M), L is M-2, productivity(X, N), N>L.
satisfactory(X) :- client_rating(X,R), good_rating(R).
satisfactory(X) :- monthly_evaluation(X, satisfactory).
```

Suppose that in addition we have the following information about average productivity, about Joe and Mary's client ratings, and about the rating

the company considers good, but not about Bill's client rating, nor about
the productivity or monthly evaluation of any employee:

```
average_productivity(40).
client_rating(joe,10).
client_rating(mary,3).
good_rating(R) :- R>5.
```

The following is a sample run of the partial evaluator on three different goals:

```
| ?- p_eval(satisfactory(bill)).
satisfactory(bill):-true,productivity(bill,_3336),_3336>38.
satisfactory(bill):-client_rating(bill,_3316),_3316>5.
satisfactory(bill):-monthly_evaluation(bill,satisfactory).

yes
| ?- p_eval(satisfactory(joe)).
satisfactory(joe):-true,productivity(joe,_3318),_3318>38.
satisfactory(joe):-true.
satisfactory(joe):-monthly_evaluation(joe,satisfactory).

yes
| ?- p_eval(satisfactory(mary)).
satisfactory(mary):-true,productivity(mary,_3336),_3336>38.
satisfactory(mary):-monthly_evaluation(mary,satisfactory).

yes
| ?-
```

We have already mentioned that this is a rather limited partial evaluator.
Although we pursue some extensions in Exercise 3.6, the reader is alerted
to the fact that partial evaluation is a complex topic. References for further
reading appear at the end of the chapter.

3.6   A breadth-first meta-interpreter

All the meta-interpreters we have discussed so far have been modifications of the basic depth-first meta-interpreter. It is possible, of course, to search the computation tree in other orders. In this section we explore a breadth-first version. The default depth-first strategy of Prolog can lead a program into an infinite loop even when a solution exists. The breadth-first strategy is guaranteed to find a solution if one exists. This method is rather extreme as it requires large amounts of time and space, but it can be applied in circumscribed cases.

General breadth-first search was discussed in the Chapter 2. Its implementation for the *and-or* computation tree will in one sense be easier, since the tree structure ensures that each node has a unique path leading to it.[4] However, the presence of variables will require maintenance of several copies of goals, each copy with differently named variables. This will make the program rather subtle.

Consider, for example, the following program:

        a(1) :- b.
        a(2) :- c.
        b :- b, d.
        c.

With the standard interpreter, the goal a(X) will lead to an infinite loop, but the breadth-first meta-interpreter will behave differently. It will start with a single-element queue [[a(X)]]. This element will then be extracted and replaced by the body of the two matching clauses, resulting in the following queue:

        [[b], [c]].

During the next step b will be expanded by the corresponding clause, leading to the following queue:

        [[c], [b,d]].

The queue will then continue to evolve as follows:

        [[b,d], [true]].
        [[true], [b,b,d]].

---

[4] Just as in the case of the standard Prolog interpreter, there is no caching of previous goals; all goals are treated as new nodes to be expanded, thus leading to a tree structure.

> [[b,b,d], [ ]].
> [[ ], [b,b,b,d]].

At this point the empty list will be taken off the queue, and the program will terminate successfully. But how will it know to return the answer X = 2? For this purpose the queue will consist not of simple conjunctions, but will instead keep with each conjunction a copy of the original goal, with the variables appropriately instantiated. A queue element will therefore be of the form conj(Conj, InstanceOfGoal), where Conj is the list of conjuncts still to be proved and InstanceOfGoal is a (possibly partially instantiated) copy of the original goal.

The findall / 3 predicate is used to create the expansion of the first element of the queue. If the first element of the queue is [A|B], then

```
findall( conj( BB, OrigGoal ),
      ( clause( A, Body ),
        mixed_append( Body, B, BB ) ),
      L )
```

creates the expansions to be put at the end of the queue (mixed_append / 3 is defined in Chapter 1 to accept one 'and' list and one regular list, and to return their concatenation as a regular list). It is important to note a side effect of the findall / 3 predicate: A different copy of free variables is created for each expansion. When a solution is found, i.e., when the list of conjuncts is empty, the original goal is unified with its copy associated with the empty conjunct list (this happens in the first b / 2 clause of the following program). Figure 3.2 shows the evolution of the queue of the breadth-first meta-interpreter for the query a(X), given the toy program above.

The following program performs breadth-first search at *or*-nodes, but retains the depth-first search at *and*-nodes; see also Exercise 3.9. For the sake of clarity, the following program does not use difference lists; see Exercise 3.7 for such an optimization.

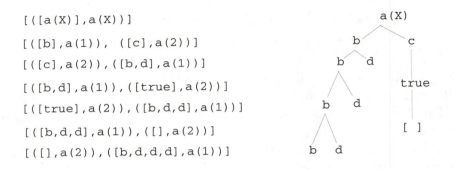

```
[([a(X)],a(X))]

[([b],a(1)), ([c],a(2))]

[([c],a(2)),([b,d],a(1))]

[([b,d],a(1)),([true],a(2))]

[([true],a(2)),([b,d,d],a(1))]

[([b,d,d],a(1)),([],a(2))]

[([],a(2)),([b,d,d,d],a(1))]
```

Figure 3.2: Computation tree and breadth-first queue evolution

```
% _____
% A breadth-first meta-interpreter
% _____


meta_bf( Goal ) :- b( [ conj( [ Goal ], Goal ) ], Goal ).


b( [ conj( [ ], InstanceOfGoal ) | _ ], InstanceOfGoal ).
b( [ conj( [ ], _ ) | S ], Goal ) :- b( S, Goal ).
b( [ conj( [ A | B ], OrigGoal ) | S ], Goal ) :-
    system( A ), A, !,
    append( S, [ conj( B, OrigGoal ) ], Newlist ),
    b( Newlist, Goal ).
b( [ conj( [ A | _ ], _ ) | S ], Goal ) :-
    system( A ), !,
    b( S, Goal ).
b( [ conj( [ A | B ], OrigGoal ) | S ], Goal ) :-
    findall( conj( BB, OrigGoal ),
            ( clause( A, Body ),
              mixed_append( Body, B, BB ) ),
          L ),
    append( S, L, Newlist ),
    b( Newlist, Goal ).


% mixed_append / 3 appends an 'and' list and a regular one; see Chapter 1.
```

3.7   A best-first meta-interpreter

We have so far explored 'blind' backward-chaining meta-interpreters – several employing a depth-first strategy, and one employing a breadth-first one. As with ordinary graphs, it is possible to employ heuristics to guide the search of the *and-or* computation tree; we discuss heuristic backward chaining in this section.

The transition from a breadth-first to a best-first meta-interpreter will resemble that transition in the case of ordinary graphs: We will replace the queue used in breadth-first search by a heuristic function that will select the most promising candidate for exploration. Note that candidates for exploration will now be conjunctions of goals (with singleton goals as special cases). In fact, since we have two kinds of nodes, *and* nodes and *or* nodes, we will use two heuristic functions: The *and* heuristic function will decide the order in which conjuncts are solved, and the *or* heuristic function will select a conjunction most likely to yield a solution. It might be tempting to use the same function for both, but they are in fact different functions. Among other distinctions, the promise of a conjunction is independent of alternative conjunctions, but the utility of selecting a particular conjunct to be solved next might well depend on the other conjuncts. Thus the *or* function will take as input the single conjunction whose value is being determined, while the *and* function will take as input all the conjuncts and return one of them.

Some examples will help clarify the roles of the two heuristic functions. The *and* heuristic function might be some combination of the following:

- Prefer a system goal to a user-defined one, if the arguments to the system goal are sufficiently instantiated (for example, an arithmetic evaluation goal (using the is operator) with the input argument completely instantiated).

- Select a conjunct with fewest solutions.

- Select the conjunct each of whose solutions leaves the least total number of solutions to the other conjuncts.

(The last two heuristics of course require additional information, which is often available.)

The *or* function might be one of the following:

- Select a shortest conjunction (one with the least number of conjuncts)

- Select the most recent conjunction derived (simulating depth-first)

- Select the least recent conjunction derived (simulating breadth-first)

It should be emphasized that the above are quite simplistic rules. It is in general quite difficult to determine the optimal search order. Such questions have generated much work within AI and the theorem-proving community. In the following implementation we simply assume these two functions as input to the meta-interpreter.

```
meta_best( Goal, AndHf, OrHf ) :-
    bs( [ 0 - conj( [ Goal ], Goal ) ], Goal, AndHf, OrHf ).


bs( [ _ - conj( [ ], InstanceOfGoal ) | _ ], InstanceOfGoal, _, _ ).
bs( [ _ - conj( [ ], _ ) | S ], Goal, AndHf, OrHf ) :-
    % Remove the last found goal, continue search
    move_smallest_to_top( S, Newlist ),
    bs( Newlist, Goal, AndHf, OrHf ).
bs( [ _ - conj( Conj, OrigGoal ) | S ], Goal, AndHf, OrHf ) :-
    call( AndHf, Conj, A ),
    remove( A, Conj, ConjRest ), !,
    expand_or_execute( A, ConjRest, OrigGoal, S, Goal, AndHf, OrHf ).


expand_or_execute( A, ConjRest, OrigGoal, S, Goal, AndHf, OrHf ) :-
    system( A ),
    A, !,
    call( OrHf, ConjRest, Val ),
    move_smallest_to_top( [ Val - conj( ConjRest, OrigGoal ) | S ], NewList ),
    bs( NewList, Goal, AndHf, OrHf ).
expand_or_execute( A, _, _, S, Goal, AndHf, OrHf) :-
    % if failed in executing system predicate A:
    system( A ), !,
    move_smallest_to_top( S, NewList ),
    bs( NewList, Goal, AndHf, OrHf ).
```

```
expand_or_execute( A, ConjRest, OrigGoal, S, Goal, AndHf, OrHf ) :-
   findall( Val - conj( NewConj, OrigGoal ),
           ( clause( A, Body ),
             mixed_append( Body, ConjRest, NewConj ),
             call( OrHf, NewConj, Val ) ),
           L ),
   append( L, S, TmpList ),
   move_smallest_to_top( TmpList, Newlist ),
   bs( Newlist, Goal, AndHf, OrHf ).

move_smallest_to_top( [ ], [ ] ).
move_smallest_to_top( [ Val - X | L ], [ S | R ] ) :-
   find_smallest( L, Val - X, S, R ).

find_smallest( [ ], T, T, [ ] ).
find_smallest( [ Val1 - X | L ], Val - T, S, [ Val - T | R ] ) :-
   Val1 < Val, !, find_smallest( L, Val1 - X, S, R ).
find_smallest( [ Val1 - X | L ], Val - T, S, [ Val1 - X | R ] ) :-
   find_smallest( L, Val - T, S, R ).
```

% call / 3, mixed_append / 3, *and* remove / 3 *appear in Chapter 1's library.*

3.8   Further reading

Initial references to the control of backward chaining include Kowalski's seminal [38], Wos et al.'s [83], and Genesereth and Nilsson's [26]. Prolog meta-interpreters are discussed in many Prolog textbooks, including Sterling and Shapiro's [77]. Most texts develop meta-interpreters in a way that follows the Prolog syntax. A more general approach is provided by O'Keefe in [61]. The literature on partial evaluation of logic programs is also substantial; initial pointers include [80, 78, 55].

3.9   Exercises

Exercise 3.1 Section 3.3 discussed a simple modification of the basic Prolog meta-interpreter, one which scans *and* nodes (that is, conjunctions) from right to left. That interpreter still scans *or* nodes (that is, clauses) from left to right (that is, from the first matching clause in the database to the last). Modify the interpreter further so that the *or* nodes too are scanned right to left.

Exercise 3.2 As demonstrated in Section 3.3, the modified meta-interpreter presented there can in some cases reverse the input-output direction of programs. However, it is certainly not foolproof. Consider the predicate abs / 2 to compute the absolute value of a number, defined in Section 3.2. Neither the standard Prolog interpreter nor the modified meta-interpreter will behave well on the query abs(X,3). Modify the meta-interpreter to handle such queries. *Hint*: Write a reversible version of the built-in is / 2 predicate.

Exercise 3.3 Section 3.4 presented two meta-interpreters, one adding an explanation facility and the second a querying mechanism. Your task here is to make them both more user friendly.

(a) Augment the explanatory meta-interpreter to write out explanations in the form

    a BECAUSE b AND c AND d
        b BECAUSE e
            e GIVEN
        c GIVEN
        d GIVEN

rather than merely return the value in tree notation.

(b) Modify the user interface in the querying meta-interpreter. Add at least the following two features: (i) Inform the user of legal input form and check that the input is indeed legal, and (ii) Rather than require that the user type the entire instance of the goal that is to succeed, prompt the user explicitly for the value of each uninstantiated variable.

Exercise 3.4 The querying meta-interpreter presented in Section 3.4 offers the user the opportunity to participate in the problem-solving activity. In that meta-interpreter the user can participate in a particular way, namely to supply new facts during runtime. The user can contribute in additional ways, even within the framework of depth-first meta-interpreters, and two of those ways are explored in this exercise.

(a) Write a meta-interpreter that, when searching for a clause to match a given goal, presents the user with the list of all untried matching clauses, and lets the user decide on the next clause to try.

(b) Write a meta-interpreter that, when processing a conjunctive query, presents the user with the remaining unproved conjuncts and lets the user decide on the next conjunct to be processed.

Exercise 3.5 Chapter 2 briefly discussed *iterative-deepening* search of ordinary graphs, in which depth-first search is performed to a bounded depth, and if no solution is found then the bound is increased; the search thus combines features of both depth-first search and breadth-first search. Similar search can be performed on *and-or* trees. Write an iterative-deepening version of the basic meta-interpreter.

Exercise 3.6 The partial evaluator given in section 3.5 is limited in a number of ways; your task here is to remove these limitations to the extent that you can.

(a) The given interpreter is limited to goals that give rise to finite computation trees; in particular, it is not appropriate for recursive programs. Remove this limitation. *Hint:* You must make sure the partial evaluator terminates. However, you can be more or less ambitious about the amount of computation performed at partial-evaluation time.

(b) The given interpreter is not designed to handle !; modify it so it does.

Exercise 3.7 The breadth-first meta-interpreter presented in Section 3.6 maintains the queue of conjunctions as a list, and thus the append operation is quite costly. Modify the implementation to maintain the queue as a difference list. *Hint:* Look at the analogous program for ordinary graphs presented in Chapter 2.

Exercise 3.8 In Section 3.4 an explanation facility was added to the standard depth-first meta-interpreter. Add a similar facility to the breadth-first meta-interpreter presented in Section 3.6.

Exercise 3.9 The implementation of the breadth-first meta-interpreter in Section 3.6 indeed searches *or* nodes of the computation tree in a breadth-first fashion, but retains the depth-first search order at *and* nodes. Modify the program so that it searches all nodes in a breadth-first fashion. (*Hint:* The change is trivial.)

Exercise 3.10 In Section 3.4 an explanation facility was added to the standard depth-first meta-interpreter. Add a similar facility to the best-first meta-interpreter presented in Section 3.7.

Exercise 3.11 The implementation of the best-first meta-interpreter given in Section 3.7 maintains the list of alternative conjunctions in the form of an ordinary list. The operation performed on this list is to find and remove a conjunction of minimal (i.e., best) heuristic value. Although convenient for exposition, regular lists are an inefficient data structure for this purpose. The ideal data structure is a *heap;* rewrite the program so that the alternative conjunctions are indeed maintained as a heap.

Chapter 4

Other Rule-Based Methods

It is common in AI to encode knowledge in the form of rules. Although they appear in different guises, all rules share the same basic *if-then* structure. Typical rules are "if the current letter in the word being read is q then the next one must be u" and "if the car overheats then check the fan belt." As even these two examples show, the meaning of the *if* and *then* parts varies among applications. One therefore encounters different names for the rules, which include the general name *if-then rules,* and more specific names such as *premise-conclusion rules* and *condition-action rules.* The rule form is popular in AI because it is natural and supports intuitively appealing problem-solving methods. Associated with these reasoning methods are rule-based programming techniques, which are the topic of this chapter.

Of course, the mere use of Prolog entails commitment to at least one set of rules, the clauses in the database, and to a particular way of using these rules, as defined by the Prolog interpreter. As discussed in Chapter 3, this use of the rules is called *backward chaining.* All the meta-interpreters presented in the previous chapter perform backward chaining. It is sometimes mistakenly argued that Prolog is inappropriate for implementing other rule-based techniques. In this chapter we discuss the Prolog implementation of another rule-based technique, *forward chaining,* and the related concept of *production systems.*

Although both forward chaining and production systems are discussed in this chapter, in fact they are quite different animals. Forward chaining is usually viewed as an automated database operation, a specific programming method to be incorporated into a broader computational framework. Production systems, in contrast, are usually presented as a stand-alone programming language in which a reasoning process is to be completely modeled, much like the Prolog interpreter. These two frameworks have enough in common to be grouped in one chapter, but, as we will see, the differences between them will be reflected in the implementations.

There is a third computational mechanism worth mentioning here, *blackboard systems*. Blackboard systems are usually thought of as an architecture for integrating different sources of knowledge in a flexible way. As such they have a status quite different from production systems, and certainly different from forward chaining. Despite the conceptual difference, however, the structure of blackboard systems is very similar to that of production systems, and therefore blackboard systems will be mentioned only briefly after the description of production systems.

4.1   Forward chaining

Consider an *if-then* rule such as

> R1. "If you believe p then believe q"[1]

One way to use this rule is to wait until a query about q is asked, and then, using the rule, replace the query by another one about p. If another rule

> R2. "If you believe both r and s then believe p"

is also present, then the query about p can be replaced by two queries about r and s, and so on, until some facts are known to be unconditionally true, or until one runs out of rules. As mentioned in Chapter 3, this goal-driven use of the rules is known as backward chaining; this is the way in which the Prolog interpreter uses the clauses in the database.

Returning to R1, however, we note that it is possible to make a different use of it. Instead of waiting until a query about q is posed, one may add to the knowledge base the fact that q is true as soon as p is known to be true. This may have further ramifications; for example, if we have a third rule

---

[1]We will discuss the reason for phrasing the rule this way, rather than simply as "if p is true then q is true," later in section 4.1.4.

R3. "If you believe q then believe t"

then as a result of the automatic addition of q, t too will be added. This data-driven process is called *forward chaining*.

The terms 'forward chaining' and 'backward chaining' suggest two symmetric processes. However, while indeed there is clearly much symmetry between them, the symmetry is not complete. As we know from the operation of Prolog, backward chaining is conservative, reducing goals to subgoals only to the extent needed to obtain a solution. Furthermore, it does not modify the database (barring Prolog-like side effects), and upon completion the results of all intermediate computation are lost. In principle, there is no reason not to perform forward reasoning in a similar fashion, deducing temporary new facts from the given ones only until some specified goal is attained (indeed, that is the subject of Exercise 4.1). However, unlike backward chaining, forward chaining is not usually used as a reasoning mechanism, but rather as an automatic database routine, to be used in conjunction with a separate problem-solving module (for example, a backward-chaining one). For this reason forward chaining does not terminate before all possible ramifications have been computed. And forward chaining does modify the database; in fact, that is its very purpose.

We have given above a rather simple example of forward chaining, and it can be extended in several ways. First, it is possible to record the dependence of the conclusion on the premise, so that if the premise is later removed from the database, so will the conclusion. So-called *reason-maintenance systems* have in fact become an important AI technique, and are discussed in Chapter 5.

Second, the automatic addition of a fact to the knowledge base as a result of adding another fact is a special case of one change triggering another: The triggering condition could be the deletion of a fact rather than its addition, and the resulting change itself could also be a deletion. Indeed, some forward-chaining systems employ two kinds of rule, *if-added rules* and *if-deleted rules*. The *if* part is a fact added (or deleted, respectively) from the database, and the *then* part is any program, which may make arbitrarily complex modifications to the database, as well as have other effects (such as notifying the user of interesting changes in the database).

In this section we start by discussing a simple version of forward chaining, the automatic addition of facts to the database as a result of adding other facts. Extensions of this system are introduced later.

4.1.1 Representing positive forward-chaining rules

To implement forward chaining, we need first to represent forward-chaining rules and label them as such. Since Prolog's ordinary backward-chaining clauses are constructed by :-, let us define a symmetric operator -: that will be used to construct forward-chaining rules:

$$op(1150, xfx, -:)$$

For now, we restrict the representation to rules that mention only facts present in the database on the left-hand side and facts to be added to the database on the right-hand side. For lack of a better term we will call such rules *positive rules*. The left-hand side of positive rules will therefore consist of an 'and' list of items, and the right-hand side of a single item. In section 4.1.4 we will define a more general form of forward-chaining rules.[2]

Thus, the three rules R1–R3 will be represented as

```
p -: q.
r, s -: p.
q -: t.
```

4.1.2 Forward chaining with positive rules, unoptimized

Now that we have the rules represented, we may implement the forward-chaining process. We have already explained that forward chaining is considered a database operation, rather than a reasoning technique. For this reason the process of forward chaining will not take a list of items as input but will instead operate directly on the database.

Given that, for now, all rules are positive, the operation to be implemented is the addition of a new item to the database and the propagation of its effects. Note that the deletion of an item from the database has no ramifications. In particular, given the rule p -: q, the addition of p will result in the addition of q. However, the subsequent deletion of p will not result in the deletion of q; such automatic deletion, which is discussed in Chapter 5, is beyond the scope of forward chaining.

---

[2]Of course there is nothing special about the -: operator, and we choose this syntax only because of the symmetry with ordinary backward-chaining clauses.

By assuming only positive rules we have already simplified our task. In addition we make two further assumptions:

1. All facts and rules are ground, that is, they contain no variables.

2. We do not mix backward and forward chaining. For example, the rule r, s -: p is acted upon only if r and s are explicitly represented in the database, and not merely derivable using Prolog's backward chaining.

We impose these restrictions so that we can discuss the efficiency issue in relative isolation. In Sections 4.1.4 and 4.1.5 we remove the restriction to positive rules, and in Section 4.1.7 we introduce variables in the rules. Mixed forward and backward chaining is discussed in the exercises.

In this section we discuss the implementation of forward chaining with positive rules, but disregard the issue of complexity; in the next section we will discuss an optimization of the implementation. Let us start with a particularly easy case, in which the *if* part of each rule contains only one condition. In this case the forward chaining can be implemented in the following way:

% if the fact is already in the database, do nothing:
add_single(X) :- clause(X, true), !.
% else assert it, find all triggered rules, and propagate:
add_single(X) :- assert(X), ((X -: B), add_single(B), fail ; true).

In the general case, in which the *if* part may contain several conditions, all these conditions must be checked before firing the corresponding rule. One way to implement this procedure is as follows:

```
add_positive_slow( X ) :- clause( X, true ), !.
```
% find all rules whose lhs contains X, *make sure all other*
% items on the lhs are in the database, and apply add_positive_slow *to their rhs's:*
```
add_positive_slow( X ) :-
    assert( X ),
    ( If -: Then ),
    amember( X, If ),
    not( ( amember( Y, If ), not( clause( Y, true ) ) ) ),
    add_positive_slow( Then ),
    fail.
add_positive_slow( _ ).
```
% amember / 2 *checks membership in 'and' lists; see Chapter 1's library*

This is obviously an inefficient implementation: when a fact is added, *all* rules are examined, and in each rule *all* the conditions in the *if* part are examined (in fact, the way the program is written some *if* conditions are examined twice). Thus each add operation requires time proportional to the size of the entire forward-chaining database! This is clearly unsatisfactory, and so we now turn to optimizing the forward-chaining procedure for positive rules.

4.1.3   Optimizing the implementation

Our aim is to reduce the complexity of each add operation so that it is proportional to the number of rules actually triggered or to some other reasonable quantity. In particular, the complexity should be independent of the total number of rules in the database or the number of conditions in those rules. To this end we modify the representation of the forward-chaining rules. Rather than represent rules directly as *if-then* pairs using the operator -:, we give each rule a name, a unique identifier (id). We then create pointers from each condition in the *if* part to this id, and from the id to the *then* part. The former are implemented by the predicate if(IfCond, Id), and the latter by the predicate then(Id, N, Then). The N represents the number of unsatisfied conditions in the *if* part of the rule Id.

Consider for example a database that is initially empty. Our three familiar rules, p -: q, r, s -: p and q -: t can be represented by the following:

```
if(p,rule1).          if(r,rule2).          if(q,rule3).
then(rule1,1,q).      if(s,rule2).          then(rule3,1,t).
                      then(rule2,2,p).
```

(Writing the forward-chaining rules in this format is somewhat tedious. In particular, it seems artificial to have to invent names for the rules – after all, we don't invent them for Prolog clauses, do we? Exercise 4.2 discusses a preprocessing procedure that automatically converts rules of the standard form used earlier to the form used here.)

Using this new representation it is possible to implement forward chaining efficiently. When adding a new fact to the database, all rules in whose *if* part that fact appears are accessed, and their counter decremented. If it reaches zero, their *then* part is added to the database. Continuing our example, the result of adding the fact r would be the following database:

```
r.
if(p,rule1).          if(r,rule2).          if(q,rule3).
then(rule1,1,q).      if(s,rule2).          then(rule3,1,t).
                      then(rule2,1,p).
```

(Notice that the counter of rule2 has been decremented by 1.) Then adding the fact q would yield the following database:

```
r. q. t.
if(p,rule1).          if(r,rule2).          if(q,rule3).
then(rule1,1,q).      if(s,rule2).          then(rule3,0,t).
                      then(rule2,1,p).
```

It was already mentioned that in the previous representation of forward-chaining rules, deletion of database items had no effect on the forward-chaining process. Under the new representation the situation is different: Just as adding elements decrements some counters, removing elements may increment them. For example, if now r is removed from the database, the second rule's counter should be incremented:

```
q. t.
if(p,rule1).          if(r,rule2).          if(q,rule3).
then(rule1,1,q).      if(s,rule2).          then(rule3,0,t).
                      then(rule2,2,p).
```

The following program implements addition and deletion:

```
add_positive( X ) :- clause( X, true ), !.
add_positive( X ) :-
   assert( X ),
   if( X, Id ),
   once( ( retract( then( Id, N, Then ) ),
          M is N-1,
          assert( then( Id, M, Then ) ) ) ),
   cond_propagate_positive( M, Then ),
   fail.
add_positive( _ ).


cond_propagate_positive( 0, Then ) :- !, add_positive( Then ).
cond_propagate_positive( _, _ ).


del_positive( X ) :- not( clause( X, true ) ), !.
del_positive( X ) :-
   if( X, Id ),
   once( ( retract( then( Id, N, Then ) ),
          M is N+1,
          assert( then( Id, M, Then ) ) ) ),
   fail.
del_positive( _ ).
```

% once / 1 is defined in Chapter 1.

What is the complexity of the program? Since, given the main functor and first argument, the Prolog interpreter locates the clauses in essentially constant time, the complexity of this implementation of add and del is proportional to the number of pointers from modified (asserted or retracted) facts to rules.

4.1.4   Representing general forward-chaining rules

So far we have considered only *positive* forward-chaining rules. In this section and the following one we relax this restriction and generalize the discussion to rules referring not only to facts present in the database ('positive conditions') but also to those absent ('negative conditions'). We still assume that all rules and facts are ground, that is, that they contain no variables. We discuss lifting this restriction in Section 4.1.7.

In order to allow for negative conditions we need to modify the form of the rules, as well as the forward-chaining process. In this section we discuss the straightforward change in representation; we simply associate with each item in the rule a *polarity*, or *status*, denoted + or –, that determines whether the rule refers to the presence or absence of the corresponding item in the database.

Consider, for example, the following modifications of the rules R1–R3 discussed in the introduction to the chapter.

> R1'(=R1). "If you believe p then believe q"
> R2'. "If you believe r and do not believe s then believe p"
> R3'. "If you believe q then do not believe t"

These will be captured in the following forward-chaining rules:

> (p,+) -: (q,+).
> (r,+),(s,–) -: (p,+).
> (q,+) -: (t,–).

Positive rules are now merely the special case in which all polarities are +.

A few words of caution are in order at this point. It is tempting to view these rules as logical sentences, with (p,–) as standing for the negation of p, and -: denoting implication. However, forward chaining, like most concepts discussed in this book, is a computational device rather than a logical one. Although there is some overlap between the intuition underlying the computational device and logic, the match is not exact. It is beyond the scope of this book to explore in detail the relationship between logic and various computational paradigms. We will only make two comments here.

First, (p,–) should not be viewed as the negation of p; rather it should be viewed as lack of evidence for p, or lack of belief in p (where lack of belief in p is a weaker notion than actual belief in the negation of p); this issue is closely related to the idea of *negation as failure* in Prolog. Forward chaining has no mechanism for representing negation.

The second comment, which is related to the first, is that the -: operator should not be viewed as standard logical implication. In fact, it should not be viewed as a logical construct at all. It is simply an instruction to modify certain beliefs on the basis of the existence and absence of certain other beliefs. In particular, rules do not contrapose; the existence of two rules (q,–) -: (t,+) and (q,–) -: (t,–) does not result in the addition of q to the database. Similarly, the absence of q from the database is perfectly consistent, although the result will be sensitive to idiosyncratic implementation details; see Section 4.1.6.

To summarize, then, the relationship between a computational device and logic is not a trivial matter. Indeed, the issue has been the subject of considerable research recently, especially in connection with *truth maintenance systems*. When we discuss truth maintenance systems in Chapter 5 we will return to the subject of representing negation and handling inconsistency, but we will not address the general issue of logical reasoning in a deep way.

4.1.5   Forward chaining with negative conditions

As in the case of positive rules, the rule representation described in the Section 4.1.4 may be optimized to facilitate more efficient algorithms. The modification of these general rules is entirely analogous to that of positive rules. For example, assuming the database initially contains only forward-chaining items s and t, the rules R1'–R3' will be represented as follows:

s. t.

if(p,+,rule1).	if(r,+,rule2).	if(q,+,rule3).
then(rule1,1,q,+).	if(s,–,rule2).	then(rule3,1,t,–).
	then(rule2,2,p,+).	

If r is added, the database will be as follows:

r. s. t.

if(p,+,rule1).	if(r,+,rule2).	if(q,+,rule3).
then(rule1,1,q,+).	if(s,–,rule2).	then(rule3,1,t,–).
	then(rule2,1,p,+).	

If now s is deleted, the ramifications will be more far-reaching: Due to the second rule p will be added, which then, due to the first rule, will lead to the addition of q. This, in turn, will lead to the deletion of t due to the third rule:

```
r. p. q.
if(p,+,rule1).           if(r,+,rule2).           if(q,+,rule3).
then(rule1,0,q,+).       if(s,−,rule2).           then(rule3,0,t,−).
                         then(rule2,0,p,+).
```

In contrast to the case of positive rules, the addition and deletion of items is clearly completely symmetric here. The following program implements both addition and deletion. In this program, the second argument to propagate / 2 is either + or −, signaling that the first argument is an item to be added or deleted, correspondingly.

```
add(X) :- clause(X, true), !.
add(X) :- assert(X), propagate(X,+).

del(X) :- not(clause(X, true)), !.
del(X) :- retract(X), propagate(X,−).


% _____
% find all rules whose lhs contains X, update their counters,
% and possibly propagate the effect onwards:
% _____

propagate( X, S ) :-
   if( X, S1, Id ),
   once( ( retract( then( Id, N, Then, S2 ) ),
           update_counter( N, S, S1, M ),
           assert( then( Id, M, Then, S2 ) ) ) ),
   cond_propagate( M, Then, S2 ),
   fail.
propagate( _, _ ).
% _____
% if polarity is as expected, decrement counter;
% otherwise increment it:
% _____
update_counter( N, S, S, M ) :- !, M is N−1.
update_counter( N, _, _, M ) :- M is N+1.
```

```
% _____
% if the counter is down to 0, propagate; else do nothing:
% _____
```

```
cond_propagate( 0, Then, +) :- !, add( Then ).
cond_propagate( 0, Then, − ) :- !, del( Then ).
cond_propagate( _, _, _ ).
```

4.1.6   Termination conditions for forward chaining

Several observations can be made about the forward-chaining procedure just
described. First, it is not hard to see that the result of the propagation may
depend on the order in which rules are examined. For example, consider the
following two rules (written, for simplicity, in the unoptimized way):

$$(p,+),(q,-) \text{ -: } (r,+).$$
$$(p,+),(r,-) \text{ -: } (q,+).$$

Assume that the database is initially empty, and that subsequently p is
added. There are two possible outcomes – either q will be added and r not,
or vice versa – depending on the order in which the two rules are processed.

In addition, general forward chaining is not guaranteed to terminate.
Indeed, it is easy to show cases in which it will not. Consider, for example,
the following two rules:

$$(p,+),(q,+) \text{ -: } (p,-).$$
$$(p,-),(q,+) \text{ -: } (p,+).$$

Assume that initially neither p nor q apears in the database. It is not
hard to see that subsequently adding q will lead to an infinite propagation,
alternating between adding and deleting p.

So in general one cannot guarantee termination of forward chaining.
There are, however, restrictions on rules that will guarantee termination.
We will not address the questions of what are the *most general* conditions
on forward chaining rules that guarantee termination. Instead, we point to
an important case that guarantees it:

> If all *then* parts of the rules have the same polarity (that is, all
> are + or all are −), then the forward-chaining is guaranteed to
> terminate.

A corollary of this property is that the update of positive rules is guaranteed to terminate.

4.1.7   Variables in forward-chaining rules

So far, we have assumed that both the database items and the forward-chaining rules are ground, that is, that neither contains variables. Now we consider relaxing the assumption and allowing variables in the rules; we will continue to assume that the database items are ground. It should be pointed out that relaxing the assumption is not a luxury we can do without; most applications require it.

We will assume that each conjunct appearing on either the left-hand side or the right-hand side of a production rule will be of the form $p(X_1, X_2, \ldots, X_n)$, where $n \geq 0$. As before, conjuncts will be associated with a polarity, + or −. When matching against items in the database, all the variables occurring in positive conjuncts on the lhs will become instantiated. Variables that are shared with the rhs will, of course, become instantiated there too. However, the rhs may contain additional variables that remain uninstantiated. These will become instantiated by a Prolog program associated with each rule, which takes as input some instantiated variables in the positive conditions on the lhs, runs further tests on them, and in the process binds the remaining uninstantiated variables in the rhs. For this reason the rhs of rules will contain not only the *then* part and its polarity (+ or −), but also a third argument, a program.

An example will help clarify the representation. Consider the following forward-chaining rule:

> R4. "If the number of people to whom you believe X is married is
> greater than one, then record the number of X's extra spouses"

This rule can be represented as:

```
(married_to( X, SpouseList ), + ) -:
    ( extra_spouses( X, N ), +, count_extras( SpouseList, N ) ).
```

where the database contains the (ordinary) clause

$$\text{count\_extras(L, N) :- length(L, M), M} > 1, \text{N is M−1.}$$

Here the program count_extras / 2 verifies a further condition on the *if* part
(namely, that X indeed has more than one spouse) and also instantiates the
remaining variable in the *then* part (N).

Thus, the added argument on the left-hand side of rules sneaks a form
of backward chaining into the forward-chaining process. This feature is
essential, but it opens the door to abuse of the system. Consider for example
the following rule:

> R5. "If you believe that X is married and
>   you do not believe he had an affair with anyone
>   then believe that X's spouse loves X"

A good way of representing this rule is:

(is_married(X), +),(affair(X, Y), −), (spouse_of(X, Z), +) -: (loves(Z, X), +, true)

A bad way of representing the rule would be:

(is_married(X), +),(affair(X, Y), −) -: (loves(Z, X), +, spouse_of(X, Z))

Assuming no clauses exist in the database for spouse_of / 2 other than
facts, this formulation would have an effect identical to that of the previous
formulation. However, moving one of the conditions to the *then* part is abusing the system; the program on the right-hand side is there in order to use
built-in predicates and similar tests not available through simple inspection
of the database.

More extreme abuses are possible. For example, there is nothing to stop
the programmer from pushing the entire activity into the backward-chaining
component, using the forward chaining as a mere trigger for the process. The
system does not prevent this abuse, but the programmer who finds himself
engaging in such a practice should question the utility of forward chaining
in this situation.

Returning from issues of usage to issues of implementation, it may seem
at first that allowing variables in rules is a minor complication in implementing forward chaining. Indeed, it is easy to write an inefficient forward-
chaining program for this generalized case. Writing an efficient program,
however, is a different matter, as the relatively simple optimized programs

we have seen so far do not extend to this case. We first present the naive implementation, and then discuss some issues relating to its optimization.

The following program is an inefficient implementation of forward chaining with variables; it is a straightforward modification of add_positive_slow / 1 from Section 4.1.2.

```
add_var_slow(X) :- clause(X, true), !.
add_var_slow(X) :- assert(X), propagate_var_slow(X,+).

del_var_slow(X) :- not(clause(X, true)), !.
del_var_slow(X) :- retract(X), propagate_var_slow(X,–).

propagate_var_slow( X, S ) :-
  ( If -: Then, S1, F ),
  amember( ( X, S ), If ),
  not( ( amember( ( Y, + ), If ), not( clause( Y, true ) ) ) ),
  not( ( amember( ( Y, – ), If ),clause( Y, true ) ) ),
  update_var_slow( Then, S1 ),
  fail.
propagate_var_slow( _, _ ).

update_var_slow(Then,+) :- add_var_slow(Then).
update_var_slow(Then,–) :- del_var_slow(Then).
```

% amember / 3 *in Chapter 1's library*

Similarly to the add_positive_slow program, this program examines the entire collection of forward-chaining rules. Although tolerable in certain applications, this practice is prohibitive in general. Unfortunately, optimizing this general case is not all that straightforward. The main reason is that a rule with variables stands for a collection of ground rules, namely the set of all its instances. Thus one cannot associate a single counter with the rule, the idea that was the key to optimizing the implementation in the ground case. Nor can one replace the rule by all its ground instances; their number is infinite.

Several approaches to the problem have been suggested. One approach does not quite result in the efficiency of the ground case, but it is a substantial improvement on the above implementation. This approach splits each

production into several 'specialized' ones: For each conjunct on the lhs of a
rule a new rule is created; this rule is accessed whenever an item matching
the conjunct is added to memory (if the polarity of the conjunct is +) or
removed from it (if the polarity is –), and the remaining conjuncts are examined for presence or absence in the database. This method prevents the
entire collection of forward-chaining rules from being explored upon each
change in the database, but examination of each rule is inefficient, and the
number of rules increases.

An alternative (and common) approach to solving the inefficiency problem is to maintain, for each rule and for each positive conjunct on the rule's
lhs, the instances of the conjunct that appear in the database. Whenever the
database is modified, the instance lists in the appropriate rules are updated.
Most importantly, whenever a list is updated, all combinations of previously
stored instances of the other items on the lhs are tested; whenever a combination turns out to satisfy the condition on the rhs, that rule instance is
triggered.

In the following, assume a single forward-chaining rule,

$$(p(X),+), (q(Y),+), (r(Y),-) -: (s(X,Y),+,X<Y)$$

and an initially empty database. The rule has two instance lists, one for
p(X) and one for q(Y), both initially empty. Now p(1) is added; the instance
list of p(X) becomes [p(1)]. Now r(1) is added, with a similar effect. Then
q(0) is added; the instance list of q(Y) is updated, but no triggering occurs: The only possible lhs-instance is ((p(1),+),(q(0),+),(r(0),–)), but it is not
satisfied since 1<0 is not satisfied. Now p(0) is added, and again no triggering occurs. Next q(1) is added. Now there are two new rhs-instances –
((p(0),+),(q(1),+),(r(1),–)) and ((p(1),+),(q(1),+),(r(1),–)) – but neither triggers (since
r(1) is in the database). Finally, q(2) is added. At this point there are two new
instances, ((p(0),+),(q(2),+),(r(2),–)) and ((p(1),+),(q(2),+),(r(2),–)), and both trigger,
leading to the addition of both s(0,2) and s(1,2).

The above description leaves open the questions of how to update the
instance lists efficiently, and how to check efficiently for satisfied instances.
The first question is straightforward, but the second less so. The best-known
method is the RETE algorithm, which was actually proposed in connection
with production systems (see the references mentioned at the end of the
chapter).

4.2   Production systems

We will discuss production systems as a programming technique, but they are more commonly thought of as a behavior-governing mechanism. Rooted loosely in behaviorism, their *if-then* rules, called *production rules,* are also often called *condition-action pairs,* the *condition* describing an aspect of the environment to be recognized and the *action* describing an action taken as a response.

4.2.1   The general structure of a production system

As a problem-solving paradigm production systems are a loaded and controversial topic, but as programming systems they are more straightforward. A production system consists of a *working memory* and a *production memory.* Working memory is a collection of *items,* an item being any datum (traditionally, items are assumed to be ground, that is, contain no variables). Production memory is a collection of production rules, or condition-action pairs. The condition consists of a list of item patterns. Item patterns may contain variables, and they refer to present or absent working-memory items (we will discuss item patterns in more detail later). The action is actually a list of individual actions. Each individual action may in principle be any program, but in fact almost always has to do with addition, deletion, or modification of working-memory items, and sometimes with addition, deletion, and modification of production memory itself.

Given these two data structures, working memory and production memory, the operation of the production memory is defined by the following cycle:

1. Determine the conflict set: Find all production rules whose left-hand side is satisfied; this set of rules is called the *conflict set.* If the conflict set is empty then halt.

2. Resolve the conflict: Select one of the rules from the conflict set, and discard the rest.

3. Act, or fire: Execute the action part of the selected rule.

4. Go to 1.

The operation of a production system is therefore similar to that of a forward chainer: Both bring about changes to the database on the basis of data already present and *if-then* rules. The most important difference is that whereas forward chaining blindly fires all rules that triggered and then quits, a production system carefully selects one rule to fire, ignores the rest, and then repeats the process. A less essential difference is that, as a matter of practicality, in production systems one usually specifies a *goal;* as soon as the goal appears as an item in working memory, the production system terminates its activity.

An example

Before we discuss the implementation of production systems, let us strengthen intuition about their use by providing a small example. Consider the implementation of a chess-playing program in a production system. One approach would represent the board position in working memory and capture the chess-playing knowledge in the form of production rules.

Thus, working memory may contain the following information:

white king on a7
white pawn on b6
black knight on c6

⋮

Similarly, the production memory may contain the following rule for escaping a check situation:

IF white king is location X
   black has piece P in location Y
   (Y,X) is a legal move for P
   Z is adjacent to X
   Z is unoccupied
   there exist no location W and piece Q such that black has Q on W
     and (W,Z) is a legal move for Q
THEN remove white king from location X
   place white king in location Z

A word about blackboards

Before we continue with the discussion of production systems, let us say a word about *blackboard systems*, a concept often confused with production systems – and for a good reason. A blackboard system consists of a central database, called the *blackboard,* and several modules, called *knowledge sources* (or KSs) that can read from and write to this database. Each KS contains a *trigger,* a test determining whether the KS is applicable at any particular moment. The BB system repeatedly selects one of the KSs that trigger (that is, whose test is satisfied), and fires it. KSs do not communicate directly, but may do so indirectly through the blackboard.

If this sounds similar to the operation of a production system, it is. The main difference between the two frameworks is that blackboard systems are thought of as integrating the activity of heterogeneous and potentially complex components, whereas production systems involve identically structured and rather simple modules. Blackboard KSs typically contain much information in addition to that in the blackboard itself, and they may engage in complex activities besides reading from and writing to the blackboard. For example, one KS may have a private database and perform backward chaining on it before deciding on the action to be taken on the blackboard. However, since the structure of an individual KS is so unconstrained, there is little to say about the implementation of blackboard systems beyond that which is discussed in connection with production systems; we will therefore not speak further of blackboard systems.

4.2.2 Implementing a generic production system

In order to implement production systems in Prolog we must first determine the representation of working memory and production memory. Let us first consider the representation of working memory. As usual, we have a choice: We can either represent working-memory items as Prolog database facts, or we can maintain them in an explicit list (or some other data structure), providing an initial list as input to the system. In the case of forward chaining we used the Prolog database, since forward chaining is viewed as a database maintenance routine. In the case of production systems the situation is less clear cut. On the one hand, production systems are used as a general reasoning tool, and the working memory, as the name suggests, consists of temporary data used in the service of some final goal. From this perspective the explicit list representation is preferable, since it is generally a bad idea to use the Prolog database to record intermediate states of computation. Indeed, general programming principles discourage the use of side effects. On the other hand, production systems constitute a rather special computational paradigm, in which the notion of a database fits very naturally. If the application involves a large number of items in memory at any given time, the implementation would naturally have to focus on querying and modifying working memory, operations that are already optimized in Prolog. Thus the choice is largely a matter of taste in this case.

Exercise 4.5 will discuss the side-effect-free implementation of production systems. Here we will discuss the implementation using side effects: Working memory will be implemented by the predicate wm / 1; that is, the working-memory item p will be represented by wm(p).

For the production rules we could use the -: / 2 operator used for forward-chaining rules. However, it will be good to keep the two categories of rule separate, and so instead we will define a new (infix) operator for production rules:

$$op(1150, xfx, --:)$$

Thus the production rule "if condition then action" will be represented by condition --: action.

Much of the treatment of production systems is inherited from the details of forward chaining. As in the case of forward chaining, we may consider increasingly complex production rules, from positive ground ones to unrestricted ground ones to ones containing variables. We will, however, assume the most general case, which allows variables (without which production systems would not be able to serve as a general reasoning framework). Typical production rules will be:

(married_to(X, SpouseList), +) --: (bigamist(X), +, (length(SpouseList, N), N > 1))
(even_and_small(X), +) --: (even_and_small(Y), +, (Y is X+2, Y < 100))
(employee(X), +),(fired(X), +),(tenured(X), −) --: (employee(X), −, true)

(Note that (bigamist(X), +, (length(SpouseList, N), N > 1)) is identical to
(bigamist(X), +, length(SpouseList, N), N > 1); we use the additional parentheses for readability.)

While the main actions of production systems are to add and remove items from working memory, production systems invariably provide the opportunity to run an arbitrary prespecified program when a rule fires. We have already allowed for that by including a program on the rhs, but, as with forward chaining, the intention is that the program be used only to bind variables not yet bound by the instantiation of patterns.

The top-level program for the production system is as follows:

```
ps( Goal ) :- wm( Goal, _ ).
ps( Goal ) :-
   conflictset( CS ),
   select( CS, Rule ),
   fire( Rule ),
   ps( Goal ).
```

In the following three sections we discuss in detail the three phases in each cycle of the production system.

4.2.3   Determining the conflict set

The conflict set is determined in exactly the same way in which forward chaining determines the rules whose left-hand sides have been satisfied (or, in other words, the *triggered* rules). As discussed in connection with forward chaining, if the rules contain no variables then the triggered rules can be found efficiently; otherwise, complications arise that may slow down the process. In this regard this phase is identical in forward chaining and production systems.

There is, however, one significant difference. Because forward chaining is a one-shot process in which all triggered rules are fired (and fired exactly once), there is no need to keep track of the fired rules. The situation is a little more complicated in production systems, where at each cycle exactly one rule is fired. At the next cycle the conflict set is recomputed, and unless we take steps to prevent it, it will usually be the case that the rule that was just fired will trigger again; furthermore, since the conflict resolution strategy is fixed, it will usually be selected again for firing. Thus, unless we are careful, we might find the production system dominated by a small set of rules.

One could imagine several ways out of this situation. For example, one could imagine a conflict resolution strategy that keeps track of fired rules and lowers their priority. The standard solution in production systems, which we will adopt, is a variation on this idea. First, the disqualified rule is not only assigned a low priority, it is in fact completely disqualified at the phase of determining the conflict set. However, rather than disqualify a general rule because one of its instances fired, we only disqualify that instance. Furthermore, we only disqualify the instance made up of the exact same working-memory items.

An example will help clarify this strategy. Suppose a rule instance with the condition p on the left-hand side has fired. Suppose also that p is later deleted, but subsequently p is added again, leading to a reinstantiation of that same rule. This new instance is considered different from the previous one.

To implement this idea each working-memory item is assigned a *tag*, or a unique identifier (id). One way to implement this is to use Prolog internal clause reference. As mentioned in Chapter 1, each clause in the database is assigned an internal reference, which can be used in the predicates assert / 2, erase / 1, and clause / 3, among others. This reference, which is incremented for each new clause, can serve as our tag. Another way is to add an argument to wm, an integer that is incremented whenever an item is added to working memory. We will use this second method in our implementation.

The test fired / 2 will take two inputs, an instantiated rhs of a rule and a list of tags corresponding to the items in the lhs of that rule, and succeed if and only if that rule fired before. (The tags will play a role not only in the determination of the conflict set but also in its resolution, as explained in the next section.) The (unoptimized) program is as follows:

```
conflictset( CS ) :-
   findall( (RevSortedTagList, Then, S ),
           ( ( If --: ( Then, S, F ) ),
             triggered( If, TagList ),
             sort( TagList, SortedTagList ),
             reverse( SortedTagList, RevSortedTagList ),
             not( fired( Then, RevSortedTagList ) ),
             not( ( amember( ( Item, - ), If ), wm( Item, _ ) ) ),
             call( F ) ),
           CS ).

triggered( ( ( Item, - ), MoreItems ), TagList ) :- triggered( MoreItems, TagList ).
triggered( ( ( Item, + ), MoreItems ), [ Tag | MoreTags ] ) :- !,
   triggered( ( Item, + ), [ Tag ] ),
   triggered( MoreItems, MoreTags ).
triggered( ( Item, + ), [ Tag ] ) ) :- !, wm( Item, Tag ).
triggered( ( _, - ), [ ] ) ).
```

The *if* parts of the instances are kept in the form (TagList-...) in order to facilitate the resolution of the conflict set; this is explained below in Section 4.2.4. The fired / 2 predicate is updated when a rule is fired, as explained subsequently in Section 4.2.5.

4.2.4 Resolving the conflict set

The resolution of the conflict is possibly the most interesting component of a production system; it is here that the programmer can encode various clever heuristics. Some general heuristics can be based on the following criteria:

1. Recency: How recently was the information added to the database?

2. Ease of satisfiability: How many patterns does the rule contain? Are these patterns often satisfied, or only rarely?

3. Support: How many instances of the same production rule are there in the conflict set?

The best-known production system is OPS5. We will follow one of the two general conflict resolution heuristics offered by OPS5, a heuristic called LEX. It incorporates three principles:

1. The *refraction* principle: The same rule instance never fires twice, where two instances are considered identical if not only have their variables been instantiated to the same values, but also their associated tags are identical.

2. The *recency* principle: Rule instances with the most recent conditions are chosen (a condition is more recent than another if its tag is higher). If the most recent conditions in two rules are identical, then the second most recent conditions are compared, and so on.

3. The *specificity* principle: If the conditions in the one rule are a proper subset of those in another rule, then the rule with the largest number of conditions is chosen.

The refraction principle has already been built into our determination of the conflict set, and its rationale has been discussed. The second principle is a 'focus of attention' mechanism, increasing the likelihood of a coherent problem-solving behavior. The third principle enforces a fairness condition, encouraging use of rules that tend to not trigger often because of the large number of conditions that need to be satisfied.

Other heuristics are possible, and some are explored in the exercises. Even LEX itself leaves some room to maneuver, since the second and third principles may be traded off against each other in different ways. The following implementation of LEX gives precedence to recency over specificity.

```
select( CS, Rule ) :- lex( CS, Rule ).


lex( [ Rule ], Rule ).
lex( [ ( TagList, RHS ) | Rules ], Rule ) :-
  lex( Rules, ( TagList1, RHS1 ) ),
  ( TagList1 @=< TagList, ! , Rule = ( TagList, RHS )
   ; Rule = ( TagList1, RHS1 ) ).
```

Since the two tag lists are sorted from largest to smallest, and since the built-in @=< /2 compares two terms (and hence two lists) lexicographically,[3] the above program is sufficient.

4.2.5   Firing a production rule

The last phase of the production-system cycle is the firing of a rule; it is also the most straightforward. Although in most production systems the *action* part of the production rule can be more complex, we have assumed that it refers either to the addition of an element to working memory or its deletion. In addition to the addition or deletion, we also record the fact that the rule instance was fired. In fact, what we record is the list of tags corresponding to the working-memory items:

```
fire( ( TagList, Then, S ) ) :- assert( fired( Then, TagList ) ), update_status( Then, S ).


update_status( Then, + ) :-
 not( clause( wm( Then, _ ), true ) ), !,
 new_wm_counter( N ),
 assert( wm( Then, N ) ).
```

---

[3]Lexicographic order is that in which words are ordered in the dictionary.

```
update_status( Then, – ) :-
  clause( wm( Then, _), true ), !,
  retract( wm( Then, _) ).
update_status( _, _ ).
```

4.3   Further reading

There is a rich body of literature about rule-based systems, especially about production systems and blackboard systems. Forgy and McDermott [24] describe the OPS production system; the manual [22] provides many more details. Forgy [23] describes a mechanism for optimizing the performance of the system; for similar discussion in the context of Prolog see Shintani [75]. Newell [56] discusses production systems in connection with the HARPY speech-understanding system. In a related publication, Lesser and Erman [42] introduce blackboard systems in connection with the HEARSAY-II speech-understanding system. Nii [58, 59] provides a detailed discussion of blackboards, and Engelmore and Morgan [19] a compilation of recent applications of blackboard systems. Finally, Hayes-Roth [31] applies the concept of blackboards to control systems.

4.4   Exercises

Exercise 4.1 As explained in this chapter, forward chaining is usually considered a database-maintenance routine. However, there is no reason not to consider a version of it that is completely symmetric with backward chaining, starting with a collection of given facts and using the rules to derive new facts, until a goal is satisfied. For example, given the fact a(1), the forward-chaining rules (a(X),+) -: (b(X),+,true) and (b(X),+) -: (c(Y),+,Y is X+1), the goal c(A) would result in first deriving the fact b(1), and then the answer c(2). Just as in the case of backward chaining, this bottom-up process can proceed in various orders – depth first, breadth first, and so on.

(a) Implement a depth-first bottom-up meta-interpreter.

(b) Implement a breadth-first bottom-up meta-interpreter.

(c) Implement a best-first bottom-up meta-interpreter.

Exercise 4.2 In this chapter we introduced two representations of forward-chaining rules: a straightforward one using -:, and an alternative representation that supports an efficient implementation of forward chaining. This second representation is somewhat unnatural and tedious, as it requires representing each forward-chaining rule by a number of database facts, associating a name with each forward-chaining rule, and initializing a counter. Write a program pre_forward / 2 that derives this representation automatically from the original, unoptimized one. For example, if file1 contains the fact b and the clause (a, +), (b, +), (c, −) --: (d, +), the goal ?- pre_forward(file1, file2) will result in file file2 containing the clauses if(a, +, rule1), if(b, +, rule1), if(c, −, rule1), then(rule1, 1, (d, +)), and b.

Exercise 4.3 This chapter presented forward chaining in isolation from other mechanisms, but mentioned that in fact the technique is generally used in conjunction with some other reasoning program. Consider the integration of backward and forward chaining. One form of integration is to use the forward chaining as a *caching* mechanism; whenever the Prolog interpreter solves a goal, whether the original goal or an auxiliary one, the forward chainer asserts the goal to the database to prevent the need for recomputation in the future. There are two versions of this idea; the caching can be done either during the computation, or only once the computation is complete. Consider the program consisting of the clauses a :- b, b :- c, and c. In both versions of caching the conjunctive goal a,a will result in adding the fact a to the database (and in other changes; see below), but while in the first version both calls to a will result in backward chaining, in the second version a will be cached already after the first call, and the second call will succeed immediately.

(a) Implement a backward-chaining meta-interpreter that caches all goals derived during computation after the computation is over, whether the top-level goal is successful or not. Note the following complications: (i) goals may have been solved along paths that ultimately failed, and (ii) when caching a goal you do not want the program to succeed twice on that goal, once by virtue of the cached result and once by virtue of the original clauses.

(b) Implement a meta-interpreter that caches results during computation.

Exercise 4.4 The discussion of production systems mentioned several criteria for selecting a rule among the conflict set. The actual implementation provided adopted a particular strategy, LEX. Your task here is to implement other strategies.

(a) Change the implementation of LEX to give precedence to specificity over recency.

(b) Modify LEX by considering the *number* of items on the left-hand side of each rule, not whether one left-hand side subsumes another.

(c) Modify LEX to increase the weight of all rules triggered but not selected (this way, a rule that triggers often will eventually be selected).

(d) Augment LEX to take into account explicit, user-supplied information about the precedence of some rules over others.

Exercise 4.5 The implementation of production systems given in this chapter uses side effects. Your task here is to implement a side-effect-free production system; you may use the database to represent the production memory, but you should implement the working memory via a data structure passed around as an argument. Make sure your program is written so as to make use of last-call optimization.

Exercise 4.6 The production system implemented in the chapter allowed only two kinds of action, addition or deletion of working-memory items.

(a) Augment the implementation to allow the addition or deletion of production rules.

(b) Augment the implementation to allow the execution of any given Prolog program.

Chapter 5

Truth Maintenance Systems

The general title of *truth maintenance systems,* or TMSs, refers to a collection of automatic methods for maintaining the coherence of a database. There are several dimensions to this coherence, and different versions of TMSs address different dimensions. (In fact, *truth* is not one of these dimensions, but we will continue to use the term truth maintenance generically since it has become so well established.) We will consider three progressively more complex versions of TMSs. The simplest are called *reason maintenance systems,* or RMSs; these systems add items to the database only when they are justified and automatically remove the items if their justification goes away. More elaborate are *consistency maintenance systems,* or CMSs. These apply in situations where, in addition to the need for reason maintenance, certain sets of items are considered contradictory and the system must make sure that the database always remains free of contradictions. Finally, the most elaborate TMSs that we will consider are so-called *assumption-based* TMSs, or ATMSs, which can be viewed as a method for capturing multiple TMSs in a single structure.

5.1   Reason maintenance

While discussing forward chaining in the previous chapter we emphasized that when a forward-chaining rule triggers, no record is kept of the triggering conditions. In particular, the effects of the rule are not undone if those conditions later change. Sometimes retaining the effects of a forward-chaining rule long after the conditions cease to be satisfied is indeed justified. Consider, for example, a robot R1 perceiving another robot R2 for the first time. If R1 has a forward-chaining rule of the form "if you perceive a robot you have never seen before then record its existence" then R1 would, appropriately, record the existence of R2. Furthermore, if R2 subsequently disappeared from sight, R1 would retain the record of R2's existence. This is clearly appropriate in this case.

There are cases, however, in which retaining inferences is inappropriate. For example, if R1's rule had been instead "if you see another robot then include it in the list of visible robots" then R1 would have been wrong to cling to the belief that R2 remained close after R2 were no longer visible. Clearly, there is a need for a different behavior of the system in this case. The role of reason maintenance systems is to provide this additional functionality. RMSs are also called *data dependency systems,* since data's presence in the database depends on whether or not other specific data are present.

5.1.1   Justifications and premises

RMS *if-then* rules are called *justifications*, for obvious reasons. We represent justifications just as we did forward-chaining rules, except for renaming the operators. The following description will therefore be short; the reader who finds it too short should reread Section 4.1.

In order to distinguish between justifications and other *if-then* rules, such as forward-chaining ones, we may define a new operator

$$op(\ xfx, \ 1150, \ \text{---}: \ )$$

We restrict the discussion here to ground justifications, that is, justifications containing no variables. Additionally, justifications never contain a negative condition on the right-hand side; since all right-hand sides are therefore positive, we omit the + sign altogether on the right-hand side. The general form of justification will therefore be:

$$(d_1, s_1), \ldots, (d_n, s_n) \text{ ---: } d$$

where the d_i's are database items and each s_i is either a + or a −. An example of a justification is

(see(robot14), +), (friendly(robot14), −) ---: threatening(robot14)

If all conditions on the left-hand side are positive the justification is called *monotonic;* otherwise it is called *nonmonotonic.* The reason for this is that if all the conditions are positive, the right-hand side is monotonic in the database: it cannot be removed as a result of *adding* items to the database.

As in the case of forward chaining and production systems, it is computationally advantageous to break each justification down into several *if* statements and one *then* statement. For example, the previous justification may be named j143, and be defined by the following:

justifier(see(robot14), +, j143)
justifier(friendly(robot14), −, j143)
justificand(j143, 1, threatening(robot14))

As discussed in Chapter 4, this more elaborate form may be derived automatically from the original representation. Note that we will use a counter for each justificand; its function is to speed the process of detecting that all the justifiers for a particular justificand are satisfied, and it works exactly like the counters in the *then* parts of forward-chaining rules. See Chapter 4 for details on these counters.

Intuitively, whereas a forward-chaining system may hold beliefs that are not supported by any forward-chaining rule, RMSs require that every belief be supported by some explicitly stated rule. All beliefs must be grounded in a justification whose justifiers are themselves justified. This recursive definition must bottom out in some beliefs that are held unconditionally; these beliefs are called *premises.* In fact, rather than designate multiple beliefs as premises, we define a single premise node, called premise, and define justifications from this premise to all the beliefs we wish to hold unconditionally. Figure 5.1 shows a sample network of justifications.

5.1.2   Operations on RMSs

In the case of forward chaining we considered the operations of adding and deleting items, while the set of forward-chaining rules was assumed fixed. In

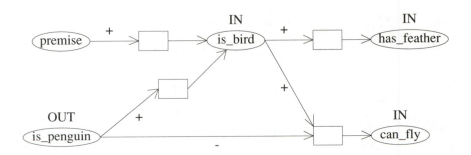

Figure 5.1: A sample RMS (IN = in database, OUT = not IN)

the case of RMSs the situation is reversed, and the *only* operations we consider are the addition and deletion of justifications. (Of course, as a special case we may add or delete a justification whose justifier is the special item premise.) These additions and deletions may ramify through the network, until all and only the justified items are in the database.

We start with an example. Consider the sample RMS from Figure 5.1. In this network, as in the other networks discussed later, the node label IN means that the corresponding item is in the database, and the label OUT means that it is not. In this figure the network is legally labeled: All and only the justified nodes are labeled IN.

Now consider Figure 5.2; it shows the changes in the database as a result of adding a justification and as a result of removing one. It is clear that adding a justification may result in removal of beliefs, since some beliefs rely on the absence of other beliefs; in other words, the set of items in the database is not a monotonically increasing function of the set of justifications. For this reason justifications with negative justifiers are called nonmonotonic.[1]

The above example may suggest that adding and removing justifications require only minor adjustments of the general procedures for forward chaining. Indeed, if the justification network contains no cycles then the following procedure for adding or removing a justification will suffice:

1. Add (resp. remove) the appropriate justification to (resp. from) the

---

[1]There is a close connection between TMSs in general and so-called *nonmonotonic reasoning* in AI, that kind of reasoning that allows for tentative conclusions that may later be retracted. However, discussion of nonmonotonic reasoning and of this connection is beyond the scope of this book.

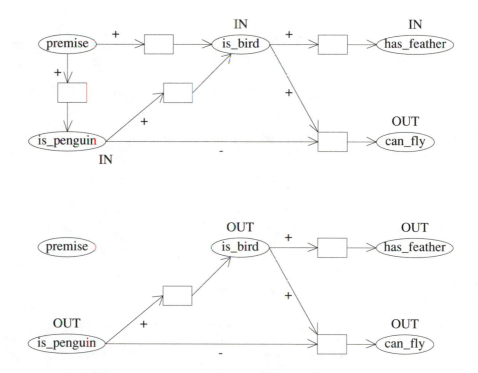

Figure 5.2: Adding and deleting justifications

database.

2. Determine whether the justificand should be in the database on the basis of the new (resp. remaining) justifications.

3. If it should (resp. should not) then add (resp. delete) the item to (resp. from) the database, treating all justifications as forward-chaining rules.

Unfortunately, in the presence of cycles the situation is not so straightforward. Even if all cycles consist of only monotonic rules, we are faced with the problem of *self justification*. Consider an initial state of a network shown in Figure 5.3. Now suppose the justification 'premise --: p' is removed. Figure 5.4 shows the resulting network, assuming that the above simple procedure is adopted; in it p and q justify each other, but are no longer grounded in the premise as required.

Cycles with nonmonotonic rules present additional problems; one is that of *underdeterminacy*. Consider the network in Figure 5.5. Should p and q

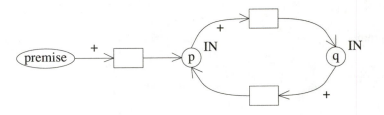

Figure 5.3: Before: a legal labeling

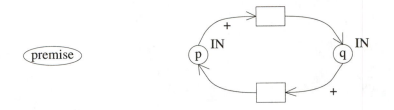

Figure 5.4: After: an illegal labeling

be IN or OUT? Clearly, there are two possibilities: either p is IN and q is OUT, or vice versa. We will assume that we may choose arbitrarily between the two consistent labelings for each underdetermined nonmonotonic cycle.

Finally, nonmonotonic justifications can present an even more troubling situation of *overdeterminacy.* Consider the network in Figure 5.6; it is not hard to see that this network has *no* consistent labeling.

Full discussion of conditions that guarantee consistent labeling is not possible here. Instead, we will assume in the following that the justification network never contains cycles with an odd number of negative justifiers. This is not always an acceptable assumption, but we will make it because such networks can be shown to always have consistent labeling; the sources cited at the end of the chapter explore this topic further.

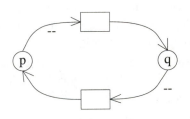

Figure 5.5: Underdeterminacy

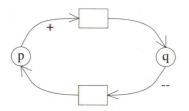

Figure 5.6: Overdeterminacy

5.1.3   An inefficient Prolog implementation

With these issues and our assumption in mind, we turn to the actual procedure for adding or removing a justification. The idea behind the procedure is simple. Whenever we either remove or add a justification, the status of its justificand (the node appearing in its right-hand side) is put in question, since it might change; we will say that in this case the node has become *contaminated*. This node may in turn contaminate other nodes, due to justifications whose left-hand side contains contaminated nodes. The procedure thus first computes the set of contaminated nodes. It then considers which contaminated nodes can be revalidated by virtue of justifications whose left-hand side contains no contaminated nodes.

Consider, for example, the network in the Figure 5.1. After adding a new justification from premise to is_penguin, the nodes is_penguin, is_bird, has_feather and can_fly become contaminated. We start the revalidation process by picking a 'decidable' node such as is_penguin (is_bird would be another), which is justified by an uncontaminated node premise. Next, we remove it from the contaminated list, update its status to be IN, and update the justifier counters of other nodes accordingly. We then do the same to is_bird. The nodes can_fly and has_feather now become decidable, and so we update them in the next rounds of the revalidation process.

In this section we discuss a straightforward, but inefficient, implementation of this idea; in the next section we optimize the implementation. Since the code is rather long, we start by spelling out the algorithm.

PROCEDURE ADD-JUST-RMS-SLOW(*if_part*, *then_part*)
add the justification (*if_part* ---: *then_part*) to the database
$C \leftarrow$ { nodes reachable from *then_part* }
REVALIDATE-RMS-SLOW(C)

PROCEDURE REVALIDATE-RMS-SLOW(C : nodelist)
while C not empty
   $(N, S) \leftarrow$ GET-DETERMINED-NODE(C)
   if GET-DETERMINED-NODE failed then
      $N \leftarrow$ an arbitrary node in C
      $S \leftarrow -$
   end if
   delete N from C
   UPDATE-NODE(N, S)
end while

PROCEDURE GET-DETERMINED-NODE(C : nodelist)
          : (node, polarity)
while C not empty
   remove a node N from C
   if N is justified by uncontaminated nodes, return $(N, +)$.
   else if N is ruled out by uncontaminated nodes, return $(N, -)$.
end while
fail

PROCEDURE ADJUST-STATUS(N : node, S : polarity)
if $S = $ '+', assert N to the database
else retract N from the database

PROCEDURE IN(N : node) : boolean
if N is in the database, return *true*
else return *false*

PROCEDURE UPDATE-NODE(N : node, S : polarity)
if $(\text{IN}(N)$ and $S = -)$ or $(\neg\ \text{IN}(N)$ and $S = +)$ then
    % N's status doesn't correspond to polarity S
    ADJUST-STATUS(N, S)
    for each justification J with N as an antecedent
        if N's polarity in J equals S then   *% N supports J*
            decrement J's justifier counter
            % If J's counter reaches zero here, we will notice and assert J in a
            % later iteration.
        else   *% N undermines J*
            increment J's justifier counter
        end if
    end for
end if

Here is the Prolog implementation of this correct, but inefficient, algorithm.

```
% _____
% Add a justification to the database, and propagate its effects.
% _____

add_just_rms_slow( If, Then ) :- exist_just_rms_slow(If,Then,_), !.
add_just_rms_slow( If, Then ) :-
   new_just_label( J ),
   findall( ( Justifier, S ),
           ( rms_amember( ( Justifier, S ), If ),
             assert( justifier( Justifier, S, J ) ),
             unsatisfied( Justifier, S ) ),
           UnSat ),
   length( UnSat, N ),
   assert( justificand( J, N, Then ) ),
   mark_contaminated_nodes_slow( Then ),
   revalidate_rms_slow.
```

```
% _____
% Delete a justification from the database, and propagate the effects of its deletion.
% _____

del_just_rms_slow( If, Then ) :-
    exist_just_rms_slow( If, Then, J ), !,
    retractall( justifier( _, _, J ) ),
    retract( justificand( J, _, _) ),
    mark_contaminated_nodes_slow( Then ),
    revalidate_rms_slow.
del_just_rms_slow( _, _).


% _____
% Find an existing justification J from a given If to a given Then.
% _____

exist_just_rms_slow( If, Then, J ) :-
    setof( ( Justifier, S ), rms_amember( ( Justifier, S ), If ), If1 ),
    justificand( J, _, Then ),
    setof( ( Justifier, S ), justifier( Justifier, S, J ), If1 ).


% _____
% To mark the contaminated nodes, perform depth-first search,
% using justifications as arcs between nodes.
% _____

mark_contaminated_nodes_slow( Node ) :-
    retractall( contaminated( _ ) ),
    retractall( contam_marked( _ ) ),
    do_all( ( contam_path( Node, Node1 ), assert( contaminated( Node1 ) ) ) ).

contam_path( Node, Node ).
contam_path( Node, Node1 ) :-
    justifier( Node, _, J ),
    justificand( J, _, NextNode ),
    not( contam_marked( NextNode ) ),
    assert( contam_marked( NextNode ) ),
    contam_path( NextNode, Node1 ).
```

```
% _____
% Examine the contaminated nodes.
% _____


revalidate_rms_slow :-
    contaminated( Node ),
    determined( Node, S ), !,
    retract( contaminated( Node ) ),
    update_node_rms_slow( Node, S ),
    revalidate_rms_slow.
revalidate_rms_slow :-
    retract( contaminated( Node ) ), !,
    update_node_rms_slow( Node, – ),
    revalidate_rms_slow.
revalidate_rms_slow.


% _____
% Perform a node update.
% _____


update_node_rms_slow( Node, S ) :- satisfied( Node, S ), !.
update_node_rms_slow( Node, S ) :-
    adjust_status( Node, S ),
    do_all( ( justifier( Node, S1, J ),
              once( retract( justificand( J, N, NextNode ) ) ),
              update_counter( S, S1, N, M ),
              assert( justificand( J, M, NextNode ) ) ) ).


update_counter( S, S, N, M ) :- M is N–1, !.
update_counter( _, _, N, M ) :- M is N+1.
```

```
%  _____
% A node is determined if its polarity is positive and it is supported by a
% justification whose justifier counter is zero, or its polarity is negative and
% every justification for it has some uncontaminated, unsatisfied justifier.
%  _____
```

```
determined( Node, + ) :-
    justificand( J, 0, Node ),
    not( ( justifier( Justifier, _, J ), contaminated( Justifier ) ) ).
determined( Node, − ) :-
    not( ( justificand( J, _, Node ),
           not( ( justifier( Justifier, S, J ),
                  unsatisfied( Justifier, S ),
                  not( contaminated( Justifier ) ) ) ) ) ).

satisfied( Item, + ) :- clause( Item, true ).
satisfied( Item, − ) :- not( satisfied( Item, + ) ).
unsatisfied( Item, S ) :- not( satisfied( Item, S ) ).

adjust_status( Node, + ) :- assert( Node ).
adjust_status( Node, − ) :- retract( Node ).

new_just_label( J ) :-
    retract( just_ctr( N ) ), M is N+1, assert( just_ctr( M ) ),
    name( j, [ Jval ] ), name( M, StrM ), name( J, [ Jval | StrM ] ), !.
```

```
%  _____
% rms_amember / 2 differs from amember / 2 because of the structure of items in the
% 'and' list of justifiers.
%  _____
```

```
rms_amember( ( X, S ), ( ( X, S ), _ ) ).
rms_amember( ( X, S ), ( ( _, _ ), Y ) ) :- !, rms_amember( ( X, S ), Y ).
rms_amember( ( X, S ), ( X, S ) ).
```

5.1.4   Optimizing the implementation

It is not hard to see that the previous implementation is not very efficient. Consider the execution of the predicate revalidate_rms_slow: Clearly, each contaminated node may be examined repeatedly in every recursive call before it is actually updated. Furthermore, each time we examine a contaminated node, we perform a costly computation, determined(Node, S).

In order to reduce the time complexity of the program, we do away with the justifier counters of the previous implementation and introduce two new types of counter in their place. With each justification J we associate a counter N, through the predicate justifier_counter(J, N). The role of this counter is similar to that of the justifier counter NN in justificand(J, NN, Justificand) used in the previous implementation. The difference is that this time we count all justifiers that are either unsatisfied or contaminated or both. Clearly, whenever this number is zero, we are guaranteed that the justified item must be in the database. However, when the number is greater than zero, the counter does not distinguish between unsatisfied justifiers and contaminated ones. For this reason we associate with each node Node a counter M, through the predicate justificand_counter(Node, M). This counter represents the number of justifications of Node *not* currently ruled out by an uncontaminated node. Consider, for example, a justification q, r ---: p . If r is neither contaminated nor in the database, we can say with confidence that this justification is ruled out, that is, that even after further processing of the network this justification will not justify p. In a way analogous to the effect of justifier_counter(J, N), if the M in justificand_counter(Node, M) is zero then the node Node must be labeled OUT.

With these two counters, we revalidate and update the node labels differently from the previous inefficient implementation. First, we pick each contaminated node whose label can be determined by one of the two counters' being zero, and start updating from that node. Whenever the result of updating a node makes another node determinable (one of the two counters becomes zero), we continue updating the latter node.

As before, we first present the algorithm in pseudo-code, and then the Prolog implementation.

PROCEDURE ADD-JUST-RMS(*if_part, then_part*)
add the justification (*if_part* ---: *then_part*) to the database
MARK-CONTAMINATED-RMS(*then_part*)
REVALIDATE-RMS

PROCEDURE MARK-CONTAMINATED-RMS(N : node)
$C \leftarrow$ { nodes reachable from N }
for all $M \in C$ mark M contaminated
for all $M \in C$ do
    set M's justificand counter to 0
    for each justification J whose rhs is M do
        set J's justifier counter to the number of J's justifiers that are
            unsatisfied or contaminated
        if J is not ruled out by an uncontaminated node then
            incremement M's justificand counter
            mark J as not ruled out
    end for
end for

PROCEDURE PROPAGATE-RMS(N : node, S : polarity)
if N is contaminated then
    mark N as not contaminated
    if (IN(N) and $S = -$) or ($\neg$ IN(N) and $S = +$) then
        % *N's status doesn't correspond to polarity S*
        ADJUST-STATUS(N, S)   % ADJUST-STATUS *as defined above*
    end if
    for each (M, J) such that M is J's rhs and N appears in J's lhs do
        if N's polarity in J equals S then
            decrement J's justifier counter
            if J's justifier counter is 0, PROPAGATE-RMS($M, +$)
        else if J is not ruled out then
            mark J as ruled out   % *This is really removing a mark from J*
            decrement M's justificand counter
            if M's justificand counter is 0, PROPAGATE-RMS($M, -$)
        end if
    end for
end if

PROCEDURE REVALIDATE-RMS
while ∃ contaminated nodes do
    while ∃ a contaminated node N satisfying DETERMINED(N, S) for
        polarity S do
        PROPAGATE-RMS(N, S)
    end while
    if ∃ a contaminated node N then   % *N is contaminated and unsupported*
        PROPAGATE-RMS(N, –)
    end if
end while

PROCEDURE DETERMINED(N : node, S : polarity)
if N is justified by uncontaminated nodes, succeed with $S = '+'$
if N is ruled out by uncontaminated nodes, succeed with $S = '-'$
otherwise, fail

Here is the Prolog implementation of this algorithm; the time complexity of this procedure is linear in the number of links between justifiers and justifications actually processed.

% _____
% *Add a new justification to the database and propagate the effects.*
% _____

```
add_just_rms( If, Then ) :- exist_just_rms( If, Then, _ ), !.
add_just_rms( If, Then ) :-
   new_just_label( J ),
   do_all( ( rms_amember( ( Justifier, S ), If ), assert( justifier( Justifier, S, J ) ), fail ) ),
   assert( justificand( J, Then ) ),
   mark_contaminated_rms( Then ),
   revalidate_rms.
```

```
% _____
% Remove a justification from the database and propagate the effects.
% _____

del_just_rms( If, Then ) :-
    exist_just_rms( If, Then, J ), !,
    retractall( justifier( _, _, J ) ),
    retract( justificand( J, _) ),
    mark_contaminated_rms( Then ),
    revalidate_rms.
del_just_rms( _, _ ).


% _____
% Succeed if and only if the database contains a justification J of the form
% If ---: Then.
% _____

exist_just_rms( If, Then, J ) :-
    setof( ( Justifier, S ), rms_amember( ( Justifier, S ), If ), If1 ),
    justificand( J, Then ),
    setof( ( Justifier, S ), justifier( Justifier, S, J ), If1 ).


% _____
% Find all the contaminated nodes, and make sure their justifier and justificand
% counters are set right.
% _____

mark_contaminated_rms( Node ) :-
    retractall( contaminated( _ ) ),
    retractall( contam_marked( _ ) ),
    do_all( ( contam_path_rms( Node, Node1 ), assert( contaminated( Node1 ) ) ) ),
    retractall( justifier_counter( _, _ ) ),
    retractall( justificand_counter( _, _ ) ),
    retractall( not_ruled_out_just( _ ) ),
    do_all( ( contaminated( Node1 ),
            compute_just_counter( Node1 ),
            compute_node_counter( Node1 ) ) ).
```

```
% _____
% Find contaminated nodes as in the inefficient program; we can't reuse the old
% code verbatim because of the different arity of justificand / 2.
% _____


contam_path_rms( Node, Node ).
contam_path_rms( Node, Node1 ) :-
   justifier( Node, _, J ),
   justificand( J, NextNode ),
   not( contam_marked( NextNode ) ),
   assert( contam_marked( NextNode ) ),
   contam_path_rms( NextNode, Node1 ).


% _____
% Compute the justifier counters for all the justifications of Node.
% _____


compute_just_counter( Node ) :-
   do_all( ( justificand( J, Node ),
            count_unsubstantiated_justifiers( J, JustifierCount ),
            assert( justifier_counter( J, JustifierCount ) ) ) ).


% _____
% A justifier is considered unsubstantiated if it is unsatisfied or contaminated.
% _____


count_unsubstantiated_justifiers( J, JustifierCount ) :-
   findall( ( Justifier, S ),
           ( justifier( Justifier, S, J ),
            ( unsatisfied( Justifier, S )
            -> true
            ; contaminated( Justifier ) ) ),
           Unsubstantiated ),
   length( Unsubstantiated, JustifierCount ).
```

```
%
% Compute the justificand counter for Node.
%
```

```
compute_node_counter( Node ) :-
  findall( J,
          ( justificand( J, Node ),
            not( ruled_out_by_uncontam_justifier( J ) ),
            assert( not_ruled_out( J ) ) ),
          Not_ruled_out ),
  length( Not_ruled_out, JustificandCount ),
  assert( justificand_counter( Node, JustificandCount ) ).
```

```
%
% A justification is ruled out if it has an unsatisfied and uncontaminated justifier.
%
```

```
ruled_out_by_uncontam_justifier( J ) :-
  justifier( Justifier, S, J ),
  unsatisfied( Justifier, S ),
  not( contaminated( Justifier ) ).
```

```
%
% The revalidation routine; note that we depend on Prolog's backtracking after the
% explicit fail for the repetitive behavior required here.
%
```

```
revalidate_rms :-
  contaminated( Node ),
  determined( Node, S ),
  propagate_rms( Node, S ),
  fail.
revalidate_rms :-
  contaminated( Node ),
  propagate_rms( Node, − ),
  fail.
revalidate_rms.
```

```
% _____
% A node is determined if its justificand counter is zero or it has a justification
% whose justifier counter is zero.
% _____


determined( Node, - ) :- justificand_counter( Node, 0 ).
determined( Node, + ) :- justificand( J, Node ), justifier_counter( J, 0 ).


% _____
% Propagate the effects of setting Node's status to S.
% _____


propagate_rms( Node, _ ) :- not( retract( contaminated( Node ) ) ), !.
propagate_rms( Node, S ) :-
   cond_adjust_status( Node, S ),
   do_all( ( justifier( Node, S1, J ),
             justificand( J, NextNode ),
             update_counter( J, S, S1, NextNode ) ) ).


% _____
% Adjusting node status is slightly different in this efficient implementation
% because adjustment may not be required.
% satisfied/2 and adjust_status/2 are as before.
% _____


cond_adjust_status( Node, S ) :- satisfied( Node, S ), !.
cond_adjust_status( Node, S ) :- adjust_status( Node, S ).


% _____
% Carry on propagating effects if a counter reached zero (and hence a
% justification's rhs may be newly determined).
% _____


cond_propagate( 0, NextNode, S ) :- !, propagate_rms( NextNode, S ).
cond_propagate( _, _, _ ).
```

```
% _____
% Update the appropriate counter according to whether or not NextNode's new
% status supports or undermines justification J.
% _____
```

```
update_counter( J, S, S, NextNode ) :-
   retract( justifier_counter( J, N ) ),
   M is N −1,
   assert( justifier_counter( J, M ) ),
   cond_propagate( M, NextNode, + ), !.
update_counter( J, _, _, NextNode ) :-
   retract( not_ruled_out( J ) ),
   retract( justificand_counter( NextNode, N ) ),
   M is N −1,
   assert( justificand_counter( NextNode, M ) ),
   cond_propagate( M, NextNode, − ), !.
update_counter( _, _, _, _ ).
```

5.2   Consistency maintenance

So far the only constraint on the TMS database was that all and only the
justified items be in it. We now introduce a further constraint, that the
database be consistent. Any collection of database items may be considered
'inconsistent' (or 'incompatible' or 'contradictory'). There are no constraints
on the sets of items that may be viewed as contradictory. We may view
friendly(robot14) and threatening(robot14) as mutually inconsistent. We may
view any two of wine, women, and song as compatible, but the three as a
forbidden combination. As a special case of binary incompatibilities, we may
wish to assume that for any item item there exists an item −item, denoting
the 'negation' of item, with the two mutually incompatible by definition.

These sets of forbidden item combinations are often called *nogood sets*,
or simply *nogoods*. The task of a consistency maintenance system (CMS)
is to look over the shoulder of the RMS and ensure that all nogoods are
respected; that is, to make sure that there does not exist a nogood all of
whose members are present in the database.

Recall that for convenience we assumed that only one premise node existed. We now similarly simplify the representation of nogood sets. We assume that there exists a unique node false (often also called $\perp$, pronounced 'bottom'), denoting an inconsistency. Now, rather than explicitly label a set of items as a nogood, we simply have that set justify the false node. For example, rather than label the set {p, −p} as inconsistent, we add a justification p, −p ---: false.

Addition and deletion of justifications in a CMS are only slightly more complex than in an RMS. First, we record all the items that were added to memory as a result of adding or deleting the justification. This requires only a minor redefinition of the adjust_status / 2 programs:

```
adjust_status( Node, + ) :- assert( Node ), mark_newly_changed( Node ).
adjust_status( Node, − ) :- retract( Node ), mark_newly_changed( Node ).
mark_newly_changed( Node ) :- newly_changed( Node ), !.
mark_newly_changed( Node ) :- assert( newly_changed( Node ) ).
```

We will assume this change henceforth.

Second, when the reason maintenance process is complete, we check all the nogoods associated with the items that were added to memory in the process and find out whether any were violated.

Finally, if any were found to be violated, we restore consistency to the network. The tools we have at our disposal are the addition and deletion of justifications. In principle we could attempt to restore consistency by adding or deleting any justification. In fact, much work has been devoted to *dependency-directed backtracking,* which attempts to locate the culprit justification(s), leaving the innocent ones unchanged. Dependency-directed backtracking schemes were among the precursors of assumption-based TMSs or ATMSs, which are discussed in the next section. Here, however, we will adopt a rather simple-minded approach. First, we will restrict the changes to the deletion, as opposed to addition, of justifications. Second, we will delete only assumptions, that is, justifications from the special item premise. Third, when several assumptions are responsible for the inconsistency, we will select at whim one for deletion. We should note that none of these simplifications are necessary; Exercise 5.1 explores some alternatives.

```
%  _____
% Add a justification to the CMS.
%  _____


add_just_cms( If, Then ) :-
   retractall( newly_changed( _ ) ),
   add_just_rms( If, Then ),
   ensure_consistency,
   retractall( newly_changed( _ ) ).


%  _____
% Remove a justification from the CMS.
%  _____


del_just_cms( If, Then ) :-
   retractall( newly_changed( _ ) ),
   del_just_rms( If, Then ),
   ensure_consistency,
   retractall( newly_changed( _ ) ).


%  _____
% If the database is inconsistent, remove premises to make it consistent.
%  _____


ensure_consistency :-
   % If false is in the database, we have inconsistency.
   clause( false, true ), !,
   bad_node( Node ),
   faulty_assumption( Node, ANode ),
   del_just_rms( ( ( premise, + ) ), ANode ),
   ensure_consistency.
ensure_consistency.
```

```
% _____
% A bad node is one that is newly changed and participates in a nogood set.
% _____

bad_node( Node ) :-
    % Find a justification that added false to the database.
    justificand( J, false ),
    justifier_counter( J, 0 ),
    justifier( Node, S, J ),
    newly_changed( Node ),
    satisfied( Node, S ).


% _____
% Find an assumption that supported the derivation of false.
% _____

faulty_assumption( Anode, Anode ) :- supported_only_by_premise( Anode ).
faulty_assumption( Node, Anode ) :-
    justificand( J, Node ),
    % Is Node in or out ?
    satisfied( Node, S ),
    justifier( Node1, S1, J ),
    contributor( Node1, S1, S ),
    faulty_assumption( Node1, Anode ).

contributor( Node, S, + ) :- !, satisfied( Node, S ).
contributor( Node, S, − ) :- unsatisfied( Node, S ).

supported_only_by_premise( Node ) :-
    clause( Node, true ),
    justificand( J, Node ),
    bagof( ( Node1, S ), justifier( Node1, S , J ), [ ( premise, + ) ] ).
```

The sample run of the program that follows is based on these rules:

$$(party, +), (have\_fun, +) \text{ ---: } drink\_beer$$
$$(go\_home, +), (have\_a\_car, +) \text{ ---: } drive$$
$$(drive, +), (drink\_beer, +) \text{ ---: } false$$

As before, we show a sample run of a modified version of the program that includes informative print statements.


```
| ?- add_just_cms(((party,+),(have_fun,+)),drink_beer).
yes
| ?- add_just_cms(((go_home,+), (have_a_car,+)),drive).
yes
| ?- add_just_cms(((drive,+), (drink_beer,+)),false).
yes
| ?- add_just_cms(((premise,+)),party),
     add_just_cms(((premise,+)),have_fun).
yes
| ?- printdb.
The facts:
premise.
party.
have_fun.
drink_beer.
| ?- add_just_cms(((premise,+)),go_home),
     add_just_cms(((premise,+)),have_a_car).
******** INCONSISTENT DATA *********
Bad Node: drive
Delete justification: (premise, +) ---: go_home
yes
| ?- del_just_cms(((premise,+)),party).
yes
| ?- add_just_cms(((premise,+)),go_home).
yes
| ?- printdb.
The facts:
premise.
have_fun.
have_a_car.
go_home.
drive.
```

5.3 Assumption-based truth maintenance

Both kinds of TMS we have discussed so far answer the following general question: "Given the following justifications and premises, is this particular conclusion warranted?" Assumption-based TMSs, or ATMSs, ask the complementary general question: "Given the following justifications, under what assumptions would the following conclusion be warranted?" This is in general a harder problem; the first question has a unique yes/no answer, while the second one could return many different sets of assumptions, each set independently warranting the conclusion. Such *abductive* reasoning, that is, the deriving of possible explanations of a given fact, is common in AI. For example, abductive reasoning arises in connection with automated diagnosis ("What could have caused this failure?"), automated planning ("What sequences of actions on my part will bring about the desired state?"), and pragmatics of natural language ("If the speaker is asking me that question, what must he be thinking?").

A simple example will clarify the operation of an ATMS. Consider a program that plans gourmet meals, including the food items and the beverages. Suppose that at some stage of the planning the program decided to have a Brazilian meal and to include quindim (a kind of dessert) and cafezinho. The program also deduced that a Brazilian dinner entails having meat, and decided to include meat. The combination of meat and dessert justifies a choice of 1969 Coca-Cola Private Reserve as beverage. In fact, the same choice of beverage is always appropriate for Brazilian meals with cafezinho. The planner records its reasoning through the following justifications:

> brazil, brazil_means_meat ---: meat.
> meat, quindim ---: coke69.
> brazil, cafezinho ---: coke69.

Later in the planning stage the program decides on an Irish theme, and decides to prepare meat stew. It turns out that 1969 Coca-Cola Private Reserve is very versatile and fits this occasion quite well. The program later considers a rack of lamb, and, sure enough, the same beverage is computed to be appropriate. The following justifications are added:

> irish ---: meat.
> irish, meat ---: coke69.
> lamb ---: coke69.

How could the planner use these justifications, say, to find out quickly whether coke69 is a good choice of beverage? The TMSs described previously would at each point maintain a set of premises (that is, a set of nodes justified by the premise node) and determine whether the label of coke69 is IN or OUT. An ATMS, in contrast, has no premises. Instead, it associates with the coke69 node all its 'explanations,' and to test whether the beverage is appropriate in a situation it searches for one explanation satisfied in that situation. But what counts as an explanation? A straightforward approach would be to accumulate all sets of nodes sufficient to justify the conclusion. Given the five justifications above, this set would include:

> {coke69}
> {meat,quindim}
> {brazil,brazil_means_meat,quindim}
> {brazil,cafezinho}
> {irish}
> {irish,meat}
> {lamb}

Notice that this list of 'explanations' is redundant; if one explanation includes another, the larger may be discarded. This reduces the list to the following:

> {coke69}
> {meat,quindim}
> {brazil,brazil_means_meat,quindim}
> {brazil,cafezinho}
> {irish}
> {lamb}

Now, there may be some facts that are to be 'taken for granted,' and which should not be specified as part of the explanation. The remaining facts, those that may appear in explanations, are called *assumptions*.[2] For example, it may be obvious that all Brazilian meals include meat, and not worthy of

---

[2]Again, it is important not to confuse premises and assumptions. The former appear in standard TMSs but not ATMSs, and denote facts taken to hold unconditionally. The latter appear in ATMSs but not in TMSs, and denote facts that may participate in an explanation. What can make it particularly confusing is that sometimes TMS facts that are supported only by a premise are also called assumptions; however these assumptions are different from ATMS assumptions.

inclusion in an explanation; the third explanation is therefore simplified to {brazil,quindim}; it is worth noting here that collapsing assumptions can lead to inclusions that were not originally present.

The next complication involves *background information*. In addition to the justifications present in the network and the identification of some of the nodes as assumption nodes, the ATMS may make use of an additional background. For example, the program may have the knowledge that lamb is a form of meat. In this case, the explanation {lamb} will be omitted, as it is subsumed by the explanation {meat} given the background theory.

The last complication involves *nogood sets,* or simply *nogoods.* Like CMSs, ATMSs contain the special false node. Intuitively, again, a justification from a set of nodes to false indicates that the set of nodes is inconsistent. ATMSs require that all explanations be consistent. For example, suppose the background theory tells us that Brazilian meals require drinking batida, and we add a justification stating that batida and cafezinho don't mix:

batida, cafezinho ---: false.

This nogood means that one of the remaining explanations must be omitted, namely {brazil,cafezinho}.

To summarize, then, in an ATMS each node is labeled not by a simple IN/OUT annotation, but rather by a *context*, representing all the possible explanations of the datum, given the justifications. ATMSs thus reverse the perspective on data and contexts: whereas in TMSs each (implicit) context determines the data, in ATMSs each datum determines the (explicit) context. We now present a more detailed description of the ATMS and its functionality.

5.3.1   The structure of an ATMS

Recall that an ordinary TMS is defined by a set of data nodes including special premise and false nodes, and a collection of justifications among the nodes. An ATMS contains all these components except for the premise node. In addition it contains a background theory and identifies some subset of the data nodes as *assumptions*. An *environment* is a set of assumptions.

An assumption can participate in more than one environment, and thus environments can overlap and even subsume one another. The set of assumptions therefore defines an *environment lattice*. Figure 5.7 shows a environment lattice, with upward links standing for inclusion.

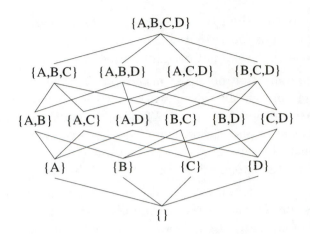

Figure 5.7: A simple environment lattice

Each environment defines a *context*. The context consists of all and only the ATMS data nodes that, given the justifications in the ATMS, can be justified entirely on the basis of the nodes in the environment. Thus, all the nodes in a given environment are also members of the derived context.[3] An ATMS can therefore embody the structure of several related ordinary TMSs, one for each context.

We can now explain the *labels* of ATMSs. The label of each ATMS data node is a set of environments, which is required to be:

Consistent: No environment in the label supports the derivation of false.

Sound: For each environment in the label it must be the case that the node is included in the context defined by that environment.

Complete: Any environment in the lattice whose context includes the node is a superset of some environment in the label. (Note that inconsistent environments have empty contexts.)

Minimal: No environment in the label is a subset of another.

Figure 5.8 shows an ATMS labeling alongside the corresponding environment lattice.

---

[3]If it is the case that no assumption is justified by any other set of nodes, then it is necessarily the case that different environments yield different contexts; otherwise different environments may in fact yield identical contexts.

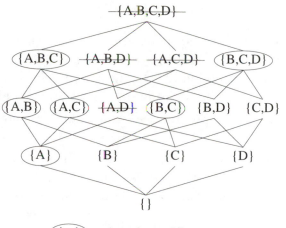

{...} - A context of P

{...} - Inconsistent environment

Label of P:{{A},{B,C}}
Nogoods: {{A,D}}

Figure 5.8: A labeled environment lattice

5.3.2   Operations on an ATMS

We consider only one type of operation on an ATMS, the addition of a justification. It might at first seem arbitrary to exclude the possibility of deleting a justification, but this exclusion has two explanations. First, the philosophy behind ATMSs is that the inferences recorded in an ATMS are *sound,* albeit only in a particular context. Since each justification records a sound inference, there is no need to retract it but only to record the context in which the inference is valid. The second explanation is related, although it is couched in more pragmatic terms: If a justification is added that might require retraction later on, one can simply add another assumption as a justifier. Later, instead of retracting that justification, one simply adds a justification from the additional assumption to false.

Another operation that one might have expected is the addition or deletion of an assumption, that is, not adding a datum node but declaring or undeclaring an existing one to be an assumption. The former operation is allowed in our ATMS definition; the latter is not.

5.3.3   An implementation of an ATMS

For simplicity's sake in our implementation, we will enforce the restriction
that all justifications in the ATMS are monotonic. Further, our implementation will not treat the notion of a background theory explicitly, although
its effects can be achieved through the standard justifications we implement.

Before we go on to the program, let us look at some predicates we use.

1. holds(Node, Env) : Node holds (or has status IN) in the environment
   Env. Node is a node in the justification network and a problem-solver
   datum. Env is an environment (a set of assumptions).

2. environment(Env, Flag) : This predicate is used as a cache to avoid
   repeatedly checking whether an environment is consistent or not. Env
   is known to be consistent if and only if Flag is true.

3. assumption(Assump, Rep) : This predicate maps an assumption Assump to
   a representation Rep of a singleton set containing Assump. This function
   has two uses: to define which nodes are assumptions and to convert
   back and forth between a real environment (the set of assumptions)
   and its representation in the program.

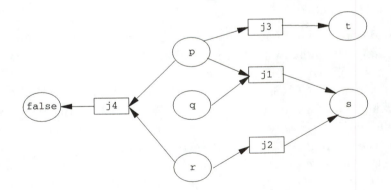

Figure 5.9: ATMS justification network

Our implementation of justifications will be much the same as before, except that for coding convenience we store a list of justifying nodes in each
justificand. Further, since all justifications must be monotonic, we dispense
with the polarity of the justifiers. An additional unnecessary restriction is

that all members of nogood sets must be declared as assumptions. Consider a normal justification network:

```
justifier(p,j1).
justifier(q,j1).
justifier(r,j2).
justifier(r,j3).
justifier(p,j4).
justifier(r,j4).
justificand(j1,s,[p,q]).
justificand(j2,s,[r]).
justificand(j3,t,[p]).
justificand(j4,false,[p,r]).
```

(Note that the justification j4 says that { p, r } is a nogood set.) We now define p, q and r to be assumptions. It will be convenient, though not necessary, to use the bit-vector representation of sets discussed in Chapter 1 and mark the assumptions by the following facts (arguments to bitvec / 1 are written in binary for clarity):

```
assumption(p,bitvec(001)).
assumption(q,bitvec(010)).
assumption(r,bitvec(100)).
```

Shown below are holds assertions and their corresponding environments.

```
holds(s,bitvec(011)).       s: p,q
holds(s,bitvec(100)).       s: r
holds(t,bitvec(100)).       t: r
holds(false,bitvec(101)).   false: p,r
```

As a by-product of computing holds, the results of checking consistency of each environment are cached.

```
environment(bitvec(011),true).
environment(bitvec(100),true).
environment(bitvec(101),fail).
```

As before, we first present the algorithm in pseudo-code and then the Prolog implementation.

PROCEDURE DECLARE-ASSUMPTION(*assump* : node)
create new bit-vector position in environment set representation
$E \leftarrow \{ \ assump \ \}$
$L \leftarrow \{$ environments in which *assump* holds $\}$
COND-UPDATE-PROPAGATE(*assump*, $L \cup \{ E \}$)

PROCEDURE ATMS-ADD-JUST(*if_part*, *then_part*)
if justification (*if_part* ---: *then_part*) not already present then
    add justification $J = ($*if_part* ---: *then_part*$)$ to the ATMS network
    NODE-UPDATE-ENV(J)
end if

PROCEDURE NODE-UPDATE-ENV(J : justification)
$N \leftarrow$ rhs of J;
if_part $\leftarrow \{$ justifiers of $J \}$
$Q \leftarrow \{$ environments in which N is known to hold $\}$
$R \leftarrow \{$ consistent environments in which all conjuncts of *if_part* hold $\}$
$S \leftarrow \{$ minimal elements of $Q \cup R \}$
if $Q \neq S$, COND-UPDATE-PROPAGATE(N, S)

PROCEDURE COND-UPDATE-PROPAGATE(N : node,
L : environment list)
retract all statements as to which environments induce N
assert that N holds in each environment in L
if $N = $ *false* then
    % Every environment in L is inconsistent
    for each $E \in L$ do
        for each $F \supseteq E$ currently marked consistent in the database do
            mark F as inconsistent in the database
            remove all facts of the form holds(Node, F)
        end for
    end for
else
    for each justification J supported by N do
        NODE-UPDATE-ENV(J)
end if

```
%
% Declare a node in the network to be an assumption node (eligible to appear in
% environments).
%
```

```
declare_assumption( Assump ):-
    new_assumption( Assump, Env ),
    gather_env( Assump, Envlist ),
    cond_update_propagate( Assump, [ Env | Envlist ] ).
```

```
%
% Add a justification to the network and calculate new labels for affected nodes.
%
```

```
atms_add_just( If, Then ) :-
    setof( N, amember( N, If ), If1 ),
    not( justificand( _, Then, If1 ) ),
    new_just_label( J ),
    do_all( ( member( InNode, If1 ), assert( justifier( InNode, J ) ) ) ),
    assert( justificand( J, Then, If1 ) ),
    node_update_env( J ).
```

```
%
% Update the environment label for the rhs of justification Just and propagate
% the effects.
%
```

```
node_update_env( Just ) :-
    justificand( Just, Node, If ),
    gather_env( Node, OldEnvlist ),
    join_assumption( If, Envlist ),
    join_env( OldEnvlist, Envlist, NewEnvlist ),
    % If the Old and New lists are different then propagate the change
    ( OldEnvlist = NewEnvlist, !
    ; cond_update_propagate( Node, NewEnvlist ) ), !.
```

```
% _____
% Get all the minimal environments in which Node is believed to hold.
% _____

gather_env( Node, OldEnvlist ) :- findall( Env, holds( Node, Env ), OldEnvlist ).


% _____
% Update the set of minimal environments in which Node is believed to hold,
% and propagate the effects to nodes justified by Node.
% _____

cond_update_propagate( Node, Envlist ):-
    retractall( holds( Node, _ ) ),
    do_all( ( member( Env, Envlist ), assert( holds( Node, Env ) ) ) ),
    ( Node = false, cond_bottom_update( Node, Envlist ), !
    ; do_all( ( justifier( Node, J ), node_update_env( J ) ) ) ).


% _____
% We have managed to introduce one or more inconsistent environments.
% Remove them from all node labels.
% _____

cond_bottom_update( false, Nogoodlist ) :- !,
    do_all( ( member(Nogoods,Nogoodlist),
            environment( Env, true ),
            bit_subset( Nogoods, Env ),
            remove_inconsistency( Env ) ) ).


% _____
% Cache the given environment as known inconsistent, and remove it from all
% node labels.
% _____

remove_inconsistency( Env ) :-
    retract( environment( Env, true ) ),
    assert( environment( Env, fail ) ),
    do_all( ( holds( Node, Env ), not( Node = false ), retract( holds( Node, Env ) ) ) ).
```

```
% _____
% Find all the minimal environments in which all the elements of If hold.
% _____


join_assumption( If, Envlist ) :-
    findall( Env, ( conjunct_env( If, Env ), check_consistency( Env ) ), Envlist ).


% _____
% Check the consistency of an environment. If we haven't already cached whether
% Env is consistent or not, we determine its consistency by whether
% it includes any nogood sets.
% _____


check_consistency( Env ) :-
    environment( Env, Flag ), !, Flag.
check_consistency( Env ) :-
    holds( false, Nogoods ),
    bit_subset( Nogoods, Env ), !,
    assert( environment( Env, fail ) ),
    fail.
check_consistency( Env ) :-
    assert( environment( Env, true ) ).


% _____
% Compute the minimal environment in which all the nodes in NodeList hold.
% Arguments: NodeList (+), Env (−)
% _____


conjunct_env( [ ], Emp ):- empty_set( Emp ).
conjunct_env( [ N | L ], Res ) :-
    holds( N, Env ),
    conjunct_env( L, Acc ),
    bit_union( Env, Acc, Res ).
```

```
% _____
% Join two environment lists, and pare out the unnecessary parts.
% _____

join_env( OldEnv, Env, NewEnv ) :-
  append( Env, OldEnv, TmpEnv ),
  minimum_env( TmpEnv, NewEnv ).


% _____
% Return a minimum list of minimal environments.
% _____

minimum_env( [ ], [ ] ).
minimum_env( [ Contx | CL ], [ Contx | Res ] ) :-
  remove_superset( Contx, CL, NewCL ), !,
  minimum_env( NewCL, Res ).
minimum_env( [ _ | CL ], Res ) :-
  minimum_env( CL, Res ).


% _____
% Remove every list element that includes S.
% Fail if S includes any element in the list.
% _____
remove_superset( _, [ ], [ ] ).
remove_superset( S, [ S2 | L ], Res ) :-
  bit_subset( S, S2 ), !, remove_superset( S, L, Res ).
remove_superset( S, [ S2 | _ ], _ ) :- bit_subset( S2, S ), !, fail.
remove_superset( S, [ S2 | L ], [ S2 | R ] ) :- remove_superset( S, L, R ).


% _____
% Generate a new justification label.
% _____
new_just_label( J ) :-
  ( retract( just_label_cnt( N ) ), ! ; N = 0 ),
  M is N+1,
  assert( just_label_cnt( M ) ),
  J = just( N ).
```

```
% _____
% Expand the set representation to include another bit position and return the
% singleton set corresponding to the new assumption.
% _____

new_assumption( Assump, bitvec( B ) ) :-
  not( assumption( Assump, _ ) ),
  ( retract( current_bit( B ) ), ! ; B = 1 ),
  NB is B << 1, % shift B left by 1
  assert( assumption( Assump, bitvec( B ) ) ),
  assert( current_bit( NB ) ).


% _____
% Bit-vector set operations
% _____


empty_set( bitvec( 0 ) ).


bit_union( bitvec( S1 ), bitvec( S2 ), bitvec( Res ) ) :- Res is S1 \/ S2.


bit_subset( bitvec( S1 ), bitvec( S2 ) ) :- S1 is S1 /\ S2.


% _____
% Inspecting the content of the ATMS
% _____
explain( X ) :-
  holds( X, _ ), !,
  nl, write('Explanation for: "'), write(X), write('"'), nl,
  do_all(( holds(X,Env), write('{'), list_env(Env,0) )).
explain( X ) :-
  nl, write('There is no way to explain "'), write(X), write('"').


list_env( bitvec(0), _ ) :- write('}'), nl, !.
list_env( bitvec(B), Shift ) :-
  B1 is (B / 1) << Shift,
  ( B1 = 0 -> true
          ;
          assumption( Assumption, bitvec(B1) ),
```

```
            write( Assumption ), write(' ') ),
     B2 is B >> 1,
     Shift2 is Shift + 1,
     list_env( bitvec(B2), Shift2 ).
```

The following is a sample run of our ATMS on the data from the Brazilian
dinner planner mentioned earlier in this section.

| ?- atms_add_just((brazil, brazil_means_meat), meat),
        atms_add_just((meat, quindim), coke69),
        atms_add_just((brazil, cafezinho), coke69),
        atms_add_just((irish), meat),
        atms_add_just((irish, meat), coke69),
        atms_add_just((lamb), coke69).
yes
| ?- explain(coke69).
There is no way to explain "coke69"
yes
| ?- declare_assumption(brazil),
        declare_assumption(brazil_means_meat),
        declare_assumption(quindim),
        declare_assumption(cafezinho),
        declare_assumption(irish),
        declare_assumption(lamb),
        declare_assumption(meat).
yes
| ?- explain(coke69).
Explanation for: "coke69"
{ irish }
{ quindim meat }
{ brazil brazil_means_meat quindim }
{ lamb }
{ brazil cafezinho }
yes
| ?- atms_add_just((brazil), meat),
        atms_add_just((lamb), meat).
yes
| ?- explain(coke69).
Explanation for: "coke69"

{ irish }
{ brazil quindim }
{ quindim meat }
{ lamb }
{ brazil cafezinho }
yes
| ?- atms_add_just((brazil), batida),
    atms_add_just((batida, cafezinho), false).
yes
| ?- explain(coke69).
Explanation for: "coke69"
{ irish }
{ brazil quindim }
{ quindim meat }
{ lamb }
yes
| ?-

5.4   Further reading

There is much literature on TMSs and their various forms. Doyle [17] is usually considered the foundational paper on 'classical' TMSs. Other important
sources are McAllester [44, 45], McDermott [47], and Goodwin [29]. De Kleer
[9] is the founding article for ATMSs. Reiter and de Kleer [68] provide clear
characterization of the functioning of ATMSs in terms of Boolean expression minimization. Descriptions of how TMSs are used in various areas of
AI, such as planning and diagnosis, are scattered throughout the literature.
We have mentioned that *nonmonotonic logics* are relevant to the theoretical
underpinnings of TMSs; initial pointers to that literature include a survey
by Reiter [67], a collection of early foundational papers edited by Ginsberg
[28], and material in Genesereth and Nilsson [26].

5.5   Exercises

Exercise 5.1 It was mentioned in the chapter that the implemented CMS consistency-restoring precedure embodies a number of some arbitrary decisions. In particular, in the implemented version when a contradiction is detected then one justification from a premise is selected at random for deletion. If that does not clear up the inconsistency, then the process is repeated.

(a) Show that the collection of justifications eliminated by this procedure is not always minimal, and modify the program so that it is.

(b) Deleting justifications is one way to restore consistency; adding justifications is another, due to the presence of nonmonotonic justifiers. Write a version of the CMS program that adopts this strategy. It should locate all the facts currently labeled OUT that participate (as nonmonotonic justifiers) in the support of the contradiction, and make as many of them IN (by adding a justification to them from the premise node) as necessary.

Exercise 5.2 At the beginning of the chapter it was explained that a TMS serves as an intelligent database to some problem solver, but in the chapter we have discussed TMSs in isolation. Your task here will be to connect TMSs and backward chaining.

(a) Modify the basic meta-interpreter from Chapter 3 so that it caches intermediate results in a CMS. The CMS-based meta-interpreter should still incorporate chronological backtracking. However, before backtracking the interpreter will always record the goals that have succeeded and their justifications. Similarly, when attempting to prove a new goal, it will always first consult the CMS to see whether that goal has a solution whose justifications currently hold, and only otherwise engage in the standard search of the computation tree. Show an example in which the new meta-interpreter performs more efficiently than the standard one.

(b) Do the same for the heuristic meta-interpreter.

(c) While introducing a certain measure of economy, the CMS-aided meta-interpreter can still perform wasteful computations; ATMSs are aimed at eliminating this waste. Show an example of such waste, and implemented an ATMS-aided meta-interpreter. *Hint:* This is a harder problem; you may want to read [9].

Exercise 5.3 All TMSs discussed in the chapter have a 'binary' nature; in RMSs and CMSs each node is labeled either IN or OUT, and in ATMSs the nodes are partitioned into assumption nodes and the rest. However, there is no reason that these binary catagorizations cannot be generalized.

(a) Let us define an n-valued RMS to be an RMS in which the labels range over n ordered values. Intuitively, the order will reflect the strength of the evidence for the fact. In the binary case, there is only the question of whether or not there is evidence for a fact; but in a three-valued RMS, for example, we might distinguish between no evidence, weak evidence, and strong evidence. Your task is to implement a general n-valued RMS. You will need to make a number of evidence-combination assumptions. For example, you may assume that the strength of a justification is the strength of its weakest link. In the case of in-justifiers that is easy: for example, if a justification has two in-justifiers, one for which there is weak evidence and another for which there is strong evidence, you may assign weak evidence to the justificand. How will you handle out-justifiers?

(b) Do the same for an n-valued CMS. You must take care here with the notion of 'strength of evidence'; there is an important difference between having no justification for a node and having that node justify false, and yet (e.g.) in the binary case they will both result in that node being labeled OUT.

(c) Here your task is to define and implement an n-valued ATMS, but the values are to be interpreted differently than in the cases of RMSs and CMSs. The value of a node here will be interpreted as 'level of criticality.' For example, in a binary (i.e., standard) ATMS, there are two levels: assumptions are critical nodes that must be taken into account when constructing explanations, and the rest are deemed sufficiently mundane to be safely ignored. Generalize ATMSs so that each node is assigned one of n possible values; the label of each node includes nodes from all levels of criticality, but the ATMS supports queries of the form "show me the label of a node with criticality level i," in response to which it constructs a minimal explanation consisting only of nodes of criticality level i or higher. *Note:* This problem is somewhat harder than might appear at first, since a node that is subsumed by another at one level of criticality may no longer be subsumed when the criticality level is increased.

Chapter 6

Constraint Satisfaction

Constraint satisfaction is a computational paradigm in which knowledge is formulated as a set of constraints on various variables. The role of constraint satisfaction algorithms is to assign values to the variables in a way that is consistent with all the constraints, or to determine that no such assignment exists. Similarly to search, discussed in Chapter 2, constraint satisfaction is a very general paradigm, encompassing many AI computational tasks. AI domains in which constraint satisfaction techniques have been applied include machine vision, temporal reasoning, scheduling, theorem proving, and diagnosis.

A simple example often used to illustrate constraint satisfaction problems (CSPs) is map coloring. Consider Figure 6.1, in which a global region is divided into five subregions. Given a collection of possible colors, the task is to assign each region a color so that no two adjacent regions are assigned the same color; the figure shows such an assignment. Figure 6.2 shows a natural graph-theoretic encoding of the same problem: the nodes in the graph represent the regions, and the arcs are annotated by the constraints between the two regions. (This is a natural example of CSPs, but don't be misled by it. Map coloring is a very special problem, which has been well studied in graph theory; constraint satisfaction methods concern networks of arbitrary constraints.)

In this chapter we will first define CSPs more precisely and informally survey techniques for solving CSPs. We will then discuss one technique –

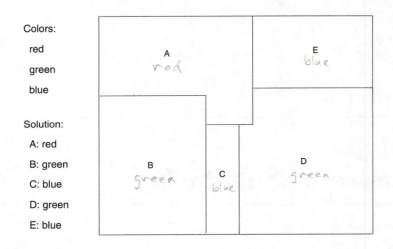

Figure 6.1: A simple map coloring problem and its solution

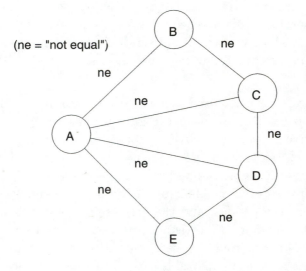

Figure 6.2: A graph representation of the map coloring problem

consistency enforcing – in more detail, and present its Prolog implementation. We will conclude with an application of consistency enforcing to temporal reasoning.

6.1   Precise definition of CSP

A *constraint network* consists of a finite set of variables $X = \{X_1, \ldots, X_n\}$, a domain D_i for each variable X_i, and a set of constraints $\{C_1, \ldots, C_m\}$. Although some work on constraint satisfaction allows infinite domains, we will assume that all the domains are finite and are explicitly enumerated. In the map coloring example above there were five variables, and they all had the same domain – {red,green,blue}. Each constraint is a predicate on some subset of the variables, say $X_{i_1}, \ldots, X_{i_j}$; the predicate defines a relation which is a subset of the Cartesian product $D_{i_1} \times \ldots \times D_{i_j}$. In English this means that each constraint restricts the values that may be simultaneously assigned to the variables participating in the constraint. In this chapter we will restrict the discussion to *binary* constraints, each of which constrains exactly two variables. For example, in the map coloring case, each "not equal" constraint applied to two nodes.

Given a subset S of the variables, an *instantiation of S* is an assignment of a unique domain value for each variable in S; it is *legal* if it does not violate any constraint that mentions only variables in S. A *solution* to a network is a legal instantiation of all variables. Typical tasks associated with constraint networks are to determine whether a solution exists, to find one or all solutions, to determine whether a legal instantiation of some of the variables can be extended to a solution, and so on. These tasks are collectively called *constraint satisfaction problems (CSPs)*. We will concentrate on the most common task, which is finding one solution to a CSP.

6.2   Overview of constraint satisfaction techniques

The most straightforward way to search for a solution, called 'generate-and-test,' is to enumerate all possible combinations of variable values and examine them one by one to see whether they satisfy all the constraints. Of course this is very inefficient. For this reason, most techniques are based

on some backtracking scheme. A typical algorithm considers the variables
in some order and, starting with the first, assigns a provisional value to
each successive variable in a way that is consistent, given the constraints,
with the values already assigned. When a dead-end is encountered, that
is, when some variable is reached none of whose values is consistent with
all the values previously assigned to other variables, backtracking occurs.
This means that a value assigned to a previous variable is replaced by a
new value from that variable's domain, and the search resumes from that
point. Usually the previous variable whose value is being reassigned is the
immediately preceding one; this so-called *chronological backtracking* is, of
course, the backtracking scheme of the Prolog interpreter.

   Constraint satisfaction techniques are aimed at speeding up this backtracking search. The major techniques can be roughly divided as follows:

1. *Consistency enforcing.* The given network is replaced by an equivalent,
   yet more explicit one; for example, some of the values in variables'
   domains are eliminated as a result of some limited consistency checks.
   Consequently, fewer bad choices of variable values are made, and less
   backtracking occurs.

2. *Constraint propagation.* This technique may be viewed as a special
   case of consistency enforcing; when a value is selected for a variable,
   this imposes a new constraint on the possible values of the remaining
   variables; this new constraint can be propagated throughout the network, resulting in the elimination of some values from some domains
   and reducing the need for subsequent backtracking.

3. *Variable ordering.* The amount of backtracking may be greatly affected
   by the order in which variables are instantiated. Typical heuristics for
   deciding on good ordering are based on the intuition that highly con-
   strained variables should be instantiated first; this idea was already
   mentioned in Chapter 3, in connection with heuristic backward chaining.

4. *Value ordering.* Just as the choice of 'next' variable is important,
   so is the choice of 'next' value for that variable. Typical heuristics
   attempt to maximize the number of consistent values for the remaining
   variables.

5. *Backjumping.* When a dead-end occurs, it is sometimes possible to

identify a set of previous choices that led to it and backtrack directly
to one of those rather than to the most recent previous choice.

6. *Nogood recording.* This technique is related backjumping; when culprit
choices that led to the dead-end (the so-called nogoods) are identified, they can be recorded so that they are not repeated in the rest of
the search. This idea underlies assumption-based truth maintenance
systems (ATMSs) discussed in the Chapter 5. The term *dependency-
directed backtracking* is sometimes used to describe methods that combine backjumping and nogood recording.

In the remainder of this chapter we will discuss consistency enforcing
(and the related technique of constraint propagation) in more detail.

6.3   Consistency enforcing

Consistency enforcing algorithms ensure that solutions to certain subnet-
works can be extended to certain other parts of the network. The most
common form of consistency is *2-consistency*, also called *arc consistency*,
which ensures that given any two nodes and any value for the first node
(from its domain), there exists at least one value for the second node (from
its domain) that is consistent with the first value, given the constraints. If
this property is not already true of the original network, the arc consistency
algorithms restrict the domains of various variables until the property holds.
Similarly, *3-consistency* means that if one picks any three nodes and assigns
two of them any values from their domains, the third node can be assigned
a value from its domain consistent with the values of the first two nodes. 3-
consistency turns out to be equivalent to another type of consistency, called
path consistency, and so we will use the two terms interchangeably. Note
that 3-consistency does not ensure that any instantiation of two nodes can
be extended to a complete solution. In general, *n-consistency* will mean that
any legal instantiation of $n - 1$ variables can be extended to any one of the
remaining variables. Clearly, any network with n nodes that is i-consistent
for all $i \leq n$ (this property is sometimes called *strong n-consistency*), has a
solution (in fact, it has at least as many solutions as the size of the largest
among the variables' domains).

Obviously, a high degree of consistency is desirable, since it reduces (or
even eliminates) the need for backtracking. Unfortunately, there is no free

lunch, and in general the complexity of achieving i-consistency is exponential in i. Empirical studies have been carried out to determine how much effort is justified in increasing the degree of consistency ahead of the search, but this is not a settled issue in AI.

In this section we will discuss arc consistency in more detail. We give two algorithms due to A. Mackworth, called respectively AC-1 and AC-3 (yes, there was an AC-2 as well). The idea in both cases is to examine each arc in turn and delete from the domain of the first node any value that does not have a matching value in the second node. In both algorithms, a deletion in one domain may necessitate deletions in other domains. AC-1 handles this in a straightforward fashion: If any change occurs during the examination of any of the arcs, all arcs are examined again. The AC-1 algorithm has the following structure:

PROCEDURE AC-1 ($network$)
$Q \leftarrow$ list of all arcs of $network$
repeat until $\neg change$
    $change \leftarrow$ false
    for each $(V_i, V_j) \in Q$ do
        $change \leftarrow$ REVISE$(V_i, V_j) \vee$ REVISE$(V_j, V_i) \vee change$
    end for
end repeat

PROCEDURE REVISE (V_i, V_j)
$flag \leftarrow$ false
for each $x \in D_i$ do
    if there is no $y \in D_j$ such that (x, y) is consistent
    then delete x from D_i, and $flag \leftarrow$ true
end for
return $flag$

(The difference between enforcing arc consistency on the entire network, as above, and propagating constraints from a given node, is simply that in the latter the queue Q is initialized to contain only arcs connecting nodes to the given node, rather than all the arcs.)

To implement the algorithm we must first decide on the representation of the constraint network. We will assume that the input is in the form of two lists, a variable list and an arc list. The members in the variable list will be pairs (*variable-name, domain*), the latter being a list of domain values. Members in the arc list will be triples (v_1, v_2, p), where v_i are variable names, and p is the name of any user-defined binary predicate. For example, in the map coloring example seen in the introduction to this chapter, the predicate name might be **ne**, and the predicate might be defined by the clause **ne(X, Y) :- not(X = Y)**. The output of the algorithm will be a list similar to the input list but with some domain values possibly removed. No domain will be empty; an empty domain for any variable will cause the procedure to fail.

With this representation, the implementation of AC-1 is as follows.

```
% _____
% ac1 / 3 ensures that the domains in the variable list are pairwise consistent
% with respect to the arc list.
% Arguments: A list of variables with associated domains (+),
a list of arcs
% with associated constraints (+), the list of variables with new domains (-)
% _____


ac1( VarList, ArcList, NewVarList ) :- !,
    ac1sub( VarList, ArcList, ArcList, 0, NewVarList ).


ac1sub( VarList, OrigArcList, ArcList, Bit, NewVarList ) :-
    remove( ( V1, V2, P ), ArcList, NewArcList ),
    revise( V1, V2, P, VarList, TmpVarList1 ),
    revise( V2, V1, P, TmpVarList1, TmpVarList2 ),
    ( Bit = 0, same_set( VarList, TmpVarList2 ) -> NewBit = 0; NewBit = 1 ),
    ( NewArcList = [ ], NewBit = 0 -> NewVarList = TmpVarList2
      ; ( NewArcList = [ ]
        -> ac1sub( TmpVarList2, OrigArcList, OrigArcList, 0, NewVarList )
         ; ac1sub( TmpVarList2, OrigArcList, NewArcList, NewBit, NewVarList ) ) ).


% _____
% revise / 5 restricts V1's domain list to that set of elements consistent with some
% element in V2's domain list.
% Arguments: V1 (+), V2 (+), consistency predicate (+),
%            old domain of V1 (+), new domain of V1 (-).
% _____
```

```
revise( V1, V2, P, VarListIn, [ ( V1, NewD1List ) | RestVars ] ) :-
  remove( ( V1, D1List ), VarListIn, RestVars ),
  member( ( V2, D2List ), RestVars ),
  ( setof( D1,
          D2^( member( D1, D1List ), member( D2, D2List ), apply( P, D1, D2 ) ),
          NewD1List )
  ; writel( [ 'no consistent assignment to ', V1 ] ), nl, !, fail ).
```

% writel / 1 writes the elements in a list; see Chapter 1.

% same_set / 3 succeeds if lists X and Y represent the same set. same_set / 3 depends
% on the fact that setof / 3 sorts the elements in its output set.

```
same_set( X, Y ) :-
  setof( Z, member( Z, X ), L1 ),
  setof( Z, member( Z, Y ), L2 ),
  L1 = L2.
```

The following is a sample run of our implementation of AC-1 on the map coloring problem from earlier in this chapter. In this run we have arbitrarily restricted node A's domain to {red} so simple permutations of the colors will not allow the domain sets to stay artificially large.

```
| ?- ac1([(a,[red]),(b,[red,green,blue]),(c,[red,green,blue]),
         (d,[red,green,blue]),(e,[red,green,blue])],
         [(a,b,ne),(a,c,ne),(a,d,ne),(a,e,ne),
          (b,c,ne),(c,d,ne),(d,e,ne)],
         X).

X = [(e,[blue,green]),(d,[blue,green]),(c,[blue,green]),
     (b,[blue,green]),(a,[red])]
| ?-
```

AC-1 is clearly a wasteful procedure; if a change in the domain of one variable occurs then all arcs are examined afresh, even if unrelated to that variable. AC-3 is more sophisticated about this reexamination. The idea behind AC-3 is that when an arc (V_i, V_j) is processed by the REVISE procedure, and the domain of V_i is made to shrink as a result, then it is enough to recheck all arcs pointing at V_i, excluding the arc from V_j (if it exists). The AC-3 algorithm uses the same REVISE procedure as above and has the following structure:

PROCEDURE AC-3 $(network)$
$Q \leftarrow$ list of all arcs of $network$
repeat until Q is empty
    remove any (V_i, V_j) from Q
    if REVISE(V_i, V_j)
       then $Q \leftarrow Q \cup \{(V_k, V_i) : (V_k, V_i)$ is an arc of $network, k \neq i, m\}$
end repeat

Assuming the earlier representation, AC-3 may be implemented as follows.

```
% _____
% ac3 / 3 ensures that the domains in the variable list are pairwise consistent
% with respect to the arc list.
% Arguments: same as in ac1 / 3
% _____

ac3( VarList, ArcList, NewVarList ) :- !,
  ac3sub( VarList, ArcList, ArcList, NewVarList ). '


ac3sub( VarList, _, [ ], VarList ) :- !.
ac3sub( VarList, OrigArcList, ArcList, NewVarList ) :-
  remove( ( V1, V2, P ), ArcList, TmpArcList ),
  revise( V1, V2, P, VarList, TmpVarList1 ),
  revise( V2, V1, P, TmpVarList1, TmpVarList2 ),
  ( same_set( TmpVarList2, VarList ) ->
    NextArcList = TmpArcList
    ;
    findall( ( V3, V1, P ),
          (member( ( V3, V1, P ), OrigArcList ),
            not( V3 = V1 ), not( V3 = V2 ) ),
          SuspectArcs ),
    union( TmpArcList, SuspectArcs, NextArcList ) ),
  ac3sub( TmpVarList2, OrigArcList, NextArcList, NewVarList ).
```

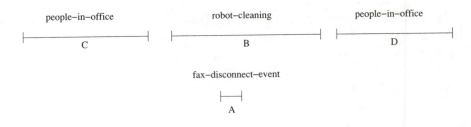

Figure 6.3: The case of the clumsy robot

% revise / 5 *and* same_set / 2 *are as above.*
% union / 3 *merges two lists, removing duplicates (see Chapter 1).*

This implementation can be optimized in a number of ways; see Exercise 6.1.

6.4   Consistency enforcing in temporal reasoning

We conclude the discussion of constraint satisfaction with an application to temporal reasoning; this material is as relevant to the chapter on temporal reasoning (Chapter 8) as it is to this chapter. Many reasoning tasks have the subtask of maintaining constraints on intervals. Consider the following narrative: "The robot started cleaning the office after everyone left, and finished before anyone returned. While cleaning the office, the robot accidentally disconnected the fax machine." Suppose that it is important to be notified whenever the fax machine is disconnected with no human in the area; how could a program be written to issue such a notification based on this narrative? One way is to draw the diagram in Figure 6.3, and note that the fax-disconnect-event (interval A) takes place *during* the robot-cleaning interval (interval B), which in turn comes *after* one people-in-office interval (interval C) and *before* another (interval D). Therefore interval A too must fall between intervals C and D. This inference is the result of constraint propagation; although no explicit constraint is given over the set {A,C,D}, such a constraint is derived from the constraints on the sets {A,B} and {B,C,D}. We are interested in a procedure to derive such seemingly obvious inferences in a systematic way.

We will discuss the influential 3-consistency (or, equivalently, path consistency) procedure due to J. Allen for maintaining knowledge about temporal intervals. To begin with, we note that two intervals may stand in one of thirteen relations to one another; these are named and shown pictorially in Figure 6.4.

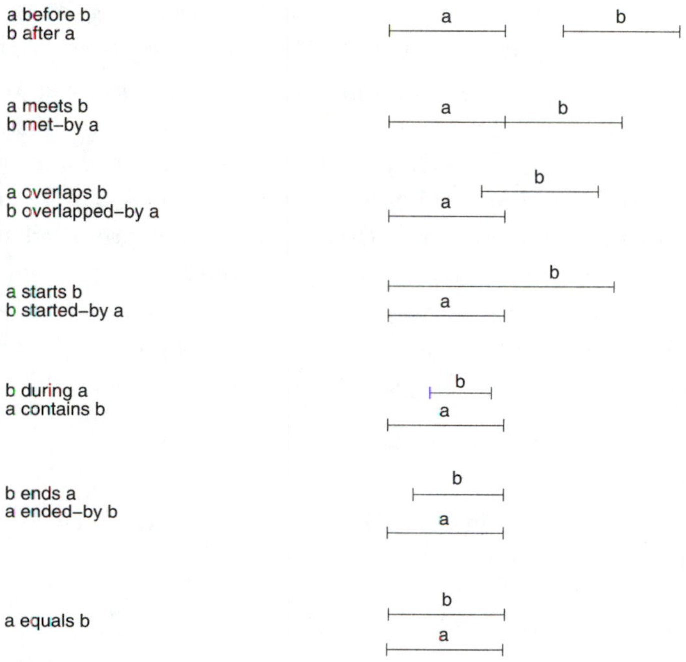

Figure 6.4: The 13 possible relations between two intervals

In the cleaning-robot example above, all constraints between pairs of intervals were in the form of one of these thirteen relations. In general, however, there may be more ambiguous information. In the following, we will allow a constraint on a pair of intervals to be any nonempty subset of the thirteen possible relations; the interpretation of the constraint will be that the two intervals must stand in one of these relations to one another. For example, the constraint {before,meets} on the pair (I,J) will mean that interval I begins before interval J, and ends either before or at the beginning of J. Similarly, the constraint {before,meets,met-by,after} on (I,J) will mean that I and J are disjoint. If the constraint contains all thirteen relations, this means that the two intervals are mutually unconstrained. (In practice, we omit these vacuous constraints and infer them from the absence of an explicit constraint between the two intervals.)

Now consider a pair of intervals (A,B). In addition to the given constraint on the possible relations between them, we may derive additional ones. For example, suppose initially no constraints are placed on this pair, but for some interval X it is known that A overlaps X and that X is during B; it follows that one of the following holds: A overlaps B, A is during B, or A starts B. Figure 6.5 depicts the full 'transitivity' table of all interval relations.

In general, if A and X can stand in one of several relations, and the same is true of X and B, then the constraints derived for the pair (A,B) consist of the *union* of all constraints derived by selecting one of the allowed relations for (A,X) and one of the allowed relations for (X,B). This is the basis for the following algorithm, which is based on an algorithm proposed by J. Allen. The input to the algorithm is a list of binary constraints on n intervals. It is given in the form of an $n \times n$ matrix N; $N(i,j)$ contains the constraint (i.e., list of possible relations) between interval i and interval j. In the subroutine CONSTRAINTS, $T(i,j)$ is the (i,j)'th entry in the transitivity table from Figure 6.5.

PROCEDURE PROPAGATE-INTERVAL-CONSTRAINTS (N: matrix)
$Q \leftarrow \{(i,j) : 1 \leq i, j \leq n, i \neq j\}$
repeat until Q is empty
    remove any (i,j) from Q
    for each interval $k \neq i, j$ do
        $N(k,j) \leftarrow N(k,j) \cap$ CONSTRAINTS($N(k,i), N(i,j)$)
        if $N(k,j)$ changed then add (k,j) to Q
        $N(i,k) \leftarrow N(i,k) \cap$ CONSTRAINTS($N(i,j), N(j,k)$)
        if $N(i,k)$ changed then add (i,k) to Q
    end for
end repeat

PROCEDURE CONSTRAINTS ($R1$, $R2$: constraints)
$R \leftarrow$ empty
for each $r1 \in R1$ and $r2 \in R2$ do
    $R \leftarrow R \cup T(r1, r2)$
end for
return R

To implement the procedure in Prolog, we must again first decide on representation. Since the matrix T is fixed once and for all, we can store it

R1 \ R2	b	a	d	di	o	oi	m	mi	s	si	e	ei
before b	b	?	b o m d s	b	b	b o m d s	b	b o m d s	b	b	b o m d s	b
after a	?	a	a oi mi d e	a	a oi mi d e	a	a oi mi d e	a	a oi mi d e	a	a	a
during d	b	a	d	?	b o m d s	a oi mi d e	b	a	d	a oi mi d e	d	b o m d s
contains di	b o m di ei	a oi di mi si	o oi d di =	di	o di ei	oi di si	o di ei	oi di si	o di ei	di	oi di si	di
overlaps o	b	a oi di mi si	o d s	b o m di ei	b o m	o oi d di =	b	oi di si	o	o di ei	o d s	di
overlapped-by oi	b o m di ei	a	oi d e	a oi di mi si	o oi d di =	a oi mi	o di ei	a	oi d e	a oi mi	oi	oi di si
meets m	b	a oi di mi si	o d s	b	b	o d s	b	e ei =	m	m	o d s	b
met-by mi	b o m di ei	a	oi d e	a	oi d e	a	s si =	a	oi d e	a	mi	mi
starts s	b	a	d	b o m di ei	b o m	oi d e	b	mi	s	s si =	d	b o m
started-by si	b o m di ei	a	oi d e	di	o di ei	oi	o di ei	mi	s si =	si	oi	di
ends e	b	a	d	a oi di mi si	o d s	a oi mi	m	a	d	a oi mi	e	e ei =
ended-by ei	b	a oi di mi si	o d s	di	o	oi di si	m	oi di si	o	di	e ei =	ei

Figure 6.5: Transitivity table for interval relations, omitting '=';
'?' denotes the set of all thirteen relations (after J. Allen)

as a collection of database facts:

```
trans(b,b,[b]).
trans(b,a,[b,a,d,di,o,oi,m,mi,s,si,e,ei]).
trans(b,d,[b,o,m,d,s]).
  .
  .
  .
trans(ei,ei,[ei]).
```

The queue Q will be maintained as a regular list. That leaves us with the need to represent the matrix N. Here we will simply assume that such a representation is given, which supports the following operations:[1]

size(+N, –Num): returns n if N is of size $n \times n$

fetch(+N, +I, +J, –Value): returns the (I,J) value of N

store(+N, +I, +J, +Value, –NewN): replaces the (I,J) value of N

With this representation, the implementation is as follows. The input is the matrix of constraints; the output is the matrix with the tighter constraints.

```
% _____
% propagate_interval_constraints / 2 accepts a matrix of given constraints as input
% and produces an output matrix of tighter constraints using the method
% described in the text.
% Arguments: input matrix (+), output matrix (–)
% _____
```

```
propagate_interval_constraints( N, NewN ) :-
    allpairs( N, Q ),                    % initialize Q
    p_i_c( N, Q, NewN, _).
```

---

[1]One, clearly suboptimal, representation is to maintain the $n \times n$ matrix by a list of rows, that is, by n lists of n elements each. For example, the matrix N would be maintained in the form

$$n([[v_{1,1},v_{1,2},\ldots,v_{1,n}], [v_{2,1},\ldots,v_{2,n}], \ldots, [v_{n,1},\ldots,v_{n,n-1},v_{n,n}]])$$

where $v_{i,j}$ is the value of the (i,j)'th entry (in our case, the constraint between intervals i and j). More efficient representations are possible, and some are available in a number of Prolog libraries.

```
% _____
% allpairs / 2 produces a list Q of all pairs that index off-diagonal elements of the
% array N.
% Arguments: N (+), Q (−)
% _____

allpairs( N, Q ) :-
    size( N, Size ), allpairs1( Size, Q ).

allpairs1( Size, Q ) :-
    halfpairs( Size, LowHalf ),
    bagof( ( X, Y ), member( ( Y, X ), LowHalf ), HiHalf ),
    append( LowHalf, HiHalf, Q ).


% _____
% halfpairs / 2 generates a list L of all below-diagonal pairs (pairs whose first
% component exceeds their second) up to and including pairs with first component
% equal to the positive integer N.
% Arguments: N (+), L (−)
% _____

halfpairs( 1, [ ] ).
halfpairs( N, L ) :-
    smaller_eq( N, Ln ),
    bagof( (M, K),
           Lm^( member( M, Ln ), smaller( M, Lm ), member( K, Lm ) ),
           L).


% _____
% smaller / 2 generates a list L of all positive integers less than the positive
% integer N.
% Arguments: N (+), L (−)
% _____

smaller( 1, [ ] ) :- !.
smaller( N, [ M | R ] ) :- M is N−1, smaller( M, R ).
```

```
% _____
% smaller_eq / 2 generates a list L of all positive integers less than or equal to the
% positive integer N.
% Arguments: N (+), L (−)
% _____
```

```
smaller_eq( N, L ) :- M is N+1, smaller( M, L ).
```

```
% _____
% p_i_c / 4 performs the outer loop of the
% PROPAGATE-INTERVAL-CONSTRAINTS algorithm. The first two
% arguments are the current matrix N of constraints and the current list Q of
% pairs whose constraints need to be propagated. The last two are the revised
% matrix and list.
% Arguments: N (+), Q (+), NewN (−), NewQ (−)
% _____
```

```
p_i_c( N, [ ], NewN, _ ) :- !, NewN = N.          % if Q is empty stop.
p_i_c( N, [ ( I, J ) | Q ], NewN, NewQ ) :-
  size( N, Size ),
  p_i_c_loop( Size, I, J, N, Q, TmpN, TmpQ ),
  p_i_c( TmpN, TmpQ, NewN, NewQ ).
```

```
% _____
% p_i_c_loop / 7 executes a single iteration of the outer loop of the
% PROPAGATE-INTERVAL-CONSTRAINTS algorithm. It propagates the
% influence of interval pair (I, J) to intervals (K, J) and (I, K) before advancing
% K and recursing.
% Arguments: K (+), I (+), J (+), N (+), Q (+), NewN (−), NewQ (−)
% _____
```

```
p_i_c_loop( K, _, _, N, Q, NewN, NewQ ) :-
  K = 0, !, NewQ = Q, NewN = N.          % If all intervals processed, stop.
p_i_c_loop( K, I, J, N, Q, NewN, NewQ ) :-
  ( K = I ; K = J ), !,          % Skip over intervals I and J themselves.
  K1 is K−1,
  p_i_c_loop( K1, I, J, N, Q, NewN, NewQ ).
```

```
p_i_c_loop( K, I, J, N, Q, NewN, NewQ ) :-
   fetch( N, K, I, ConKI ),
   fetch( N, I, J, ConIJ ),
   constraints( ConKI, ConIJ, ConKJ ),
   fetch( N, K, J, Nkj ),
   intersect( Nkj, ConKJ, NewKJ ),
   ( NewKJ = [ ], !, write( 'Network not satisfiable' ), nl,
     writel( [ 'No assignment for ', K, ', ', J,
              ' inferring from ', I ] ), nl,
     show_array( N ), fail ; true ),
   ( same_set( Nkj, NewKJ ) -> ( Tmp1N = N , Tmp1Q = Q )
    ; ( store( N, K, J, NewKJ, Tmp1N ), Tmp1Q = [ ( K, J ) | Q ] ) ),
   fetch( Tmp1N, J, K, ConJK ),
   constraints( ConIJ, ConJK, ConIK ),
   fetch( Tmp1N, I, K, Nik ),
   intersect( Nik, ConIK, NewIK ),
   ( NewIK = [ ], !, write( 'Network not satisfiable' ), nl,
     writel( [ 'No assignment for ', I, ', ', K,
              ' inferring from ', J ] ), nl,
     show_array( Tmp1N ), fail ; true ),
   ( same_set( Nik, NewIK ) -> ( Tmp2N = Tmp1N , Tmp2Q = Tmp1Q )
    ; ( store( Tmp1N, I, K, NewIK, Tmp2N ), Tmp2Q = [ ( I, K ) | Tmp1Q ] ) ),
   K1 is K-1,
   p_i_c_loop( K1, I, J, Tmp2N, Tmp2Q, NewN, NewQ ).
```

```
% _____
% constraints / 3 computes the list Con3 of constraints consistent with those in the
% lists Con1 and Con2 through a single transitivity computation in the matrix
% represented by trans / 3.
% Arguments: Con1 (+), Con2 (+), Con3 (-)
% _____
```

```
constraints( Con1, Con2, Con3 ) :-
   constraints1( Con1, Con2, Con2, [ ], Con3 ).
constraints1( [ ], _, _, TmpCon, Con3 ) :- !, Con3 = TmpCon.
constraints1( [ _| Con1 ], [ ], OrigCon2, TmpCon, Con3 ) :- !,
   constraints1( Con1, OrigCon2, OrigCon2, TmpCon, Con3 ).
constraints1( [ R1 | Con1 ], [ R2 | Con2 ], OrigCon2, TmpCon, Con3 ) :-
```

```
trans( R1, R2, Con4 ),
union( TmpCon, Con4, NewTmpCon ),
constraints1( [ R1 | Con1 ], Con2, OrigCon2, NewTmpCon, Con3 ).
```

% intersect / 3 *intersects two lists (see Chapter 1);* union / 3 *is as above.*
% show_array / 1 *is assumed to display the current matrix of domain lists.*

It can be shown that since the unions and intersections take constant time, and if the matrix operations also took constant time, then the time complexity of the algorithm would be $O(n^3)$, where n is the number of intervals. In connection with this, see Exercise 6.5.

Below, we show input and output for two sample runs of our implementation, assuming the array representation discussed in the footnote on page 156; the first run uses the cleaning-robot example.

```
| ?- All=[ b,a,d,di,o,oi,m,mi,s,si,e,ei,= ],
      propagate_interval_constraints( [ [ [ = ], [ d ], All,   All ],
                                        [ [ di ], [ = ], [ a ], [ b ] ],
                                        [ All,   [ b ], [ = ], [ b ] ],
                                        [ All,   [ a ], [ a ], [ = ] ] ], N ).

N = [[[=],[d],[a],[b]],
     [[di],[=],[a],[b]],
     [[b],[b],[=],[b]],
     [[a],[a],[a],[=]]]


| ?- All=[ b,a,d,di,o,oi,m,mi,s,si,e,ei,= ],
      propagate_interval_constraints( [ [ [ = ], [ d ], All,   All ],
                                        [ [ di ], [ = ], [ a ], [ b ] ],
                                        [ All,   [ b ], [ = ], [ b ] ],
                                        [ All,   [ a ], [ b ], [ = ] ] ], N ).

    Network not satisfiable
    No assignment for 2, 3 inferring from 4
    [=][d][b,a,d,di,o,oi,m,mi,s,si,e,ei,=][b,a,d,di,o,oi,m,mi,s,si,e,ei,=]
    [di][=][a][b]
    [b,a,d,di,o,oi,m,mi,s,si,e,ei,=][b][=][b]
    [b,a,d,di,o,oi,m,mi,s,si,e,ei,=][a][b][=]


    no
| ?-
```

6.5   Further reading

Good general surveys of constraint satisfaction techniques are provided by
Dechter [13], Mackworth [43], and Kumar [40]; these surveys contain references to earlier foundational publications, as well as to more recent advances
in the area. Allen's influential paper appeared in [1]. Since then there have
been many additions and refinements; a recent article, by Dechter et al. [14]
includes reference to many recent results in this area. Finally, constraint
satisfaction has come to play an important role within logic programming
itself. For a discussion of constraint satisfaction techniques in the context of
logic programming, see Van Hentenryck [33] and Jaffar and Lassez [34].

6.6   Exercises

Exercise 6.1 The implementation of the AC-3 algorithm given in the chapter is wasteful in a number of ways. Let e be the number of arcs in the network, and k the size of the largest domain.

(a) Modify the program so that it runs in time $O(ek^3)$.

(b) Modify the program so that it runs in time $O(ek^2)$ (hard).

Exercise 6.2 Being only a 3-consistency method, the interval constraint propagation procedure described in the chapter is not complete. That is, there are networks that imply stricter constraints than those derived by the procedure. In particular, there are networks that are inconsistent without the procedure ever discovering the fact; can you show such a network?

Exercise 6.3 Consider maintaining information about time points rather than time intervals. There are only three possible relations between two points – before, equal, and after – as opposed to thirteen in the case of intervals. There are therefore only $2^3 = 8$ possible binary constraints on points as opposed to the 2^{13} for intervals.

(a) Construct the transitivity table for points.

(b) Adapt the constraint propagation program from intervals to points.

(c) Is the new program complete? In particular, if the network is inconsistent, is the procedure guaranteed to discover this fact?

Exercise 6.4 The interval constraint propagation procedure can become quite unwieldy when many intervals are involved. For this reason, J. Allen introduced the notion of *reference intervals*, which provide a natural form of abstraction. For example, when asked whether your trip to the zoo in eighth grade overlapped with the period of being in love with Sara in eleventh grade, you need not compare them directly; it is enough to know that they belong to two disjoint reference intervals, 'eighth grade' and 'eleventh grade.' These two reference intervals may in turn belong to higher-level reference interval 'school years,' which is disjoint from the interval 'university years.'

Adapt the interval constraint propagation procedure so that two intervals are comparable only if they belong to the same reference interval, or else the relationship between them is deducible from the relationship between the reference intervals.

Exercise 6.5 The interval constraint propagation procedure can be made faster by representing each constraint as a 13-bit string; in this way the union and intersection operations can be done more efficiently. Modify the program to accommodate this representation. *Hint:* See the discussion of bit strings in Chapter 1.

Chapter 7

Reasoning with Uncertainty

All the methods discussed so far have applied to categorical information: Items were either in the database or out of it, conclusions were either sanctioned by the system or not. Yet in many AI applications, as in real life, finer shades of certainty exist; we are quite certain of some facts, less certain of others, and clueless about yet others. Consider medical diagnosis, for example. On the basis of some symptoms a doctor may diagnose a certain illness. For a number of reasons, however, this diagnosis is merely a hypothesis that is not guaranteed to be correct: Medicine provides only a partial account of the functioning of the human body, the data obtained from the patient is partial and error-prone, and so on. Nonetheless, the diagnosis is more than a wild guess; it provides *some* assurance that the diagnosed illness is the actual one. We often have a sense of how good the hypothesis is, either in absolute terms or in comparison with other candidate hypotheses.

Uncertainty arises in most areas of AI. This is definitely the case in many expert systems, in automated planning, and in machine learning, to name only a few. In fact, some in AI have argued that *all* AI problems should be couched in some calculus of uncertainty (the leading candidate being probability theory, discussed below). Although such sweeping claims about the nature of AI are probably unwarranted, uncertainty does play an important role in AI.

It is in principle possible to take any reasoning technique and augment it with some notion of uncertainty, and this is definitely true of the reasoning techniques discussed so far – backward chaining, forward chaining, and truth maintenance. We will concentrate here on backward chaining. To incorporate uncertainty into backward chaining, we need to represent uncertainty in the Prolog database and to modify the meta-interpreter accordingly. In the first section, therefore, we discuss the representation of uncertainty in Prolog. In the second section we present a general meta-interpreter. This general meta-interpreter leaves open the question of how to combine uncertainties, a topic addressed in the remainder of the chapter. In the third section we briefly review the main concepts of probability theory. In the fourth section we describe a number of probability-combination functions, and in the fifth section we discuss the combination of certainty factors in the well-known MYCIN program. The combination methods discussed in these last two sections are merely heuristic and are not grounded firmly in probability theory. The final section of this chapter explores more rigorous methods for computing certainties, as embodied in *Bayesian networks*.

7.1   Representing uncertainty in the database

To represent uncertainty, we will associate with each Prolog clause a measure representing its certainty. To do so, we will make use of the internal references of Prolog clauses, which were reviewed in Chapter 1. For example, to represent the fact that it is 'likely' that the connection

$$\text{head :- goal}_1, \ldots, \text{goal}_n.$$

holds, we will assert a fact cert(*ref*, likely), where *ref* is the database reference of the clause. This is a natural representation, but others are possible as well. If a particular Prolog implementation does not support internal references, one may represent the certainty of the clause in the body itself, for example by the format

$$\text{head :- cert}(certainty\_measure), \text{goal}_1, \ldots, \text{goal}_n.$$

and modify the cclause / 3 and cassert / 2 predicates, described below, accordingly.

The meaning of likely is yet to be clarified. In fact, at this stage we do not specify the range from which the certainty is taken; it may be all the floating-point numbers in the range [0,1] (for example, when we interpret certainty measure as probabilities – see Section 7.5), or the numbers in the range [-1,1] (as in the case of MYCIN – see Section 7.4), or the set {impossible,unlikely,possible,likely,certain}. The general scheme of the meta-interpreter will allow all these.

We will use the following two utility predicates.

```
cassert( Clause, Certainty ) :- assert( Clause, Ref ), assert( cert( Ref, Certainty ) ).
cclause( Head, Body, Certainty ) :- clause( Head, Body, Ref ), cert( Ref, Certainty ).
```

7.2   A general meta-interpreter with uncertainty

The operation of the meta-interpreter in the presence of uncertainty requires combining uncertainties at various stages. It is tempting to view this as a minor complication, merely requiring accumulation of uncertainty while performing the standard backward chaining. However, the situation is more complex. In the absence of uncertainty, each rule may be treated in a context-free fashion. Consider, for example, the following diagnostic rule, stating that if the patient has high fever, has recently been in the jungle, and has not taken malaria pills, then the person is suffering from malaria

```
malaria :- high_fever, recently_in_jungle, not( took_pills ).
```

If the *if* part is satisfied, we may conclude that the *then* part holds, no matter what other rules and facts are in the database. However, if we associate a measure of certainty with facts and rules, the certainty of having malaria is not computable solely on the basis of this rule, even if the *if* part is known to hold with certainty. There may be other confirming or disconfirming evidence, such as results of a blood count, which will either increase or decrease the certainty of the diagnosis. If the certainty of this rule is 'likely,' then its correct reading is "Given *only* the information that the patient has a high fever, was recently in a jungle area, and did not take malaria pills, it is a likely that he is suffering from malaria." The somewhat disturbing conclusion is that this rule cannot be used on its own to infer the likelihood of the patient's suffering from malaria; other relevant rules must be considered as well.

We might start by considering three uncertainty-combination functions:

'Rule' combination: How is the contribution of the clause to the certainty
of the head computed from the certainty of the body and the certainty
of the clause itself?

'Serial' or 'and' combination: What is the certainty of a body of a clause,
given the certainties of its individual conjuncts?

'Parallel' or 'or' combination: If a goal appears as the head of several
clauses, how is its certainty computed from the contribution of the
various clauses?

It turns out to be hard to provide efficient combination functions that are
grounded firmly in some calculus of uncertainty. Indeed, various combination
functions that had been used in AI were later shown to be unsound, at
least relative to their plausible interpretation. In the following sections we
will explore several choices, but let us assume here that these choices have
already been made. Specifically, let us assume three functions, comb_fn_rule / 2,
comb_fn_serial / 2 and comb_fn_parallel / 2; each of these will accept as input a list
of certainty values and will return the combined certainty.

Below we give the general meta-interpreter; the input to the interpreter is
a goal, and the output is the certainty of the goal. In addition to the combination functions, we assume two other functions. The predicate highest_certainty / 1
depends on the range of certainty values; it may succeed for the argument 1,
for the argument certain, and so on. Similarly, complement / 2 will depend on
the uncertainty values; it might convert .3 to .7, likely to unlikely, and so on.

```
certainty( not( A ), Cert ) :- !, certainty( A, Cert1 ), complement( Cert1, Cert ).
certainty( true, Cert ):- highest_certainty( Cert ), !.
certainty( ( A, B ), Cert ):- !,
   findall( Cert1, ( amember( X, ( A, B ) ), certainty( X, Cert1 ) ), CertList ),
   comb_fn_serial( CertList, Cert ).
certainty( A, Cert ):-
   findall( Cert3,
        ( cclause( A, B, Cert1 ),
          certainty( B, Cert2 ),
          comb_fn_rule( [ Cert1, Cert2 ], Cert3 ) ),
        CertList ),
   comb_fn_parallel( CertList, Cert ).
```

An example is in order at this point. Let us assume that the certainty values are taken from the set { impossible, highly_unlikely, unlikely, possible, likely, highly_likely, certain }. The goal highest_certainty(X) will therefore succeed with X = certain. Now consider the following database. The first rule is the familiar one: If the patient has a high fever, was recently in the jungle and did not take malaria pills, it is likely that he is suffering from malaria. The second rule states that it is unlikely that if the patient has dysentery then he also has malaria. The third rule identifies a condition for hypothesizing dysentery, albeit weakly. The other rules are similarly self-explanatory.

```
malaria :- high_fever, recently_in_jungle, not(took_pills). (highly_likely)
malaria :- dysentery. (unlikely)
dysentery :- recently_in_third_world. (possible)
recently_in_third_world :- recently_in_guatemala. (certain)
recently_in_jungle :- recently_in_guatemala. (highly_likely)
recently_in_guatemala. (certain)
high_fever. (certain)
took_pills. (highly_unlikely)
```

In order to be able to use this information we must still specify the complementation function and the three combination rules. Although we will use the symbolic terms, it will be useful to translate them internally to the integers 1,2,...,7: impossible will be translated into 1, highly_unlikely into 2, and so on.

```
number( impossible, 1 ). number( highly_unlikely, 2 ). number( unlikely, 3 ).
number( possible, 4 ). number( likely, 5 ). number( highly_likely, 6 ). number( certain, 7 ).
```

Complementation will be defined as symmetry around the uncertainty value possible, or the value 4:

```
complement( A, B ) :- number( A, Na ), Nb is 8 – Na, number( B, Nb ).
```

Finally, let us adopt the following combination rules:

Rule combination: Bias the certainty away from the value possible, that is, the value 4, in proportion to the certainty of the body and the certainty of the rule.

Serial combination: Select the minimum.

Parallel combination: Select the maximum.

These may be implemented as follows:

```
comb_fn_rule( [ A, B ], C ) :-
   number( A, Na ),number( B, Nb ),
   Nc is 4 + ( ( Na − 4 ) * Nb // 7 ), % // is integer division
   number( C, Nc ).

comb_fn_serial( [ ], certain ).
comb_fn_serial( [ A | B ], C ) :-
   number( A, Na),
   comb_fn_serial( B, B1 ),
   number( B1, Nb ),
   ( Na < Nb, !, C = A ; C = B1 ).

comb_fn_parallel( [ ], possible ) :- !.
comb_fn_parallel( [ A ], A ) :- !.
comb_fn_parallel( [ A | B ], C ) :-
   number( A, Na ),
   comb_fn_parallel( B, B1 ),
   number( B1, Nb ),
   ( Na < Nb, !, C = B1 ; C = A).
```

(The utility predicates amember / 2 and not / 1 are given in Chapter 1.)

Do these combination functions seem reasonable? The following first run might suggest that they are (in the following sessions, print commands were added to the certainty / 2 predicate):

| ?- certainty(malaria,C).

Certainty of high_fever = certain
Certainty of recently_in_guatemala = certain
Certainty of recently_in_jungle = highly_likely
Certainty of took_pills = highly_unlikely
Certainty of not(took_pills) = highly_likely
Certainty of high_fever,recently_in_jungle,not(took_pills) = highly_likely
Certainty of recently_in_guatemala = certain
Certainty of recently_in_third_world = certain
Certainty of dysentery = possible
Certainty of malaria = likely

C = likely

| ?-

If we reduce the certainty of the first malaria clause from highly_likely to likely, the certainty of malaria will drop from likely to possible; so far, so good. However, if instead we set the certainties of the first and sixth rules to be impossible, and the certainties of the other six rules to be certain, we observe the following behavior:

| ?- certainty(malaria,C).

Certainty of high_fever = certain
Certainty of recently_in_guatemala = impossible
Certainty of recently_in_jungle = possible
Certainty of took_pills = certain
Certainty of not(took_pills) = impossible
Certainty of high_fever,recently_in_jungle,not(took_pills) = impossible
Certainty of recently_in_guatemala = impossible
Certainty of recently_in_third_world = possible
Certainty of dysentery = likely
Certainty of malaria = highly_likely (!!!!!)

C = highly_likely

| ?-

Clearly something is quite wrong here. The one piece of positive evidence for malaria, dysentery, is only likely. The other potential evidence, the conjunction of the three factors, would appear to contribute nothing: Both the *if*-part and the rule itself are deemed impossible. And yet malaria is judged to be *highly* likely!

Evidently, we must be more careful about the meaning of uncertainties, and about the ways we combine them. These issues are in fact still subjects of debate within AI; in the remainder of the chapter we examine a number of proposals made in the literature.

7.3 Informal heuristics

In this section we consider specializations of the general scheme of the interpreter for uncertainties that lie in the range $[0, 1]$. This suggests a probabilistic interpretation of these certainties. However, probability theory requires more than merely ensuring that certainty values lie between 0 and 1. In the last two sections of the chapter we discuss rigorous probabilistic reasoning; in both this section and the next one we discuss methods that have been used in AI without formal justification and that are in general unjustified from the standpoint of probability theory.

Independence heuristic

Under this assumption, whose name is based loosely on the notion of conditional independence (see section 7.5), we take the certainties of different goals to be independent of one another.

Serial combination of A and B: $Pr(A)Pr(B)$

Parallel combination of A and B: $Pr(A) + Pr(B) - Pr(A)Pr(B)$

These combination rules can easily be extended to the general case:

Serial combination of $A_1, \ldots, A_n$: $Pr(A_1)Pr(A_2) \cdots Pr(A_n)$

Parallel combination of $A_1, \ldots, A_n$: $1 - (1 - Pr(A_1)) \cdots (1 - Pr(A_n))$

Maximal disjointness heuristic

Under this assumption, we adopt the minimum possible likelihood that the combined goals can be simultaneously achieved. For two arguments, this assumption leads to the following serial and parallel combination functions:

Serial combination of A and B: $max(\{Pr(A) + Pr(B) - 1, 0\})$

Parallel combination of A and B: $min(\{Pr(A) + Pr(B), 1\})$

These can be generalized as follows:

Serial combination of $A_1, \ldots, A_n$: $max(\{Pr(A_1) + \cdots + Pr(A_n) - n + 1, 0\})$

Parallel combination of $A_1, \ldots, A_n$: $min(\{Pr(A_1) + \cdots + Pr(A_n), 1\})$

Inclusion heuristic

If one goal entails the other, serial combination is determined by the weakest link, and parallel combination by the strongest:

Serial combination of $A_1, \ldots, A_n$: $min\{Pr(A_1), Pr(A_2), \ldots, Pr(A_n)\}$

Parallel combination of $A_1, \ldots, A_n$: $max\{Pr(A_1), Pr(A_2), \ldots, Pr(A_n)\}$

Note that if a particular heuristic serial combination function is adopted, it is not necessary to adopt the corresponding parallel combination function; different variables may participate in each function. Thus, one can construct examples in which independence is warranted in the serial combination, but maximal disjointness in the parallel combination.

Prolog implementation

The Prolog implementation of the three sets of serial and parallel combination functions is straightforward:

```
serial_indep( [ A ], B ) :- !, A = B.
serial_indep( [ A | B ], Cert ) :- serial_indep( B, BB ), Cert is A * BB.
```

```
parallel_indep( [ A ], B ) :- !, A = B.
parallel_indep( [ A | B ], Cert ) :-
   parallel_indep( B, CertB ),
   Cert is ( 1 – A ) * CertB.

serial_inc( Args, Cert ) :- minimal( Args, Cert ).
parallel_inc( Args, Cert ) :- maximal( Args, Cert ).
serial_maxdis( Args, Cert ) :-
   length( Args, N ),
   add( Args, Sum ),
   Sum1 is Sum – N + 1,
   maximal( [ 0, Sum1 ], Cert ).
parallel_maxdis( Args, Cert ) :- add( Args, Sum ), minimal( [ 1, Sum ], Cert ).

minimal( [ X ], X ).
minimal( [ X | Y ], M ) :-
   minimal( Y, M1 ),
   ( X < M1, !, M = X ; M = M1 ).

maximal( [ X ], X ).
maximal( [ X | Y ], M ) :-
   maximal( Y, M1 ),
   ( X > M1, !, M = X ; M = M1 ).
```

The add / 2 program is as follows:

```
add( [ ], 0 ).
add( [ A | B ], Sum ) :- add( B, Sum1 ), Sum is A + Sum1.
```

Still to be defined is the rule-combination function. It is common to adopt the simple heuristic of assuming independence of the certainty of the rule from the certainty of its body, and simply multiply the two probabilities. This is again grounded only in imprecise intuition, rather than in probability theory.

```
rule_simple( [ ClauseCert, BodyCert ], C ) :- C is ClauseCert * BodyCert.
```

Let us now return to the medical example given earlier. First, we modify the database to reflect the new range of uncertainties:

malaria :- high_fever, recently_in_jungle, not(took_pills). (0.85)
malaria :- dysentery. (0.3)
dysentery :- recently_in_third_world. (0.6)
recently_in_third_world :- recently_in_guatemala. (1)
recently_in_jungle :- recently_in_guatemala. (0.9)
recently_in_guatemala. (1)
high_fever. (0.95)
took_pills. (0.2)

We also modify highest_certainty(X) to succeed with X = 1, and define complement(X, Y) to instantiate Y to 1 − X. The following first run assumes inclusion in both serial and parallel combination:

| ?- cert(malaria,C).

Certainty of high_fever = 0.95
Certainty of recently_in_guatemala = 1
Certainty of recently_in_jungle = 0.9
Certainty of took_pills = 0.2
Certainty of not(took_pills) = 0.8
Certainty of high_fever,recently_in_jungle,not(took_pills) = 0.8
Certainty of recently_in_guatemala = 1
Certainty of recently_in_third_world = 1
Certainty of dysentery = 0.6
Certainty of malaria = 0.68

C = 6.8E-01

| ?-

We now adopt different assumptions; we still assume inclusion for parallel combination, but maximal disjointness for serial combination:

| ?- cert(malaria,C).

Certainty of high_fever = 0.95
Certainty of recently_in_guatemala = 1
Certainty of recently_in_jungle = 0.9
Certainty of took_pills = 0.2
Certainty of not(took_pills) = 0.8
Certainty of high_fever,recently_in_jungle,not(took_pills) = 0.65
Certainty of recently_in_guatemala = 1
Certainty of recently_in_third_world = 1
Certainty of dysentery = 0.6
Certainty of malaria = 0.5525

C = 5.525000000000003E-01

| ?-

Once again, we emphasize that in this section we have adopted the various assumptions merely as heuristics, which will in fact be justified only in limited circumstances. In section 7.6 we discuss a rigorous framework for computing probabilities, but first we take a quick look at the uncertainty calculus that was employed in the well-known MYCIN program.

7.4   Certainty factors in MYCIN

Among the earliest and best-known expert systems to reason with uncertainty is the MYCIN program. In MYCIN the certainty values were taken from the range $[-1, 1]$; informally, they are thought of as 'degrees of confirmation.' The precise grounding of this intuition in probability theory is the subject of some debate, which we will avoid here.

MYCIN's serial combination function adopts the total dependence assumption discussed earlier and simply returns the minimum certainty value. The parallel function, in contrast, is a variation on the parallel combination function corresponding to the total independence assumption. The parallel combination function is slightly complicated by the presence of positive and negative values, and it is computed as follows:

$$
c(A, B) = \begin{cases}
c(A) + c(B) - c(A)c(B) & c(A), c(B) \geq 0, \\[2mm]
\dfrac{c(A)+c(B)}{1-min(|c(A)|,|c(B)|)} & c(A), c(B) \text{ of opposite sign}, \\[2mm]
c(A) + c(B) + c(A)c(B) & c(A), c(B) < 0.
\end{cases}
$$

As the serial combination function is identical to the one yielded by the dependence assumption, there is no need to recode it. The parallel combination rule is implemented by the following Prolog clauses:

```
or_mycin( [ A ], A ).
or_mycin( [ A | B ], CF ):-
  or_mycin( B, C ),
  or_mycin_aux( A, C, CF ).


or_mycin_aux( A, C, CF ):- A > 0, C > 0,
  CF is A + C - A * C.
or_mycin_aux( A, C, CF ):- A < 0, C < 0,
  CF is A + C + A * C.
or_mycin_aux( A, C, CF ):-
  abs( A, AA ), abs( C, CC ),
  minimal( [ AA, CC ], Z ),
  CF is ( A + C ) / ( 1 - Z ).
```

The MYCIN certainty scheme differs also in its rule-combination function. In Section 7.3 this function was implemented by the product of the certainties associated with the hypothesis and with the rule. In MYCIN, only the clauses with a positive certainty value affect the certainty of the hypothesis. Therefore, the rule-combination scheme can be expressed by the following function:

$$
Z = \begin{cases}
WX & W \geq 0 \\
0 & W < 0
\end{cases}
$$

where W is the certainty associated with the clause, and X is the certainty associated with the body. The corresponding Prolog predicate is defined below:

```
rule_mycin( [ ClauseCert, BodyCert ], C ):-
   maximal( [ ClauseCert, 0 ], CertMax ),
   C is BodyCert * CertMax.
```

7.5   A review of probability theory

None of the methods discussed so far have been anchored firmly in probability theory, despite the fact that some methods used uncertainties in the
range [0, 1]. In Section 7.6 we discuss rigorous probabilistic reasoning; in
this section we provide a very brief review of the main concepts involved in
probability theory. For more thorough treatment, the reader should consult
texts mentioned at the end of the chapter.

A *joint probability distribution* over a set $V = v_1, \ldots, v_n$ of discrete random variables is a function

$$\mathrm{Pr} : \mathrm{Val}(v_1) \times \mathrm{Val}(v_2) \times \cdots \times \mathrm{Val}(v_n) \to [0,\ 1]$$

where $Val(v_i)$ is the set of values the variable v_i may take. We denote this
joint probability distribution by $\mathrm{Pr}(v_1, \ldots, v_n)$. We will consider only the
special case in which variables are boolean, that is, may take the values true
and false. We define the *atoms* of V by

$$\mathrm{Atoms}(V) = \{\{l_1, l_2, \ldots, l_n\} : l_i = v_i \text{ or } l_i = \neg v_i\}$$

The joint probability distribution is then simply $\mathrm{Pr} : \mathrm{Atoms}(V) \to [0,1]$.
The probability distribution is required to satisfy the following property:

$$\sum_{a \in \mathrm{Atoms}(V)} \mathrm{Pr}(a) = 1.$$

The probability function is easily extended to apply to any subset of the
variables (this operation is called *marginalizing* the joint distribution to the
subset of variables):

$$\mathrm{Pr}(\{l_{i_1} l_{i_2} \ldots l_{i_m}\}) = \sum_{a : a \in \mathrm{Atoms}(V) \wedge l_{i_j} \in a} \mathrm{Pr}(a)$$

For convenience, we omit the curly braces in the notation. For example,
given a joint distribution over a, b and c, we have that $\mathrm{Pr}(ab) = \mathrm{Pr}(abc) +
\mathrm{Pr}(ab\neg c)$.

The special case, in which the probability function is applied to a single variable, defines the *prior* probability of that variable:

$$\Pr(v) = \sum_{\substack{a \in \mathrm{Atoms}(V) \\ v \in a}} \Pr(a)$$

For any two $A, B \subseteq V$, the *conditional probability of A given B*, written $\Pr(A \mid B)$, is defined by

$$\Pr(A \mid B) = \frac{\Pr(A \cap B)}{\Pr(B)}$$

Bayes' rule is easily derived:

$$\Pr(A \mid B \cap C) = \frac{\Pr(B \mid A \cap C)\Pr(A \mid C)}{\Pr(B \mid C)}$$

or, as a special case,

$$\Pr(A \mid B) = \frac{\Pr(B \mid A)\Pr(A)}{\Pr(B)}$$

A is said to be *conditionally independent* (or simply *independent*) *of B given evidence E* if the following holds:

$$\Pr(A \mid B \cap E) = \Pr(A \mid E)$$

In this case we have as a consequence the important property that the joint probability of two independent events is equal to the product of their respective probabilities:

$$\Pr(A \cap B \mid E) = \Pr(A \mid E)\Pr(B \mid E)$$

In the special case in which E is empty we simply say that A is independent of B, and have:

$$\Pr(A \mid B) = \Pr(A)$$

$$\Pr(A \cap B) = \Pr(A)\Pr(B)$$

7.6   Bayesian networks

We have emphasized that merely adopting certainty values in the interval [0, 1] does not guarantee reasoning that makes formal sense. In this section we discuss *Bayesian networks*, which offer an uncertainty representation and a calculation method that are sound from the perspective of probability theory and are applicable in a wide class of situations.[1]

The first potential problem in representing probabilistic information, which Bayesian networks tackle successfully, is that not every collection of (prior and conditional) probability statements is consistent, in the sense that there may exist no legal probability distribution satisfying all the statements. For example, the statements $\Pr(y) = .8$, $\Pr(x \mid y) = .7$, and $\Pr(y \mid x) = .5$ are mutually inconsistent, since

$$\Pr(x) = \Pr(y)\Pr(x \mid y)/\Pr(y \mid x) = .8 \times .7/.5 > 1$$

Fully representing a joint distribution over a collection of n variables can be expensive. The representation would in general require $\Omega(2^n)$ amount of storage; one possible representation would explicitly store the probability of $2^n - 1$ of the atoms (the probability of the last atom is determined, since the probabilities of all atoms sum to 1).

To understand how Bayesian networks reduce this cost, it is helpful to look at a simple example. Consider the following toy database, which is not unlike the malaria example given earlier.

symptom1 :- illness1.
symptom2 :- illness1.
illness1 :- cause1.
illness1 :- cause2.

This database corresponds to the structure in Figure 7.1. What are the dependencies among the variables in the graph? Intuitively speaking, given no evidence in addition to the graph, we must conclude that cause1 affects the

---

[1]Bayesian networks are called also *belief networks, probabilistic networks,* and *causal networks.* The related term *influence diagrams* is usually reserved for a slightly more complex construct, involving not only probabilities but also utilities, which is not covered in this book.

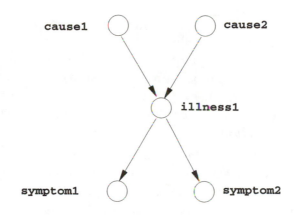

Figure 7.1: A simple Bayesian network

likelihood of all of other variables, including, for example, that of symptom1. In other words, symptom1 and cause1 are not conditionally independent:

$$\Pr(\text{symptom1} \mid \text{cause1}) > \Pr(\text{symptom1})$$

However, if we are given the additional evidence that illness1 is present, the two become conditionally independent:

$$\Pr(\text{symptom1} \mid \text{cause1 illness1}) = \Pr(\text{symptom1} \mid \text{illness1})$$

Intuitively, this is because the only reason the cause might affect the symptom is by affecting the likelihood of the illness; if we are told independently whether or not the illness is present, the cause becomes irrelevant to the symptom.

This is precisely the idea behind Bayesian networks. Bayesian networks are directed, acyclic graphs. The nodes in the graphs represent random variables, and the structure of the graph implies certain independence properties. The precise condition is as follows. Denote the set of nodes by V, the parents of a node v by $\text{Pa}(v)$, and the (not necessarily immediate) descendents of v by $\text{Desc}(v)$. The assumption embodied in the network is that for any node v and $S \subseteq V \setminus \text{Desc}(v)$,

$$\Pr(v \mid \text{Pa}(v) \cup S) = \Pr(v \mid \text{Pa}(v))$$

This independence assumption results in convenient properties. Given this implicit independence assumption, in order to specify the joint distribution of all the variables in the network it is sufficient to specify the probability of every node conditioned on its parents. In the last example, for the node illness1 it is sufficient to store the values of Pr(illness1 | cause1 cause2), Pr(illness1 | cause1 ¬cause2), Pr(illness1 | ¬cause1 cause2), and Pr(illness1 | ¬cause1 ¬cause2). It turns out that if for each node one specifies such a set of conditional probabilities, these probabilities are guaranteed to be globally consistent, and in fact they induce a unique joint distribution on all the nodes in the network. Specifying these conditional probabilities is called *quantifying the network*.

In addition to assuring soundness, Bayesian networks save storage space: Rather than represent an exponential number of probabilities, we specify only $O(n2^d)$ values, where d is the maximal number of parents for any node. For example, if each node has at most two parents, we need specify only $4n$ values.

The structure of Bayesian networks also helps in reasoning about the probabilities. The computational problem we consider is the computation of $Pr(v \mid S)$ for any node v and set of nodes S. More informally, we will ask for the probability of v given the 'evidence' S. Of course, if $S \subseteq \mathrm{Pa}(v)$ then the answer is computed directly from the conditional probabilities given for that node. However, we are interested in computing the conditional probability of a node given *any* evidence, and so a more complex procedure is called for. Computing such conditional probabilities turns out to be quite hard in general (specifically, it is NP-complete). One must therefore either limit the problem under consideration or resort to inexact methods. Both approaches appear in the literature. We will briefly discuss the former. Specifically, we will discuss the computation of conditional probabilities under the following restrictions:

1. Each node in the network has at most one incoming edge.

2. The evidence nodes are all boundary nodes, that is, nodes with either no incoming edges or no outgoing edges.

The second restriction is not severe, and is made for reasons of exposition. The first restriction is essential to the procedure and quite limiting in practice. It is not too hard to generalize the algorithm to the case in which the network is a *polytree*, or a *singly connected DAG* (this means that a node may have more than one parent, but there is at most one directed path between any two nodes). For general Bayesian networks, as we have said, the problem is thought to be unsolvable in polynomial time; most common techniques transform the problem to an equivalent tree-like problem, a process that uses exponential time in the worst case. We will not discuss this process further.

The algorithm for computing the probabilities in tree-like Bayesian networks is based on a message-passing scheme. Each node repeatedly communicates information with its parent and children, and updates its own probability as a result of messages received. When the process terminates, the network has settled on the (unique) correct probability distribution.

When node V receives a message from node N, where N is either the parent or one of the children of V, V checks that the arrived message is different from the last message received from N. If it is, V updates its probability (also called its 'strength of belief'), and sends messages to its parent as well as to all of its children, excluding the node N itself. To understand how a node computes its own probability, note that every internal node V divides the tree into two parts: the subtree under V and the rest of the tree. Let the subset of the evidence residing in the node's subtree be e_V^-, and let the evidence from the rest of the tree be e_V^+. Denote $\lambda(V) = \Pr(e_V^- \mid V)$, and $\pi(V) = \Pr(V \mid e_V^+)$. Using this notation we can compute the probability of V given all the evidence in the graph as:

$$
\begin{aligned}
\Pr(V \mid e_V^+, e_V^-) &= \Pr(e_V^- \mid V)\Pr(V \mid e_V^+)/\alpha \\
&= \lambda(V)\pi(V)/\alpha
\end{aligned}
$$

where α is a normalizing constant :

$$
\alpha = \sum_{v \in \{0,1\}} Pr(e_V^- \mid V = v)\Pr(V = v \mid e_V^+)
$$

To compute $\lambda(V)$ we divide e_V^- into disjoint subsets, $e_{V_i}^-$, each corresponding to the evidence that resides in V_i, a child of V.

$$
\begin{aligned}
\lambda(V) &= \Pr(e_V^- \mid V) \\
&= \Pr(e_{V_1}^-, \ldots, e_{V_n}^- \mid V) \\
&= \prod_{i=1}^{n} \Pr(e_{V_i}^- \mid V) \\
&= \prod_{i=1}^{n} \lambda_{V_i}(V)
\end{aligned}
$$

where $\lambda_{V_i}(V)$ is a message passed to V from its child V_i.
We compute $\pi(V)$ using the message $\pi_V(U) = \Pr(U \mid e_V^+)$ from the parent

of V, U.

$$
\begin{aligned}
\pi(V) &= \Pr(V \mid e_V^+) \\
&= \sum_{u \in \{0,1\}} \Pr(V \mid e_V^+, U = u)\Pr(U = u \mid e_V^+) \\
&= \sum_{u \in \{0,1\}} \Pr(V \mid U = u)\Pr(U = u \mid e_V^+) \\
&= \sum_{u \in \{0,1\}} \Pr(V \mid U = u)\pi_V(U = u)
\end{aligned}
$$

We now formulate the messages that node V sends to its parent U and to each of its children V_i upon update. Each such message is a pair of conditional probabilities: the probability given that the condition holds and the probability given that it does not. The message from V to the parent U, $\lambda_V(U)$, is

$$
\begin{aligned}
\lambda_V(U) &= \sum_{v \in \{0,1\}} \Pr(e_V^- \mid U, V = v)\Pr(V = v \mid U) \\
&= \sum_{v \in \{0,1\}} \Pr(e_V^- \mid V = v)\Pr(V = v \mid U) \\
&= \sum_{v \in \{0,1\}} \lambda(V = v)\Pr(V = v \mid U)
\end{aligned}
$$

and the message from V to its child V_j is

$$
\begin{aligned}
\pi_{V_j}(V) &= \Pr(V \mid e_{V_i}^+) \\
&= \Pr(V \mid e_V^+, e_{V_1}^-, \ldots, e_{V_{i-1}}^-, e_{V_{i+1}}^-, \ldots, e_{V_n}^-) \\
&= \beta \left(\prod_{j \neq i} \Pr(e_{V_i}^- \mid V, e_V^+) \right) \Pr(V \mid e_V^+) \\
&= \beta \left(\prod_{j \neq i} \Pr(e_{V_i}^- \mid V) \right) \Pr(V \mid e_V^+) \\
&= \beta \left(\prod_{j \neq i} \lambda_{V_i}(V) \right) \pi(V)
\end{aligned}
$$

where β is a normalizing constant (needed so that the probabilities add up to 1).

Messages from the root to its children or from leaf nodes to their parents require special treatment.

- Root node: $(\pi(root), \pi(root))$, where $\pi(root)$ is the prior probability of the root.

- Leaf nodes: when we know that the fact represented by the node holds then we set its λ to $(1,0)$, and if we know that the fact does not hold then we set it to $(0,1)$. If we have no information either way we set it to $(1,1)$; this setting will cause no change in the parent's probabilities.

We are now ready to implement Bayesian networks. For every node V with parent U in the network, we will require the following data structures:

- Conditional probability matrix describing $P(V \mid U)$. Since we are considering the boolean case here, these will be 2×2 matrices: the (i,j) entry will contain the conditional probability of V being true (if $i = 1$) or false (if $i = 2$) given that U is true (if $j = 1$) or false (if $j = 2$). For the root node, all values in the matrix will be its prior probability.

- The last message received from U, $\pi_V(U)$,

- The last message received from every child of the node, $\lambda_{V_i}(V)$

Of course, in addition we need to represent the structure of the network (in our case, a tree).

We will first give a pseudo-code description of the procedures, and follow that with a Prolog implementation. The procedures we will discuss are the initialization of the graph, given the input described above, and its update. The Prolog implementation follows the pseudo code.

PROCEDURE GraphInit (N: network)
for every node $V \in N$ do
   V.Matrix $\leftarrow$ conditional probability of V given its parent (a pair)
   V.Parent.Message $\leftarrow$ (0 0)
   for every child of V do
      V.Child.Message $\leftarrow$ (1 1)
   end for
end for
PropagateDn(Root, (1 0));
END

```
PROCEDURE PropagateUp ( V, Sender : nodes; Message: prob_vector )
if V.Sender.Message ≠ Message then do
    V.Sender.Message ← Message { Update the child message }
    NodePi ← Pi(V.Matrix, V.Parent.Message)
    NodeLambda ← Lambda(V)
    if Parent(V) ≠ null then { Propagate change to parent}
        UpMessage ← Up_Message(V.Matrix, NodeLambda)
        PropagateUp(Parent(V), V, UpMessage)
    end if
    { Propagate change to children }
    for every child of V ≠ Sender do
        TempLa[1] ← NodeLambda[1] / V.Child.Message[1]
        TempLa[2] ← NodeLambda[2] / V.Child.Message[2]
        ChildPi ← Belief(NodePi, TempLa)
        PropagateDn(V.Child, V, ChildPi )
    end for
end if


PROCEDURE PropagateDn ( V, Sender:node; Message:prob_vector )
if V.Parent.Message ≠ Message then do
    V.Parent.Message ← Message { Update the parent message }
    NodePi ← Pi(V.Matrix, Message)
    NodeLambda ← Lambda(V)
    for every child of V do
        TempLa[1] ← NodeLambda[1] / V.Child.Message[1]
        TempLa[2] ← NodeLambda[2] / V.Child.Message[2]
        ChildPi ← Belief(NodePi, TempLa)
        PropagateDn(V.Child, V, ChildPi )
    end for
end if


PROCEDURE add_evidence ( V : node; Evidence : boolean )
if Evidence = true
    then NodeLambda ← (1 0)
    else NodeLambda ← (0 1)
end if
{ Propagate change to parent}
UpMessage ← Up_Message(V.Matrix, NodeLambda)
PropagateUp(Parent(V), V, UpMessage)
```

PROCEDURE remove_evidence(V : node)
NodeLambda ← (1 1);
{ Propagate change to parent}
UpMessage ← Up_Message(V.Matrix, NodeLambda)
PropagateUp(Parent(V), V, UpMessage)

PROCEDURE Belief(NodePi, NodeLambda : prob_vectors): prob_vector
NodeBel[1] ← NodeLambda[1] * NodePi[1]
NodeBel[2] ← NodeLambda[2] * NodePi[2]
{Normalize}
Alpha ← NodeBel[1] + NodeBel[2]
NodePi[1] ← NodeBel[1] / Alpha
NodePi[2] ← ModeBel[2] / Alpha
return NodeBel

PROCEDURE Up_Message(M: prob_matrix ;
                          Lambda : prob_vector) : prob_vector
UpMessage[1] ← Lambda[1]*Matrix[1,1] + Lambda[2]*Matrix[1,2]
UpMessage[2] ← Lambda[2]*Matrix[1,2] + Lambda[2]*Matrix[2,2]
return UpMessage

PROCEDURE Pi(M : prob_matrix; Message : prob_vector) : prob_vector
NodePi[1] ← Message[1]*Matrix[1,1] + Message[2]*Matrix[2,1]
NodePi[2] ← Message[1]*Matrix[1,2] + Message[2]*Matrix[2,2])
return NodePi

PROCEDURE Lambda(V : node) : prob_vector
NodeLambda[1] ← NodeLambda[2] ← 1
for child Child of V do
    NodeLambda[1] ← NodeLambda[1] * V.Child.Message[1]
    NodeLambda[2] ← NodeLambda[2] * V.Child.Message[2]
end for
return NodeLambda

When implementing this pseudo code in Prolog, we must decide whether the network and associated data structures are to be passed around as arguments or represented explicitly in the database. As we have seen before in this book, both approaches are justified in certain cases. For purity of code, and for the possibility of speeding up the implementation by optimizing the data structures, it is preferable to pass around the information as arguments. On the other hand, if the Bayesian network is to be used as a database to be queried and modified on occasions and by programs that are not fixed in advance, explicit representation in the database is sensible. We will take this latter route, and store all data structures explicitly in the database; see Exercise 7.1 for the alternative implementation.

The following annotated Prolog program is a direct implementation of the above pseudo code; it is followed by an example.

```
% _____
% Propagate evidence up the tree. If the arriving message is the same as the
% previous message then there is nothing to propagate.
% _____

propagateUp( N, Sender, Message ) :-
    struct( N, _, ChildList, _ ),
    same_message( ChildList, Sender, Message ), ! .
propagateUp( N, Sender, Message ) :-
    retract( struct( N, Pmessage, ChildList, Matrix ) ),
    replace_message( ChildList, Sender, Message, NewChildList ),
    assert( struct( N, Pmessage, NewChildList, Matrix ) ),
    pi( N, Pi ),
    lambda( N, La ),
    arc( Pname, N ),
    ( Pname = null, !
    ; % Send message to parent
      up_message( Matrix, La, UpMessage ),
      propagateUp( Pname, N, UpMessage ) ),
    % Send messages to children
    remove_sender( NewChildList, Sender, SendList ),
    send_to_child( SendList, La, Pi ).
```

```
% _____
% Check if the new message received from the Sender is the same as the
% previous message received from it.
% _____

same_message( [ [ Sender, M1, M2 ] | _ ], Sender, [ M1, M2 ] ).
same_message( [ [ Sender, _, _ ] | _ ], Sender, _ ) :- !, fail.
same_message( [ _| More ], Sender, Message ) :-
   same_message( More, Sender, Message ).


% _____
% Replace the old message from Sender with the new one.
% _____

replace_message( [ [ Sender, _, _ ] | More ], Sender, [ M1, M2 ], [ [ Sender, M1, M2 ] | More ] ).
replace_message( [S | More ], Sender, Message, [ S | Res ]) :-
   replace_message( More, Sender, Message, Res ).


% _____
% Remove sender from the list.
% _____

remove_sender([[Sender, _, _] |More], Sender, More).
remove_sender([Child | More], Sender, [Child | Res]) :- remove_sender(More, Sender, Res).


% _____
% Send message to every child.
% _____

send_to_child( [ ], _, _ ).
send_to_child( [ [ Child, M1, M2 ] | More ] , [ La1, La2 ], Pi ) :-
   T1 is La1 / M1, T2 is La2 / M2,
   belief( Pi, [ T1, T2 ], Bel ),
   ( Child, Bel ),
   send_to_child( More, [ La1, La2 ], Pi ).
```

```
% _____
% Propagate messages down the tree. If the message from the parent is the
% same as the previous message then ignore it.
% _____

propagateDn( N, [ M1, M2 ] ) :-struct( N, [ M1, M2 ], _, _ ).
propagateDn( N, [ M1, M2 ] ) :-
  retract( struct( N, _, ChildList, Matrix ) ),
  assert( struct( N, [ M1, M2 ], ChildList, Matrix ) ),
  pi( N, Pi ),
  lambda( N, La ),
  send_to_child( ChildList, La, Pi ). % Send messages to children
% _____
% Record new evidence. Evidence can be recorded for leaf nodes only.
% _____

add_evidence( N, _ ) :-
  arc( N, _ ),
  write('Error. Evidence can be recorded for leaf nodes only.'), nl, !, abort.
add_evidence( N, Evidence ) :-
  retractall( evidence( N, _) ),
  assert( evidence( N, Evidence ) ),
  arc( Parent, N ),
  struct( N, _, _, Matrix ),
  ( Evidence = true, !, Lambda = [ 1, 0 ] ; Lambda = [ 0, 1 ] ),
  up_message( Matrix, Lambda, Message ), !,
  propagateUp( Parent, N, Message ).


% _____
% Remove node evidence.
% _____

remove_evidence( N ) :-
  retractall( evidence( N, _) ),
  arc( Parent, N ),
  struct( N, _, _, Matrix ),
  up_message( Matrix, [ 1, 1 ], Message ), !,
  propagateUp( Parent, N, Message ).
```

```
% _____
% Calculate the Pi value of N. If N is the root then Pi is the prior
% probability of N.
% _____

pi( N, [ Pi1, Pi2 ] ) :-
   struct( N, [ P1, P2 ], _, [ M11, M21, M12, M22 ] ),
   Pi1 is P1*M11 + P2*M21,
   Pi2 is P1*M12 + P2*M22 .




% _____
% Calculate the Lambda value of the node.  There are three cases :
% 1.  N is an uninstantiated leaf: La = [1,1]
% 2.  N is instantiated an leaf: there is evidence about N
%     La = [1,0] if (Evidence = true), else [0,1])
% 3.  N is not a leaf: compute La.
% _____

lambda( N, [ 1, 1 ] ) :-
   not( arc( N, _ ) ),
   not( evidence( N, _ ) ), !.
lambda( N, La ) :-
   not( arc( N, _ ) ), !,
   evidence( N, Evidence ),
   ( Evidence = true, !, La = [ 1, 0 ] ; La = [ 0, 1 ] ).
lambda( N, La ) :-
   struct( N, _, ChildList, _ ),
   lambda1( ChildList, La ).


lambda1( [ ], [ 1, 1 ] ).
lambda1( [ [ _, ChildLambda1, ChildLambda2 ] | More ], [ La1, La2 ] ) :-
   lambda1( More, [ Temp1, Temp2 ] ),
   La1 is ChildLambda1 * Temp1,
   La2 is ChildLambda2 * Temp2.
```

```
% _____
% Calculate a node's belief strength (or probability), given its Lambda and Pi
% values.
% _____

belief( [ Pi1, Pi2 ], [ La1, La2 ], [ B1, B2 ] ) :-
    T1 is La1 * Pi1,
    T2 is La2 * Pi2,
    N is T1+T2,
    B1 is T1 / N,
    B2 is T2 / N.



% _____
% Calculate a node's belief strength, given its name.
% _____

state( N, Bel ) :-
    evidence( N, Evidence ), !,
    ( Evidence = true, !, Bel = [ 1, 0 ] ; Bel = [ 0, 1 ] ).
state( N, Bel ) :-
    pi( N, Pi ),
    lambda( N, La ),
    belief( Pi, La, Bel ).


% _____
% Calculate message to parent.
% _____

up_message( [ M11, M12, M21, M22 ], [ La1, La2 ], [ Up1, Up2 ] ) :-
    Up1 is La1*M11 + La2*M12,
    Up2 is La1*M21 + La2* M22.
```

We conclude this section with an example of Bayesian networks in operation. The simple network we consider is depicted graphically in Figure 7.2. It represents the dependence among events associated with Mary's upcoming salary: Her getting a bonus will affect her having or not having money; her having money will encourage her to move to a new house, which in turn would increase the chances of her having wild parties; by contrast, her not

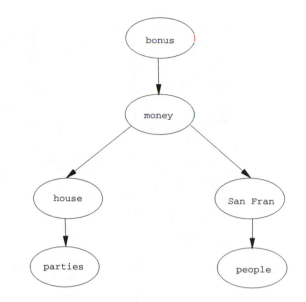

Figure 7.2: Mary's social and economic future

having money would tend to encourage her to stick around San Francisco, which in turn would make it highly likely that she will encounter strange people.

The probability of Mary's getting a bonus (the prior) is .6; the other, conditional probabilities are given in the following tables:

- Having money

	Pr(money | bonus)	
	bonus	no bonus
money	0.8	0.3
no money	0.2	0.7

- Moving to a new house

	Pr(house | money)	
	money	no money
house	0.7	0.1
no house	0.3	0.9

- Having wild parties

	Pr(parties | house)	
	house	no house
parties	0.75	0.2
no parties	0.25	0.8

- Roaming San Francisco

	Pr(SF | money)	
	money	no money
SF	0.2	0.5
no SF	0.8	0.5

- Meeting strange people

	Pr(people | SF)	
	SF	no SF
people	0.95	0.6
no people	0.05	0.4

We will implement these probabilities via the following database and auxiliary routines:

```
init :-
   retractall( struct( _, _, _, _ ) ),
   retractall( evidence( _, _ ) ),
   arc( null, Root ),
   create_structure( Root ),
   propagateDn( Root, [ 1, 0 ] ).

create_structure( N ) :-
   findall( [ Child, 1, 1 ],
           ( arc( N, Child ), create_structure( Child ) ),
           ChildList ),
   matrix( N, Matrix ),
   assert( struct( N, [ 0, 0 ], ChildList, Matrix ) ), !.


display_probabilities :-
   show( [ bonus, money, hawaii, san_francisco, surf, people ] ).
```

```
show( [ ] ).
show( [ N | L ] ) :-
        state( N, [ B1, _ ] ),
        write( 'Probability of ' ), write( N ), write( ': ' ), write( B1 ), nl,
        show( L ).


arc( null, bonus ).
arc( bonus, money ).
arc( money, house ).
arc( house, parties ).
arc( money, san_francisco ).
arc( san_francisco, people ).


matrix( bonus, [ 0.6, 0.4, 0.6, 0.4 ] ).
matrix( money, [ 0.8, 0.2, 0.3, 0.7 ] ).
matrix( house, [ 0.7, 0.3, 0.1, 0.9 ] ).
matrix( parties, [ 0.75, 0.25, 0.2, 0.8 ] ).
matrix( san_francisco, [ 0.2, 0.8, 0.5, 0.5 ] ).
matrix( people, [ 0.95, 0.05, 0.6, 0.4 ] ).
```

The following is the result of a sample run:
| ?- init, display_probabilities.
Probability of bonus: 0.6
Probability of money: 0.6
Probability of house: 0.46
Probability of san_francisco: 0.32
Probability of parties: 0.453
Probability of people: 0.712

yes
| ?- add_evidence(people,true), display_probabilities.
Probability of bonus: 0.582303
Probability of money: 0.564607
Probability of house: 0.438764
Probability of san_francisco: 0.426966
Probability of parties: 0.44132
Probability of people: 1

```
yes
| ?- add_evidence(parties,true), display_probabilities.
Probability of bonus: 0.674212
Probability of money: 0.748425
Probability of house: 0.745656
Probability of san_francisco: 0.366431
Probability of parties: 1
Probability of people: 1

yes
| ?- remove_evidence(people), display_probabilities.
Probability of bonus: 0.687417
Probability of money: 0.774834
Probability of house: 0.761589
Probability of san_francisco: 0.26755
Probability of parties: 1
Probability of people: 0.693642

yes
| ?- add_evidence(house,true), display_probabilities.
Error. Evidence can be recorded for leaf nodes only.
! Execution aborted

| ?-
```

7.7   Further reading

There exist numerous texts on probability theory. Within AI, Pearl offers a comprehensive coverage of probabilistic reasoning in the field [63] as well as a more concise overview of the area [64]. Neapolitan provides a clear explanation of Bayesian networks [54]. Charniak provides a particularly gentle introduction to Bayesian networks [6]. Other good sources are Heckerman [32], Geffner [25], Dean and Wellman [12] and Shachter [72].

7.8   Exercises

Exercise 7.1 The implementation of Bayesian networks presented in this chapter assumed an explicit representation of the network in the database, and thus used side effects. Re-implement the procedure with no side effects, assuming the Bayesian networks as an additional input and producing the revised network as output.

Exercise 7.2 For ease of exposition, both the discussion and implementation of Bayesian networks assumed binary values for each variable. However, neither the theory nor the implementation is complicated in any essential way by allowing any fixed number of possible values for each variable. Modify the implementation to allow such values.

Exercise 7.3 Removing all clauses that make reference to malaria from the *malaria* example on page 175 induces a tree-structured network. Quantify this network, and use the Bayesian network program to add the given evidence; what are the resulting probabilities?

Note: The following two exercises require that you read additional material on Bayesian networks; Pearl [63] and Neapolitan [54] are two good sources.

Exercise 7.4 The implementation of Bayesian networks given in this chapter handles tree-structured networks. Generalize the program so that it handles polytree-structured networks.

Exercise 7.5 If the clause

```
recently_in_jungle :- recently_in_guatemala. (0.9)
```

is omitted from the *malaria* example on page 175, the example induces a polytree-structured network. Quantify the network, and use the program of Exercise 7.4 to add the given evidence; what are the resulting probabilities?

Chapter 8

Planning and Temporal Reasoning

In one way or another, every area of AI has to do with time: Medical diagnosis systems reason about the time at which the virus infected the blood system; device troubleshooting systems reason about the time it takes to saturate a capacitor; in automatic programming the time at which a variable becomes bound is important; in robot planning one wants to achieve one goal before another and to meet deadlines; and so on. Even in domains that seem inherently atemporal, such as mathematical theorem proving, meta-level reasoning about how long to continue along a line of proof involves time.

We have already encountered a general technique to reason about time, the interval constraint propagation described in Chapter 6. In this chapter we will start by concentrating on a particular task in temporal reasoning, automated planning. We will first discuss basic automated planning techniques developed in AI, which fall under the category of *linear planning,* presenting two such planners in detail. We will then discuss *nonlinear planners* and present one such planner. Finally, we will discuss a general scheme for maintaining temporal information, centered around the notion of *time maps.*

8.1   Basic notions

8.1.1   Plan and action libraries

Most automated planning methods rely on the notion of a *plan library,* some representation of basic building blocks out of which more complex plans may be built. While in some systems these basic building blocks are themselves quite complex, we will assume that the plan library consists of simple *action rules,* each consisting of four components:

- – action name

- – preconditions

- – add-list

- – delete-list

Rules in this form, often called 'STRIPS rules' after the STRIPS planner that used them (see Section 8.2.1), have the following intuitive meaning: If the action is taken in a situation in which its preconditions hold, then in the resulting situation the facts in the action's add-list hold and the facts in its delete-list do not.

The Prolog representation of STRIPS rules is demonstrated in the following example:

```
strips_rule( paint( Object, NewColor ),
          [ paint-on-brush, neg( oily( Object) ), color_of( Object, OldColor ) ],
          [ color_of( Object, NewColor ) ],
          [ color_of( Object, OldColor ) ] )
```

Other representations are possible, naturally. Our programs will require the predicates preclist / 2, prec / 2, addlist / 2, adds / 2, dellist / 2, and dels / 2. In the current representation, those are defined as follows (in all clauses either of the two arguments may be an output argument):

```
preclist( Action, Plist ) :- strips_rule( Action, Plist, _, _ ).
prec( Action, Cond ) :- preclist( Action, Plist ), member( Cond, Plist ).
addlist( Action, Alist ) :- strips_rule( Action, _, Alist, _ ).
```

```
adds( Action, Cond ) :- addlist( Action, Alist), member(Cond, Alist ).
dellist( Action, Dlist ) :- strips_rule( Action, _, _, Dlist ).
dels( Action, Cond ) :- dellist( Action, Dlist), member( Cond, Dlist ).
```

The reader is invited to devise other, more efficient, representations, so long as these six operations are supported.

8.1.2 The blocks world

It is common in AI to illustrate planning issues and properties of specific planners in a simple domain called the *blocks world*. This domain involves moving blocks around and creating towers of various kinds. One may define quite complex blocks worlds, but our simple blocks world will be defined by the following plan library:

```
strips_rule( stack(X,Y), % place X on Y
          [ clear(Y), holding(X) ],
          [ on(X,Y), clear(X), handempty ],
          [ clear(Y), holding(X) ] )

strips_rule( unstack(X,Y), % remove X from on top Y
          [ on(X,Y), clear(X), handempty ],
          [ clear(Y), holding(X) ],
          [ on(X,Y), clear(X), handempty ] )

strips_rule( pickup(X), % pick up X from the table
          [ ontable(X), clear(X), handempty ],
          [ holding(X) ],
          [ ontable(X), clear(X), handempty ] )

strips_rule( putdown(X), % put X down on the table
          [ holding(X) ],
          [ ontable(X), clear(X), handempty ],
          [ holding(X) ] )
```

8.1.3 Planning problems

Given a plan library (that is, a collection of STRIPS rules), the input to a planning problem consists of a description of an initial state and a description

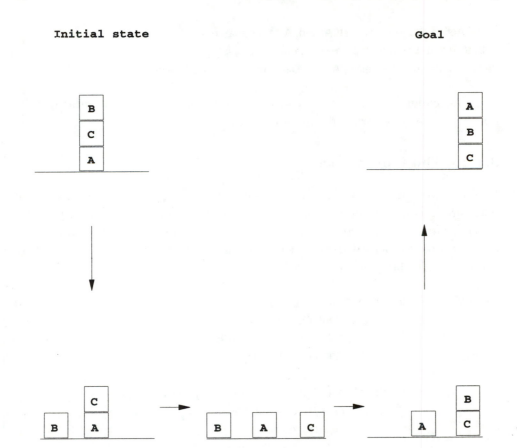

Figure 8.1: A planning problem and its solution

of a goal state; the output is a sequence of actions taken from the library that leads from the initial state to the goal state. Figure 8.1 depicts a simple planning problem and its solution; in the next sections we will discuss a number of classical methods to produce such solutions automatically.

8.2   Linear planning

All planners develop plans in stages, usually starting with the empty plan and ending (if successful) with the final plan. The final plan is usually, but not always, a linear sequence of actions. In between the empty initial plan and the final one, planners maintain *partial plans*, which are repeatedly extended, refined, and otherwise modified. The term 'linear planners' refers to planners whose partial plans in these intermediate stages are linear sequences of actions. Early AI planners were all linear; we discuss two such planners below.

8.2.1   STRIPS

The planning problem is easily seen as a search problem: The nodes of the graph are the possible states, and the arcs (each labeled by an action name) represent actions that transform one state into another.[1] Since the planning problem can be viewed as a search problem, standard search techniques may be applied to it. In particular, we may perform backward chaining.

One of the earliest automated planners in AI is the STRIPS planner; it performs precisely such backward chaining.[2] Notice, however, that there are two 'orders' associated with the process of planning: The order of search in the space of partially developed plans and the temporal ordering of actions within plans. STRIPS performs backward chaining, but does not compute the actions from latest to earliest. Rather, it starts by computing the actions backward in time, but only until it encounters an action whose preconditions are satisfied in the initial state; in this case it simulates the action in that state, and generates a new initial state.

STRIPS uses a stack to keep track of the goals it needs to achieve. It also maintains the 'current' state, initialized to the given initial state. The stack is initialized to the given goal. STRIPS stops with a solution when the stack is empty; at that time the goal is satisfied in the 'current' state. In between, STRIPS repeatedly examines the top of the stack. If the top of the stack is a goal that is satisfied in the current state description, it is ignored and the next goal is examined. Otherwise, STRIPS searches for an action that contains the goal in its add-list. It then forms a plan to establish the action's preconditions by calling itself recursively. When such a plan is found, STRIPS applies the action to the 'current' state, by deleting all the

---

[1] Note a certain subtlety: Each STRIPS rule really defines a *collection* of arcs, since the preconditions, add-lists and delete-lists of any rule refer to only some of the facts about the domain. For example, the **move** action does not refer to the color of the blocks.

[2] STRIPS was inspired by another, earlier planner called the General Problem Solver, or GPS, due to A. Newell and H. Simon.

facts in the action's delete-list from the 'current' state, and adding all the facts in the action's add-list. It then appends the plan for achieving the action's preconditions as well as the action itself to the existing intermediate plan, and calls itself recursively with the new state and new intermediate plan. In this recursive call the original goal list is given, since, although some parts of it may have been achieved already, they may become undone later on.

The main procedure in the STRIPS algorithm is as follows (in the following '+' denotes concatenation):

PROCEDURE STRIPS (GoalList, InitialState, PartialPlan)
Plan ← PartialPlan
CurrentState ← InitialState
while there is a goal G in GoalList that is unsatisfied in CurrentState do
    find an operator A with G in its add list; else backtrack
    Preconditions ← A's preconditions
    APlan ← STRIPS(Preconditions, CurrentState, PartialPlan)
    CurrentState ←
            the result of executing APlan in CurrentState
            + A's add list
            − A's delete list
    Plan ← Plan + APlan + A
end while
return Plan

The algorithm contains two nondeterministic selection points. The first is the selection order among conjuncts of a compound goal. The second is the selection of an action to achieve a given atomic goal. One may bring to bear any search technique at this point; however, the following STRIPS planner adopts a simple depth-first strategy. To compensate for the risk of following infinite paths, the planner is forbidden to apply any particular operator more than once in any plan. While eliminating infinite loops, this prohibition obviously precludes the solution of problems that necessitate repeating an operator.

```
% _____
% strips / 3 is the main STRIPS program
% Arguments: initial state (+), goal list (+), plan (-)
% _____
strips( InitState, GoalList, Plan ) :-
  strips1( InitState, GoalList, [ ], [ ], _, RevPlan ),
  reverse( RevPlan, Plan ).


% Arguments to strips1 / 6: current state (+), goal list (+), current plan (+),
% operators forbidden in current stage of planning (+), new state (-), new plan (-)
strips1( State, GoalList, Plan, _, State, Plan ) :-
  subset( GoalList, State ).
strips1( State, GoalList, Plan, ForbiddenActions, NewState, NewPlan ) :-
  member( Goal, GoalList ),
  not( member( Goal, State ) ), % find an unsatisfied goal
  adds( Ac, Goal ), % find an operator that achieves it
  % (next line may be omitted, at the risk of infinite loops)
  not(member(Ac, ForbiddenActions)), % do not repeat operators
  preclist( Ac, PrecList ), % find its preconditions
  % achieve preconditions:
  strips1( State, PrecList, Plan, [Ac | ForbiddenActions], TmpState1, TmpPlan1 ),
  apply_rule( Ac, TmpState1, TmpState2 ). % update state
  strips1( TmpState2, GoalList, [Ac|TmpPlan1], ForbiddenActions, NewState, NewPlan ).


% Arguments to apply_rule / 3: operator (+), current state (+), next state (-)
apply_rule( Ac, State, NewState ):-
  nl, write('doing '), write(Ac), ttyflush,
  dellist( Ac, DelList ),
  subtract( State, DelList, TmpState ),
  addlist( Ac, AddList ),
  union( AddList, TmpState, NewState ).
```

Here is an example of STRIPS in operation:

```
| ?- strips(
     [clear(a),clear(b),clear(c),ontable(a),ontable(b),ontable(c),handempty],
     [on(b,c), on(a,b)],
     Plan).
```

doing pickup(b)
doing stack(b,c)
doing pickup(a)
doing stack(a,b)

Plan = [pickup(b),stack(b,c),pickup(a),stack(a,b)]

| ?-

What a clever little planner it is! Unfortunately, it performs less spectacularly on other problems. For example, in the following run STRIPS is given the task of inverting a stack of size three. It finds a plan, but one that is decidedly awkward:

```
| ?- strips([clear(c),ontable(a),on(b,a),on(c,b),handempty],
         [on(a,b),on(b,c)],
         Plan).
```

doing unstack(c,b)
doing putdown(c)
doing unstack(b,a)
doing putdown(b)
doing pickup(b)
doing stack(b,a)
doing unstack(b,a)
doing putdown(b)
doing pickup(a)
doing stack(a,b)
doing unstack(a,b)
doing putdown(a)
doing pickup(b)
doing stack(b,c)

doing pickup(a)
doing stack(a,b)

Plan =

       [unstack(c,b),putdown(c),unstack(b,a),putdown(b),pickup(b),
        stack(b,a),unstack(b,a),putdown(b),pickup(a),stack(a,b),
         unstack(a,b),putdown(a),pickup(b),stack(b,c),pickup(a),stack(a,b)]

| ?-

On other problems, STRIPS can be lured into an infinite loop. Here is one example:

| ?- strips(
    [clear(a),clear(b),ontable(a),ontable(b),handempty],
    [on(a,b), on(b,a)],
    Plan).

doing pickup(a)
doing stack(a,b)
doing unstack(a,b)
doing putdown(a)
doing pickup(b)
doing stack(b,a)
doing unstack(b,a)
doing putdown(b)
doing pickup(a)
doing stack(a,b)
doing unstack(a,b)

    ⋮

8.2.2   Goal protection and goal regression

Clearly, one limitation of STRIPS is that even if one subgoal is achieved, subsequent planning may violate it; this destructive occurrence is called the *clobbering* of one goal by another. A natural solution is to 'protect' goals in the plan from the spot at which they are established until the spot where they are needed (they may be needed as a precondition to some action or as part of the top-level goal).

While conceptually simple, this idea is in fact quite tricky to realize. A number of increasingly complex issues surface: When do we protect a goal, and when do we remove the protection? How do we detect protection violation? What do we do once such a violation is detected? The last question is the trickiest of all. One easy answer is to drop the entire plan developed so far whenever a protection violation occurs. In most cases, however, this amounts to throwing out the baby with the bathwater; much work may have gone into the plan so far, and often simple tweaks to the existing plan eliminate the protection violation. The most important tweak is to reorder the plan, moving an offending goal to an earlier point in the plan so that it does not interfere with later stages. Of course, those later stages may now interfere with the newly positioned goal, a situation to be avoided as much as possible. Moving goals to earlier points in the plan is called *goal regression*.

We will explore these issues by presenting a specific planner that employs goal protection and goal regression, called RSTRIPS, adapted from a planner by that name due to N. J. Nilsson. Since the operation of RSTRIPS is complex, we will explain it in stages. First, we will explain its essentials and demonstrate them through a partial example. We will then present a heavily annotated Prolog program implementing the planner. Even so, the reader will do well to trace closely the execution of the program on a planning problem, in order to appreciate the subtle issues that arise in the process of planning.

RSTRIPS maintains an ordered list. The list contains all goals and sub-goals generated so far, as well as operations selected so far. It also contains additional information relevant to the planning. To start, with each goal we will associate a *conjunction number* (or *cnumber*), a number that will be used to maintain correct goal protection. The cnumber of the top-level goals will be 1; then, whenever a new operator is selected (and thus added with its preconditions to the list), the cnumber will be incremented; the new cnumber will be associated with the operator and each of its preconditions. In addition, at all times during planning, a 'current' marker will separate the list into two: Everything before (or, in the drawings to come, above) it will be considered completely planned, whereas everything after (below) it will be at best partially planned. At the beginning of planning the 'current' marker will be placed at the beginning (or top) of the list; upon successful completion of planning it will move to the end (or bottom) of the list. We will use the term 'current state' to mean the state resulting from taking the (possibly empty) sequence of operations that is above the 'current' marker, starting from the initial state.

Let us consider a concrete planning example. Suppose the initial state is one in which three blocks – a, b, and c – are on the table, and the robot's hand is empty. If the top-level goal is the conjunction on(a,b) & some_goal, then the list will be be initialized as follows:

$$
\begin{array}{lll}
current \rightarrow & & \\
goal & 1 & \text{on(a,b)} \\
goal & 1 & \text{some\_goal}
\end{array}
$$

Now planning will commence. The first goal following the 'current' marker is on(a,b). RSTRIPS will note that the operator stack(a,b) achieves this goal, and will insert the operator with its preconditions into the list. The list will now look as follows:

$$
\begin{array}{lll}
current \rightarrow & & \\
goal & 2 & \text{holding(a)} \\
goal & 2 & \text{clear(b)} \\
op & 2 & \text{stack(a,b)} \\
goal & 1 & \text{on(a,b)} \\
goal & 1 & \text{some\_goal}
\end{array}
$$

Now the first goal following the 'current' marker is holding(a). RSTRIPS will notice that the operator pickup(a) achieves it, and will insert the operator with its preconditions into the list. The list will now look as follows:

$$
\begin{array}{lll}
current \rightarrow & & \\
goal & 3 & \text{ontable(a)} \\
goal & 3 & \text{clear(a)} \\
goal & 3 & \text{handempty} \\
op & 3 & \text{pickup(a)} \\
goal & 2 & \text{holding(a)} \\
goal & 2 & \text{clear(b)} \\
op & 2 & \text{stack(a,b)} \\
goal & 1 & \text{on(a,b)} \\
goal & 1 & \text{some\_goal}
\end{array}
$$

Now the first goal below the 'current' marker is ontable(a). This goal happens to hold in the current state, and so the no_op operation will be

inserted right before it, and the 'current' marker will be moved past the
ontable(a) goal. However, in order to prevent later stages from clobbering
this goal, protection will be placed on it. The list will now look as follows
(protection is denoted by ∗):

op			no_op
goal	3	∗	ontable(a)
current →			
goal	3		clear(a)
goal	3		handempty
op	3		pickup(a)
goal	2		holding(a)
goal	2		clear(b)
op	2		stack(a,b)
goal	1		on(a,b)
goal	1		some_goal

Next the same procedure is repeated for the ensuing two goals, and the
result is the following list:

op			no_op
goal	3	∗	ontable(a)
op			no_op
goal	3	∗	clear(a)
op			no_op
goal	3	∗	handempty
current →			
op	3		pickup(a)
goal	2		holding(a)
goal	2		clear(b)
op	2		stack(a,b)
goal	1		on(a,b)
goal	1		some_goal

Now below the 'current' marker there is an operator, followed by the
goal it achieves. RSTRIPS will move the marker past both and place protection on the new goal, but remove protection from the preconditions of the
operator. The list will look as follows:

op			no_op
goal	3		ontable(a)
op			no_op
goal	3		clear(a)
op			no_op
goal	3		handempty
op	3		pickup(a)
goal	2	*	holding(a)
current →			
goal	2		clear(b)
op	2		stack(a,b)
goal	1		on(a,b)
goal	1		some_goal

Now let us skip ahead, to a point at which the list looks as follows:

op			no_op
goal	3		ontable(a)
⋮			⋮ rest of plan for on(a,b)
op	2		stack(a,b)
goal	1	*	on(a,b)
⋮			⋮ partial plan for some_goal
current →			
goal	17		some_sub_goal
⋮			⋮ partial plan for some_goal, cont.
op	8		some_operator
goal	1		some_goal

At this point RSTRIPS will search for an operator to achieve some_sub_goal.
It will first seek an operator that does not violate protected goals in the portion of the list that is above the 'current' marker (in our example, we have
only one – on(a,b)). Suppose such an operator does not exist. RSTRIPS will
now pick an operator that achieves some_sub_goal and will find the lowest protected goal above the 'current' marker that is violated by it (again, in our example, there is only one). It will then attempt to regress some_sub_goal all the
way back above the operator achieving the violated goal. We say "attempt,"
since while some_sub_goal is regressed back through the list, RSTRIPS must
make sure that no new violations are introduced. Consider an operator Op

through which some_sub_goal is regressed; this includes the operator achieving the violated goal and all other operators along the way. If some_sub_goal is in the delete-list of Op, then there is no point in regressing some_sub_goal through it. For example, if some_sub_goal is clear(b), it is no use regressing it past stack(a,b). Similarly, it is futile to regress some_sub_goal past a goal G such that G and some_sub_goal are mutually inconsistent; this futility might be discovered anyway (sometimes at great expense) by subsequent planning, but domain-specific information about inconsistency allows us to avoid this useless direction early on.

If some_sub_goal can indeed be regressed all the way back above the violated goal, then it will be moved there, and protection will be removed from on(a,b) and placed back on the preconditions of stack(a,b). The list will look as follows:

op			no_op
goal	3	*	ontable(a)
⋮			⋮ rest of plan for on(a,b)
current →			
goal	17		some_sub_goal
op	2		stack(a,b)
goal	1		on(a,b)
⋮			. partial plan for some_goal
			⋮ as above, minus protections
op	8		some_operator
goal	1		some_goal

However, what should RSTRIPS do if some_sub_goal cannot be regressed all the way beyond the violated goal? It is tempting to say that in this case RSTRIPS should simply fail and backtrack to the previous choice point. This, however, will not do. For example, suppose some_sub_goal is clear(b), some_operator is stack(b,c), and some_goal is on(b,c). Since clear(b) cannot be moved ahead of stack(a,b), we would like one of the higher-level goals to be moved there; but if we simply backtrack, that 'there' will be lost. Rather than fail, therefore, RSTRIPS will search down the list for the first higher-level goal that can be regressed to the desired point; in our example it will be the top-level goal on(b,c) itself. (This is where the cnumbers will come in handy, since they encode the goal-subgoal relationships.) RSTRIPS will now move on(b,c) above the stack(a,b) operation, but there is one last additional complication: The partial plan for achieving on(b,c) already developed is now potentially obsolete. Rather than attempt to revalidate it, RSTRIPS simply discards this plan from the list (again, the cnumbers are used to determine which part of the list is the partial plan for on(b,c)).

This example explains the essential ways in which RSTRIPS makes use of goal protection and regression. The operation of RSTRIPS is by no means straightforward, and we have suppressed some of the details. To fully explain the details, we now present a heavily annotated Prolog program. The annotation is self-contained; the only part requiring additional explanation is the representation of the list maintained by RSTRIPS. We implement this list by two 'back-to-back' stacks: Tstack will contain all items above the 'current' marker in reverse order, and Bstack will contain all items below the 'current' marker in regular order. The 'current' marker will be implicit in these stacks and will not be represented explicitly. Here is an example explaining the representation:

RSTRIPS list				Prolog representation	
op			no_op	Tstack:	[pro(goal(ontable(a)), 2),
goal	2	*	ontable(a)		op(no_op, 2)]
current →					
goal	2		clear(a)	Bstack:	[goal(clear(a), 2),
goal	2		handempty		goal(handempty, 2),
op	2		pickup(a)		op(pickup(a), 2),
goal	1		holding(a)		goal(holding(a), 1)]

With this, we turn to the actual program. Despite the heavy annotation, some aspects of RSTRIPS will become clearer by tracing its execution. For this reason, the program is followed by a short sample run.

```
% _____
% rstrips / 3 is the main RSTRIPS program.
% Arguments: initial state (+), goal list (+), plan (-)
% _____
rstrips( InitState, GoalList, Plan ) :-
    add_cnumber(1, GoalList, Bstack),        % add the cnumber '1' to top-level goals
    rstrips1( InitState, Bstack, [ ], 1, Plan ),
    display_plan( InitState, InitGoal, Plan ).


% _____
% Arguments to rstrips1 / 5: initial state (+), Bstack (+), Tstack (+),
%                            cnumber counter (+), plan (-)
% _____
% Case 1: Bstack is empty
rstrips1( _, [ ], Tstack, _, Plan ) :- extract_plan( Tstack, Plan ).

% Case 2: top of Bstack is an operator followed by a goal
rstrips1( InitState, [op(Op,OpCnum), goal(Goal, GoalCnum) | MoreBstack],
        Tstack, Ctr, Plan ) :- !,
    display_prec_accomplished( Goal, Op ), % (for trace purposes)
    remove_protection( OpCnum, Tstack, NewTstack),
    rstrips1( InitState, MoreBstack,
            [pro(goal(Goal, GoalCnum)), op(Op,OpCnum) | NewTstack], Ctr, Plan ).


% Case 3: top of Bstack is a satisfied goal
rstrips1( InitState, [goal(Goal, GoalCnum) | Bstack], Tstack, Ctr, Plan ) :-
    rstrips_holds( Goal, Tstack, InitState), !, % goal already holds
    display_no_op_selection( Goal ), % (for trace purposes)
    NewCtr is Ctr + 1, % increment cnumber counter
    rstrips1( InitState, Bstack, [pro(goal(Goal, GoalCnum)), op(no_op,NewCtr) | Tstack],
            NewCtr, Plan ).
```

% Case 4: top of Bstack is an unsatisfied goal

% Subcase 4a: an operator is found that achieves the goal without violating
% protected goals; the operator and its preconditions are added to Bstack
```
rstrips1( InitState, [goal(Goal, GoalCnum) | Bstack], Tstack, Ctr, Plan ) :-
  adds( Op, Goal ), % operator achieves the goal
  % as in STRIPS, the following line may be omitted, risking infinite loops:
  not( member( op(Op, _), Bstack ) ), % no operator repetition
  preserves_protection( Op, Bstack, Tstack ), % no protection violation
  preclist( Op, Prec ), % find action's preconditions
  display_op_selection( Goal , Op, Prec ), % (for trace purposes)
  NewCtr is Ctr+1, % increment cnumber counter
  add_cnumber( NewCtr, Prec, OpPrec ), % attach cnumber to preconditions
  % append the new operator and its preconditions to Bstack:
  append( OpPrec, [op(Op,NewCtr), goal(Goal, GoalCnum) | Bstack], NewBstack ),
  rstrips1( InitState, NewBstack, Tstack, NewCtr, Plan ).
```

% Subcase 4b: an operator is found that achieves the new goal but which
% violates a previous, protected goal; the new goal is regressed past the
% operator achieving the protected goal
```
rstrips1( InitState, [goal(Goal, GoalCnum) | MoreBstack], Tstack, Ctr, Plan ) :-
  adds( Op, Goal ), % operator achieves the goal
  % again, the following may be omitted, risking infinite loops
  not( member( op(Op, _), Bstack ) ),
  % find the violated goal:
  find_violated_goal( Op, Bstack, Tstack, Vgoal, VgoalCnum, Vop, VopCnum ),
  find_goal_to_regress( Goal, GoalCnum, VgoalCnum,
                [goal(Goal, GoalCnum) | MoreBstack],
                Rgoal, RgoalCnum, Tmp1Bstack ),
  display_regression( Goal, GoalCnum, Vop, VopCnum ), % (for trace purposes)
  reverse( Tmp1Bstack, Tmp1BstackRev ),
  remove_subplan( Tmp1BstackRev, CnumList, Tmp2BstackRev, NewCnumList ),
  reverse( Tmp2BstackRev, Tmp2Bstack ),
  remove_subplan( Tstack, NewCnumList, Tmp2BstackRev, _ ),
  regress( Rgoal, RgoalCnum, Vgoal, VgoalCnum, Tmp2Bstack, Tmp2Tstack
        NewBstack, NewTstack ), % regress, generating new stacks
  rstrips1( InitState, NewBstack, NewTstack, Ctr, Plan ).
```

```
% _____
% add_cnumber / 3 assign cnumber to the elements of the list.
% Arguments: cnumber (+), list of goals (+), list of cnumbered goals (-)
% _____
add_cnumber( _, [ ], L ) :- !, L = [ ].
add_cnumber( Cnum, [X | MoreX], [goal(X,Cnum) | MoreL] ) :-
    add_cnumber(Cnum, MoreX, MoreL).


% _____
% remove_protection / 3 removes protection in Tstack of goals with specified
% cnumber.
% Arguments: cnumber (+), Tstack (+), new Tstack (-)
% _____
remove_protection( _, [ ], [ ]) :- !.
remove_protection(Cnum, [pro(goal(Cond, Cnum)) | MoreTstack],
                  [goal(Cond, Cnum) | NewMoreTstack] ) :- !,
    remove_protection( Cnum, MoreTstack, NewMoreTstack ).
remove_protection(Cnum, [ X | MoreTstack], [ X | NewMoreTstack] ) :-
    remove_protection( Cnum, MoreTstack, NewMoreTstack ).


% _____
% preserves_protection / 3 verifies that an operator does not delete any goal which
% is protected (in Tstack). For every condition in the delete list of the operator,
% it checks that one of the following is true: (1) the condition is not protected,
% or (2) it is protected, but the deletion is only temporary, meaning that there
% is an operator later in the same execution scope that reinstates the condition.
% Arguments: operator (+), Bstack (+), Tstack (+)
% _____
preserves_protection( _, _, [ ] ) :- !.
preserves_protection( Op, Bstack, [pro(goal(Goal, GoalCnum)) | More] ) :- !,
    ( not(dels(Op, Goal)) ; temporary_viol( Bstack, Goal, GoalCnum) ), !,
    preserves_protection( Op, Bstack, More ).
preserves_protection( Op, Bstack, [_ | More] ) :- preserves_protection( Op, Bstack, More ).
```

```
% _____
% temporary_viol / 3 verifies that a goal protection violation is only temporary; this
% is so whenever there is another operator later in the execution context with the
% goal in its add list (a so-called white knight).
% Arguments: Bstack (+), violated goal (+), violated goal's cnumber (+)
% _____
temporary_viol( [op(Op, Cnum) | _], Goal, Cnum) :- !, adds( Op, Goal ).
temporary_viol( [op(Op,_) | _], Goal, _ ) :- adds( Op, Goal ), !.
temporary_viol( [_ | MoreBstack], Goal, Cnumber ) :-
   temporary_viol( MoreBstack, Goal, Cnumber ).
```

```
% _____
% find_violated_goal / 7 finds the violated goal in Tstack.
% Arguments: operator violating protected goal (+), Bstack (+), Tstack (+),
%                  violated goal (-), violated goal's cnumber (-),
%                  operator preceding violated goal (-), that operator's cnumber (-)
% _____
find_violated_goal(Op, Bstack, [pro(goal(Goal, Cnum)), op(Op1,Op1Cnum) | _],
                 Goal, Cnum, Op1, Op1Cnum) :-
  dels( Op, Goal ),
   not( temporary_viol( Bstack, Goal, Cnum) ), !.
find_violated_goal( Op, Bstack, [_ | MoreTstack], Rgoal, RgoalCnum, Vop, VopCnum ) :-
  find_violated_goal( Op, Bstack, MoreTstack, Vgoal, VgoalCnum, Vop, VopCnum ).
```

```
% _____
% find_goal_to_regress / 8 first returns 'current' goal (the one on top of Bstack),
% and then increasingly higher-level goals farther down Bstack
% Arguments:  current goal (+), its cnumber (+), violated goal's cnumber (+),
%             Bstack (+), goal to be regressed (-), its cnumber (-),
%             list containing cnumbers of all goals participating in the subplan
%             developed so far for the goal to be regressed (-)
% _____


% the extra input argument to the _aux predicate is a list of goal cnumbers:
find_goal_to_regress( Goal, GoalCnum, VgoalCnum, Bstack, Rgoal, RgoalCnum,
                MoreBstack, CnumList ) :-
    find_goal_to_regress_aux( Goal, GoalCnum, VgoalCnum, [ ], Bstack, Rgoal,
                RgoalCnum, MoreBstack, CnumList ).


% first, return current goal:
find_goal_to_regress_aux( Goal, GoalCnum, _, CnumList,
                [goal(Goal, GoalCnum) | MoreBstack],
                Goal, GoalCnum, MoreBstack, CnumList ).
% if current goal and violated goal have the same cnumber, and if the operator
% for which they are preconditions has been reached in Bstack, then fail:
find_goal_to_regress_aux( _, GoalCnum, VgoalCnum, _, [op(_, OpCnum) | _], _, _, _, _) :-
                VgoalCnum = OpCnum, GoalCnum = OpCnum, !, fail.
% otherwise, find the operator for which the current goal is a precondition,
% and return the goal following it in Bstack:
find_goal_to_regress_aux( _, GoalCnum, VgoalCnum, CnumList,
                [op(Op,OpCnum), goal(Goal1, Goal1Cnum) | MoreBstack],
                Rgoal, RgoalCnum, [op(Op,OpCnum) | NewBstack], NewCnumList ) :-
    GoalCnum = OpCnum, !,
    find_goal_to_regress_aux( Goal1, Goal1Cnum, VgoalCnum, [GoalCnum | CnumList],
                [goal(Goal1, Goal1Cnum) | MoreBstack],
                Rgoal, RgoalCnum, NewBstack, NewCnumList ).
find_goal_to_regress_aux( Goal, GoalCnum, VgoalCnum, CnumList, [X | MoreBstack],
                Rgoal, RgoalCnum, [X | NewBstack], NewCnumList ) :-
    find_goal_to_regress_aux( Goal, GoalCnum, VgoalCnum, CnumList, MoreBstack,
                Rgoal, RgoalCnum, NewBstack, NewCnumList ).
```

```
%  _____
% remove_subplan / 8 accepts a stack (either Bstack or Tstack) and a list of
% cnumbers, and returns the stack without all partial plans for achieving the
% goals with specified cnumbers; it also returns an augmented list of cnumbers,
% which includes the given cnumbers as well as the cnumbers in all
% subgoals encountered.
%  _____
remove_subplan( [ ], CnumList, NewStack, NewCnumList ) :- !,
   NewStack = [ ], NewCnumList = CnumList.
remove_subplan( [goal(_,GoalCnum), op(_,OpCnum) | MoreStack],
               CnumList, NewStack, NewCnumList ) :-
   member( GoalCnum, CnumList ), !,
    remove_subplan( MoreStack, [OpCnum | CnumList], NewStack, NewCnumList ).
remove_subplan( [pro(goal(_,GoalCnum)), op(_,OpCnum) | MoreStack],
               CnumList, NewStack, NewCnumList ) :-
   member( GoalCnum, CnumList ), !,
    remove_subplan( MoreStack, [OpCnum | CnumList], NewStack, NewCnumList ).
remove_subplan( [goal(_,GoalCnum) | MoreStack], CnumList, NewStack, NewCnumList ) :-
   member( GoalCnum, CnumList ), !,
    remove_subplan( MoreStack, CnumList, NewStack, NewCnumList ).
remove_subplan( [pro(goal(_,GoalCnum)) | MoreStack],
               CnumList, NewStack, NewCnumList ) :-
   member( GoalCnum, CnumList ), !,
    remove_subplan( MoreStack, CnumList, NewStack, NewCnumList ).
remove_subplan( [op(_,OpCnum) | MoreStack], CnumList, NewStack, NewCnumList ) :-
   member( OpCnum, CnumList ), !,
    remove_subplan( MoreStack, CnumList, NewStack, NewCnumList ).
remove_subplan( [X | MoreStack], CnumList, [X | NewStack], NewCnumList ) :-
   remove_subplan( MoreStack, CnumList, NewStack, NewCnumList ).


%  _____
% regress / 8 regresses the goal violating protection through the operator that
% achieves the protected goal.
% Arguments: regressed goal (+), regressed goal's cnumber (+), violated goal (+),
%            violated goal's cnumber (+), Bstack minus regressed goal (+),
%            Tstack (+), new Bstack (-), new Tstack (-)
%  _____
```

% if the violated goal in Tstack is reached, and it was achieved by a no_op,
% then remove the no_op *and the goal protection, and halt:*
regress(Rgoal, RgoalCnum, Vgoal, VgoalCnum, Bstack,
        [pro(goal(Vgoal,VgoalCnum)), op(no_op,_) | MoreTstack],
        NewBstack, NewTstack) :- !,
    not(inconsistent(Vgoal, Rgoal)),
    NewBstack = [goal(Rgoal,RgoalCnum), goal(Vgoal,VgoalCnum) | Bstack],
    NewTstack = MoreTstack.
% if the violated goal in Tstack is reached, and it was achieved by a regular
% operator, then remove protection from violated goal, place it on preceding
% action's preconditions, and halt:
regress(Rgoal, RgoalCnum, Vgoal, VgoalCnum, Bstack,
        [pro(goal(Vgoal,VgoalCnum)), op(Vop,VopCnum) | MoreTstack],
        NewBstack, NewTstack) :- !,
    not((dels(Vop, Rgoal) ; inconsistent(Vgoal, Rgoal))),
    NewBstack =
        [goal(Rgoal,RgoalCnum), op(Vop,VopCnum), goal(Vgoal,VgoalCnum) | Bstack],
    protect(VopCnum, MoreTstack, NewTstack).
% for all other goals do the same, but continue to process remaining Tstack:
regress(Rgoal, RgoalCnum, Vgoal, VgoalCnum, Bstack,
        [pro(goal(Goal,GoalCnum)), op(no_op,_) | MoreTstack],
        NewBstack, NewTstack) :- !,
    not(inconsistent(Goal, Rgoal)),
    regress(Rgoal, RgoalCnum, Vgoal, VgoalCnum,
            [goal(Goal,GoalCnum) | Bstack],
            MoreTstack, NewBstack, NewTstack).
regress(Rgoal, RgoalCnum, Vgoal, VgoalCnum, Bstack,
        [pro(goal(Goal,GoalCnum)), op(Op,OpCnum) | MoreTstack],
        NewBstack, NewTstack) :- !,
    not((dels(Op, Rgoal) ; inconsistent(Goal, Rgoal))),
    regress(Rgoal, RgoalCnum, Vgoal, VgoalCnum,
            [op(Op,OpCnum), goal(Goal,GoalCnum) | Bstack],
            MoreTstack, NewBstack, NewTstack).

```
regress( Rgoal, RgoalCnum, Vgoal, VgoalCnum, Bstack,
         [goal(Goal,GoalCnum), op(no_op,_) | MoreTstack],
         NewBstack, NewTstack ) :-
   not( inconsistent(Goal, Rgoal) ),
   regress( Rgoal, RgoalCnum, Vgoal, VgoalCnum,
            [goal(Goal,GoalCnum) | Bstack],
            MoreTstack, NewBstack, NewTstack ).
regress( Rgoal, RgoalCnum, Vgoal, VgoalCnum, Bstack,
         [goal(Goal,GoalCnum), op(Op,OpCnum) | MoreTstack],
         NewBstack, NewTstack ) :-
   not(( dels(Op, Rgoal) ; inconsistent(Goal, Rgoal) )),
   regress( Rgoal, RgoalCnum, Vgoal, VgoalCnum,
            [op(Op,OpCnum), goal(Goal,GoalCnum) | Bstack],
            MoreTstack, NewBstack, NewTstack ).


% _____
% protect / 3 adds protection to goals with given cnumber in Tstack.
% Arguments: cnumber to protect (+), Tstack (+), new Tstack (−)
% _____
protect( _, [ ], NewTstack ) :- !, NewTstack = [ ].
protect( Cnum, [goal(Goal, Cnum) | MoreTstack], NewTstack ) :- !,
   protect( Cnum, MoreTstack, TmpTstack ),
   NewTstack = [pro(goal(Goal, Cnum)) | TmpTstack].
protect( Cnum, [X | MoreTstack], [X | MoreNewTstack] ) :-
   protect( Cnum, MoreTstack, MoreNewTstack ).


% _____
% extract_plan / 2 collects all non-no_op operators from Tstack in reverse order.
% Arguments: Tstack (+), plan (−)
% _____
extract_plan( Tstack, Plan ) :- extract_plan1( Tstack, [ ], Plan ), !.
extract_plan1( [ ], Plan, Plan).
extract_plan1( [op(X,_) | MoreTstack], RevPlan, Plan ) :-
   not( X = no_op ),
   extract_plan1( MoreTstack, [X | RevPlan], Plan ).
extract_plan1( [_| More], RevPlan, Plan ) :- extract_plan1( More, RevPlan, Plan ).
```

```
%
% rstrips_holds / 3 verifies that a goal holds in the 'current' state; this is so iff
% one of the following is true: (1) the current state is the initial state (i.e.,
% empty Tstack), and the goal is true in it; (2) the immediately preceding
% operator added the goal; (3) the immediately preceding operator did not delete
% the goal, and (recursively) the goal held right before it.
% Arguments: Goal (+), Tstack (+), initial state (+)
%
rstrips_holds( Goal, [ ], InitState ) :- !, member( Goal, InitState ). % case (1)
rstrips_holds( Goal, [op(Op,_) | _], _) :- adds( Op, Goal), !. % case (2)
rstrips_holds( Goal, [op(Op,_) | MoreTstack], InitState ) :- !, % case (3)
   not( dels( Op, Goal ) ),
   rstrips_holds( Goal, MoreTstack, InitState ).
% otherwise, top of Tstack is not an operator; ignore it
rstrips_holds( Goal, [_ | MoreTstack], InitState ) :-
   rstrips_holds( Goal, MoreTstack, InitState ).




%
% NOTE: all remaining predicates display information, but do not affect planning
%




%
% display_plan / 3 displays the completed plan.
% Arguments: initial state (+), Goal (+), Plan (+)
%
display_plan( I, G, P ) :-
   nl, write( '- - - - - - - - - - - - - - - - - - - - - - - - - - - - - -' ),
   nl, write( 'PLANNING IS NOW COMPLETE;' ),
   nl, write( 'to get from' ), nl, tab(2), write( I ),
   nl, write( 'to the goal' ), nl, tab(2), write( G ),
   nl, write( 'execute the following sequence:' ),
   nl, tab( 2 ), writeplan1( P ).


writeplan1( [ ] ).
writeplan1( [A | B] ) :- write( A ), write( ' ; ' ), writeplan1( B ).
```

```
%
% display_prec_accomplished / 2 notifies when an operator's preconditions have been
% accomplished.
%
display_prec_accomplished( Goal, Op ) :-
    nl, writel( ['Preconditions of operator ', Op, ' have been accomplished;']),
    nl, tab(2), writel( [Op, ' and ', Goal, ' are moved to Tstack;'] ),
    nl, tab(2), writel( ['protection is lifted from the preconditions of ', Op] ),
    nl, tab(2), writel( ['protection is placed on ', Goal] ).
display_prec_accomplished( _, Op ) :- % execute upon backtracking
    nl, writel( ['** Backtracking to operator ', Op] ),
    fail.


%
% display_op_selection / 3 notifies of operator selection.
%
display_op_selection( Goal, Op, Prec ) :-
    nl, writel( ['Operator ', Op, ' added to stack, in order to achieve ', Goal, ';'] ),
    nl, tab(2), writel( ['it is preceded by its preconditions, ', Prec] ).
display_op_selection( Goal, Op, _ ) :- % execute upon backtracking
    nl, write('** Backtracking:'),
    writel(['operator ', Op, ' de-selected for goal ', Goal]),
    fail.


%
% display_no_op_selection / 1 notifies when a condition happens to hold in the
% current state, and is thus achievable by the no_op operator.
%
display_no_op_selection( Goal ) :-
    writel( ['Goal ', Goal, ' holds in the current state, so no_op is sufficient;']),
    nl, tab(2), writel( ['protection is placed on ', Goal] ).
display_no_op_selection( Goal ) :- % execute upon backtracking
    nl, writel(['** Backtracking past the (sub)goal ', Goal, ' ;']),
    nl, tab(3), write('the no_op plan is removed'),
    fail.
```

```
% _____
% display_regression / 2 prints regression steps.
% _____
display_regression( Rgoal, RgoalCnum, Vop, VopCnum ) :-
    writel( ['>> attempting to regress ', Rgoal, ' (cnumber = ', RgoalCnum, ' )'] ),
    tab(3), writel( ['all the way through ' , Vop, ' (cnumber = ', VopCnum, ' )] ).
display_regression( Rgoal, _, Vop, _) :- % execute upon backtracking
    nl, write('** Backtracking: '),
    nl, tab(3), writel( ['attempting to regress, ', Rgoal, ' through ',
                    Vop, ' did not lead to a solution'] ),
    fail.


% _____
% This is the end of the RSTRIPS program
% _____
```

We have thus far explained the procedure employed by RSTRIPS through a partial example and presented the annotated program. Actually tracing the execution of the program provides additional insights. Here is a sample run of the program on three planning problems, but with all print commands suppressed:

```
| ?- restrips([clear(c),ontable(a),on(c,a),ontable(b), clear(b),handempty],
            [on(a,b),on(b,c)],
            Plan).
Plan = [pickup(b),stack(b,c),pickup(a),stack(a,b)]
yes
| ?- restrips([clear(c),ontable(a),on(c,a),ontable(b), clear(b),handempty],
            [on(a,b),on(b,c)],
            Plan).
Plan = [unstack(c,a),putdown(c),pickup(b),stack(b,c),pickup(a),stack(a,b)]
yes
| ?- restrips([clear(a),on(a,b),on(b,c),ontable(c),handempty],
            [on(a,b),on(b,a)],
            Plan).
no
| ?-
```

While RSTRIPS appears to work well on these problems, it requires much effort to achieve this triumph; if we were to include a full printout, the above trace would run over twenty pages! The reader is encouraged to experiment with the program to gain a deeper understanding of its strengths and weaknesses.

8.3   Nonlinear planning

Both planners discussed so far – STRIPS and RSTRIPS – are linear planners: In both, any partial plans under development consists of a linear sequence of actions. AI researchers recognized early on that the linear sequences might be an unnecessary limitation. For example, suppose a construction robot has a goal of placing a container at an elevated level. One plan would be to build a ramp, build a platform, and use the ramp to place a container on the platform. Obviously, both the platform and the ramp must be built before the container is moved, but it is unimportant (as far this goal goes) which is built first. Why then not delay this decision until a later point in planning, where it might make a difference? If we do delay the decision, we end up with only a partial order among the plan steps and, hence, a nonlinear plan.

Delaying the order among plan steps is a form of *least-commitment* planning. Another form of the same principle exists, and it has to do with instantiation of variables. Suppose a two-handed robot needs to grasp a given object with its hand. Rather than commit to using one hand or the other, why not delay this commitment, so that if a future planning step calls for the use of a particular hand simultaneously with the grasping then at that point the other hand will be selected for the grasping. It should be added that, although least commitment is a natural notion, the extent to which it speeds up planning is still a matter of debate; Section 8.5 points to relevant literature on this topic.

One notion investigated in connection with planning, and emphasized in the context of nonlinear planning, is that of *planner completeness*. A planner is complete if it is guaranteed to produce a solution, if one exists. The first nonlinear planner shown to be complete was called TWEAK, due to Chapman; we will present a more recent planner, due to McAllester and Rosenblitt (see Section 8.5 for references). This planner is not particularly clever in the way in which it searches for a plan; in fact it is quite useless as a practical planner. However, what the planner lacks in smarts it makes up in systematicity; it never generates the same plan more than once, and eventually generates all legal plans. Furthermore, it can be modified to embody clever search heuristics.

The planner maintains a symbol table, which is a mapping of plan-step names to actual operators. A partial ordering on the plan-step names is represented separately in the form of *safety conditions* and *causal links*. A safety condition is merely a statement that a particular instance of one action precedes another particular instance of some (possibly identical) action. A typical safety condition could be "Step5 (in which the robot picks up block b) precedes Step2 (in which the robot unstacks block c from block d)." We use the symbol $<$ to denote a safety condition, as in 'Step5 $<$ Step2'. A causal link is a stronger relation between pairs of plan-step names; it not only implies an ordering of the two steps in the plan, but also supplies logical information about why the planner decided to impose the ordering. Specifically, a causal link between two steps means that some precondition p of the later step is caused by (i.e., appears in the add-list of) the earlier step. The causal link is labeled not only with the two steps it relates, but with this precondition, as in 'Step5 $\xrightarrow{p}$ Step2'.

Before we explain the operation of the planner, it is convenient to introduce two special steps: begin and end, and two STRIPS rules:

strips_rule(begin, [ ], *initial state*, [ ]).

strips_rule(end, *goal*, [ ], [ ]).

The step begin is defined to precede all other steps that will ever exist in the plan, and the step end to follow them.

The planner starts with an initial partial plan; the partial plan may be the null one, which consists only of the steps begin and end. The planner then repeatedly refines and modifies its partial plan, until an acceptable plan is achieved. A plan is acceptable if it satisfies the following condition:

> for every precondition p of every plan step s2
> there is another plan step s1
> such that s1 $\xrightarrow{p}$ s2
>   and such that
>   for any other s3 in the plan

with p in either its add or delete list
(a so-called *threat*),
either s3 < s1 or s2 < s3.

In order to achieve this condition, the operations available to the planner are the addition of a safety condition, the addition of a causal link between two steps already in the plan, and the addition of a plan step. The operation of the planner is as follows:

PROCEDURE FIND-COMPLETION (P: a partial plan)

1. If P is acceptable, return P.

2. If the safety conditions in P are inconsistent then fail and backtrack.

3. If there is a causal link s $\xrightarrow{p}$ w in P and a threat v to this causal link in P such that neither v < s nor w < v are in P, then add either v < s or w < v to P and go to 1.

4. Otherwise, there must be a step w in P with precondition p such that there is no causal link of the form s $\xrightarrow{p}$ w in P. In this case do one of the following:

    (a) Find a step s in P that adds p and add s $\xrightarrow{p}$ w to P.

    (b) Find an operator o that adds p, create a new entry s in the symbol table which maps to o, and add s $\xrightarrow{p}$ w to P.

Go to 1.

The Prolog implementation below uses the following representation:

The symbol table is a list of (Name, Op) pairs.

The safety conditions are represented by a list of (A, B) pairs, interpreted as 'A precedes B.'

The causal links are represented by a list of (S, P, W) triples, where S and W are step names, and P is the condition which is in the add-list of S and precondition list of W.

The procedure above contains a number of choice points. The implementation below opts for systematicity over efficiency. Systematicity is achieved by conducting an iterative-deepening search, exhaustively checking all plans of less than n steps before increasing n. The result is a planner that is complete (see Exercise 8.5), but impractical for all but the most trivial cases. Exercise 8.6 explores other, more clever search orders.

```
% _____
% non_lin_plan / 4 is the top-level program which calls the planner with an empty
% initial plan and a bound on the plan cost, and returns the plan (i.e., symbol
% table, safety conditions, and causal links) generated by the planner.
% _____

non_lin_plan( MaxCost, SymbolTable, Safety, CausalLinks ) :-
    find_completion( [ ( start, begin ), ( finish, end ) ], [ ( start, finish ) ], [ ], MaxCost,
                SymbolTable, Safety, CausalLinks ).


% _____
% find_completion / 7 finds a completion, if one exists, for the partial plan
% described by SymbolTable, Safety, and CausalLinks. Only partial plans with
% cost at most MaxCost are considered. The resulting plan is returned in
% NewSymbols, NewSafety, and NewCausals.
% Arguments: SymbolTable (+), Safety (+), CausalLinks (+), MaxCost (+),
%            NewSymbols (–), NewSafety (–), NewCausals (–)
% _____

find_completion( SymbolTable, Safety, CausalLinks, MaxCost,
                NewSymbols, NewSafety, NewCausals ) :-
  order_consistent( Safety ),
  plan_cost( CausalLinks, C ), C =< MaxCost,
  ( complete( SymbolTable, Safety, CausalLinks ),
    NewSymbols = SymbolTable,
    NewSafety = Safety,
    NewCausals = CausalLinks
  ; ( member( ( S, P, W ), CausalLinks ),
      step_threat( SymbolTable, V, S, P, W ),
      not( member( ( V, S ), Safety ) ),
      not( member( ( W, V ), Safety ) ),
      ( TmpSafety = [ ( V, S ) | Safety ]
```

```
      ; TmpSafety = [ ( W, V ) | Safety ] ),
    find_completion( SymbolTable, TmpSafety, CausalLinks, MaxCost,
                     NewSymbols, NewSafety, NewCausals ) )
  ; ( prec_unsatisfied( SymbolTable, CausalLinks, W, P ),
    ( step_adds( SymbolTable, S, P ),
      TmpSymbols = SymbolTable,
      member( ( S, O ), SymbolTable )
    ; adds( O, P ), O \ = = begin,
      make_step_op( SymbolTable, O, S, TmpSymbols ) ),
    ( member( ( S, W ), Safety ), TmpSafety = Safety
    ; TmpSafety = [ ( S, W ) | Safety ] ),
    find_completion( TmpSymbols, TmpSafety, [ ( S, P, W ) | CausalLinks ], MaxCost,
                     NewSymbols, NewSafety, NewCausals ) ) ).
```

```
%  _____
% step_threat / 5 succeeds exactly when V threatens the causal link ( S, P, W ).
% Arguments: SymbolTable (+), V (?), S (+), P (?), W (+)
%  _____


step_threat( SymbolTable, V, S, P, W ) :-
  ( step_adds( SymbolTable, V, P )
  ; step_dels( SymbolTable, V, P ) ),
  V \== S, V \== W.
```

```
%  _____
% step_adds / 3 succeeds exactly when P appears in the add-list of the action
% taken at step Name.
% Arguments: SymbolTable (+), Name (?), P (?)
%  _____


step_adds( SymbolTable, Name, P ) :-
  step_op( SymbolTable, Name, Op ), adds( Op, P ).
```

```
%  _____
% step_dels / 3 succeeds exactly when P appears in the delete-list of the action
% taken at step Name.
% Arguments: SymbolTable (+), Name (?), P (?)
%  _____
```

```
step_dels( SymbolTable, Name, P ) :-
  step_op( SymbolTable, Name, Op ),
  dels( Op, P ).
```

```
% _____
% step_op / 3 succeeds exactly when the action taken at step Name is Op.
% Arguments: SymbolTable (+), Name (?), Op (?)
% _____
```

```
step_op( SymbolTable, Name, Op ) :- member( ( Name, Op ), SymbolTable ).
```

```
% _____
% prec_unsatisfied / 4 succeeds when the action taken at step Name has a
% precondition Prec that is not justified for Name by any causal link.
% Arguments: SymbolTable (+), CausalLinks (+), Name (?), Prec (?)
% _____
```

```
prec_unsatisfied( SymbolTable, CausalLinks, Name, Prec ) :-
  member( ( Name, Op ), SymbolTable ),
  prec( Op, Prec ),
  not( member( ( _, Prec, Name ), CausalLinks ) ).
```

```
% _____
% make_step_op / 4 adds a new step that takes action Op to the symbol table.
% We use numbers to name all steps except start and finish, hence we label the
% new step with an integer one greater than the current maximum step name.
% Arguments: SymbolTable (+), Op (+), NewStepName (−), NewSymbolTable (−)
% _____
```

```
make_step_op( SymbolTable, Op, Step, [ ( Step, Op ) | SymbolTable ] ) :-
  max_step( SymbolTable, Max ),
  Step is Max+1.
```

```
% _____
% max_step / 2 computes the maximum step name in the SymbolTable, giving special
% consideration to the special steps start and finish.
% Arguments: SymbolTable (+), MaxName (−)
% _____
```

```
max_step( [ ], 0 ).
max_step( [ ( StepName, _ ) | Symbols ], Max ) :-
    max_step( Symbols, TailMax ),
    ( StepName = start, Max = TailMax
    ; StepName = finish, Max = TailMax
    ; TailMax > StepName, Max = TailMax
    ; Max = StepName ), !.
```

```
% _____
% order_consistent / 1 succeeds exactly when the Safety conditions contain no
% cycles, no step precedes start, and no step follows finish.
% Arguments: Safety (+)
% _____
```

```
order_consistent( Safety ) :-
    not( member( ( _, start ), Safety ) ),
    not( member( ( finish, _ ), Safety ) ),
    acyclic( Safety ).
```

```
% _____
% acyclic / 1 succeeds exactly when Arcs contains no cycles. We use
% depth-first search to determine whether or not there are any cycles.
% Arguments: Arcs (+)
% _____
```

```
acyclic( Arcs ) :- not( has_cycle( Arcs ) ), !.

has_cycle( Arcs ) :-
    member( ( X, X ), Arcs ).

has_cycle( Arcs ) :-
    member( ( X, Y ), Arcs ),
    ( member( ( Y, X ), Arcs )
    ; path( Y, X, Arcs, [ ] ) ).

path( A, A, _, _ ).
```

```
path( A, B, G, Used ) :-
    member( ( A, C ), G ),
    not( member( C, Used ) ),
    path( C, B, G, [ C | Used ] ).
```

```
% _____
% plan_cost / 2 returns the cost of CausalLinks in Cost. We have defined the
% cost of a partial plan to be the number of causal links, so only the causal
% links are required. Any change in the definition of partial plan cost may
% necessitate a change in the arguments to this predicate, as well as to its body.
% Arguments: CausalLinks (+), Cost (−)
% _____
```

```
plan_cost( [ ], 0 ).
plan_cost( [ _ | More ], Cost ) :-
    plan_cost( More, SubCost ),
    Cost is SubCost+1.
```

```
% _____
% complete / 3 succeeds precisely when the plan described by its arguments
% is complete.
% Arguments: SymbolTable (+), Safety (+), CausalLinks (+)
% _____
```

```
complete( SymbolTable, Safety, CausalLinks ) :-
        all_prereq_satisfied( SymbolTable, CausalLinks ),
        all_threats_defused( SymbolTable, Safety, CausalLinks ).
```

```
all_prereq_satisfied( [ ], _ ).
all_prereq_satisfied( [ ( Name, Op ) | SymbolTable ], CausalLinks ) :-
        % get the list of prerequisites for this operator:
        preclist( Op, OpPrec ),
        % make sure there is a causal link for every precondition:
        not(( member(Prec, OpPrec), not( member((_, Prec, Name), CausalLinks) ) ))
        all_prereq_satisfied( SymbolTable, CausalLinks ).
```

```
all_threats_defused( _, _, [ ] ).
all_threats_defused( SymbolTable, Safety, [ ( S, P, W ) | CausalLinks ] ) :-
```

```
findall( V, step_threat( SymbolTable, V, S, P, W ), Threats ),
these_threats_defused( Threats, S, W, Safety ),
all_threats_defused( SymbolTable, Safety, CausalLinks ).
```

```
these_threats_defused( [ ], _, _, _ ).
these_threats_defused( [ Threat | Threats ], S, W, Safety ) :-
    ( member( ( Threat, S ), Safety ) ; member( ( W, Threat ), Safety ) ),
    these_threats_defused( Threats, S, W, Safety ).
```

The following is a sample run in which we use the same database of
STRIPS rules as before, and we ask the planner to complete a plan to invert
a stack of two blocks. The partial plan we give the planner contains all but
one step, namely stacking block a on top of block b. The planner introduces
the required step and adds the necessary safety conditions and causal links
to complete the plan. Because of the gargantuan number of partial orders
on even so few steps, several days of computer time were unfortunately in-
sufficient to devise this plan from scratch (again, see Exercise 8.6 for turning
this cautious planner into a practical one).

```
| ?- find_completion([[(start,begin),(finish,end),(1,unstack(b,a)),
                 (2,putdown(b)),(3,pickup(a))],
              [(start,finish),(start,1),(start,2),(start,3),
               (1,2),(1,3),(2,3)],
              [(start,on(b,a),1),(start,handempty,1),
               (start,clear(b),1),(start,ontable(a),3),
               (1,holding(b),2),(1,clear(a),3),
               (2,handempty,3)],
              10, NSym, NS, NC ).
```

```
NSym = [(4,stack(a,b)),(start,begin),(finish,end),(1,unstack(b,a)),
        (2,putdown(b)),(3,pickup(a))],
NS = [(2,4),(3,4),(1,4),(4,finish),(start,finish),(start,1),(start,2),(start,3),
      (1,2),(1,3),(2,3)],
NC = [(3,holding(a),4),(2,clear(b),4),(4,on(a,b),finish),(start,on(b,a),1),
      (start,handempty,1),(start,clear(b),1),(start,ontable(a),3),
      (1,holding(b),2),(1,clear(a),3),(2,handempty,3)]
```

```
| ?-
```

8.4   Time map management

So far in this chapter we have discussed one type of task involving the passage of time, namely planning, and this task motivated the representation employed, namely STRIPS rules. However, planning is by no means the only task involving time; it is no less important in AI to be able to *predict* the outcome of given processes or to *explain* observed occurrences. In this section we discuss a general tool to aid in temporal reasoning, one that is not specific to one type of reasoning.

We have already explored one such general technique – the interval constraint satisfaction procedure in Chapter 6. That technique supported reasoning about the relationship between the endpoints of time intervals, but it did not support reasoning about what was true and false in those intervals. The technique discussed here does just that; it amounts to a temporal database management scheme, or a method for maintaining information about time. This technique has been used in modern-day planners, but it is also useful for other tasks that involve temporal reasoning. The technique we describe is based on the concept of *time map management* and is closely related the notion called the *event calculus*.

Suppose we want to maintain information about all points in time: Who was the US president in 1994, is the robot operational throughout a certain interval, and so on. Clearly we cannot maintain a separate database for each time point. Instead, a common approach is to store, for each fact, the time points at which its truth value changes. Thus we might say that the robot became operational at time point t_1, that it was brought in for service at some later time t_2, and from this information infer *by default* that it was operational at all times between t_1 and t_2. This idea is the basis for time maps. Figure 8.2 illustrates this idea graphically; solid lines represent time intervals, dotted lines represent temporal coincidence, and the dashed arrows represent temporal precedence.

To make the notion of time map management more precise, we start by assuming a certain language for making assertions. The precise language is not important; what is important is that we have an easily computable criterion for determining when two assertions in the language are *inconsistent,* or *contradictory*. Assertions in this language are called *facts;* from now on we take facts to be ground Prolog terms. Examples of facts are president(usa, bill_clinton) and operational(robot17). We also assume a predicate

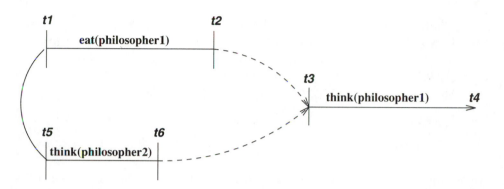

Figure 8.2: A simple time map: solid lines represent time intervals, dotted lines coincidence in time, and dashed arrows temporal precedence (after T. Dean)

contradicts / 2 that determines which pairs of facts are contradictory. For example, we may decide that contradicts(president(usa, X), president(usa, Y)) holds for any two distinct ground terms X and Y. Similarly, we may decide that contradicts(X, neg(X)) and contradicts(neg(X), X) hold for any ground term X; intuitively, neg represents negation. (Here we restrict contradiction to hold only between pairs of facts, but in a more expressive setting we may declare larger collections of facts contradictory; see Exercise 8.7.) To capture the symmetry of contradiction, we will use the following predicate:

contradiction(Fact1, Fact2) :- contradicts(Fact1, Fact2) ; contradicts(Fact2, Fact1).

The statements about contradiction capture general domain knowledge; the time map itself represents specific temporal information. It consists of two components:

- A collection of *(potential) fact tokens.* Each potential fact token will be of the form potential_fact_token(t1, t2, fact). Intuitively, this potential fact token represents the assertion that fact is guaranteed to hold at t1, and to continue to persist through t2, or until the first time point at which a contradictory fact holds; in the latter case we say that the fact token was *clipped* before its natural termination. fact may also hold up to t1 and past t2, but this is not guaranteed by this fact token. The time points will be any atoms. As a special case, however, we will use the time point infinity to represent unbounded persistence. (The only place where this symbol is accorded special status in the programs below is in predicates to compute temporal relations between time points.)

- A collection of *binary temporal constraints*: Each constraint constrains the relationship between two time points, and is in one of two forms:

  precedes(t1, t2): t1 is strictly earlier than t2.

  coincident(t1, t2): the two time points coincide.

We assume that the constraints are consistent (for example, that the precedes statements do not form cycles; see Exercise 8.8). In more complex time maps, in addition to these ordinal constraints one can specify metric ones; see Exercise 8.9 for such an extension. For a given potential_fact_token(t1, t2, fact) we will not require the assertion that t1 precedes t2; that will be assumed. We will use the following predicate to capture the symmetry of coincidence:

coincident_point(T1, T2) :- coincident(T1, T2) ; coincident(T2, T1).

8.4.1   The basic time map manager

The job of the basic time map manager is to support ground queries of the form

$$tm\_holds(t1, t2, fact)$$

whose intuitive meaning is that, despite the merely partial ordering on the time points, the time map guarantees that fact holds over the interval (t1, t2). It does so via the following program:

```
% _____
% tm_holds / 3 succeeds exactly when the database guarantees that Fact holds over
% time interval ( T1, T2 ).
% Arguments: T1 (+), T2 (+), Fact (+)
% _____
```

```
tm_holds( T1, T2, Fact ) :-
    potential_fact_token( T3, T4, Fact ),
    is_before_or_coincident( T3, T1 ),
    is_before_or_coincident( T2, T4 ),
    not( ( contradiction( Fact, Fact1 ),
        potential_fact_token( T5, _, Fact1 ),
        not( ( is_before( T5, T3 )
            ; is_before_or_coincident( T2, T5 ) ) ) ) ).
```

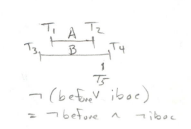

In other words, a fact is guaranteed to hold over an interval A exactly when there is an enclosing interval B throughout which it potentially holds, and this default persistence is not clipped before the end of interval A: any other contradictory fact in the database is guaranteed to have started either before the beginning of interval B or not before the end of interval A.

The roles of is_before_or_coincident / 2 and is_before / 2, whose arguments are time points, are obvious from the names. is_before_or_coincident is implemented simply by performing a search from the first time point to the second, using the precedence relations implied by potential fact tokens as well as coincident / 2 and precedes / 2 assertions as arcs. is_before / 2 is implemented in terms of is_before_or_coincident / 2 in the obvious way. The following implementation of is_before_or_coincident / 2 uses depth-first search; it is a direct adaptation of the depth_first_search / 3 program of Chapter 2.

```
% _____
% is_before / 2 succeeds exactly when the constraints in the database
% guarantee that T1 is before T2.
% Arguments: T1 (+), T2 (+)
% _____

is_before( Time, infinity ) :- Time \== infinity.
is_before( T1, T2 ) :-
    ( precedes( T3, T4 ) ; potential_fact_token( T3, T4, _ ) ),
    is_before_or_coincident( T1, T3 ),
    is_before_or_coincident( T4, T2 ).
```

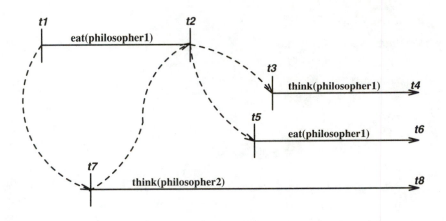

Figure 8.3: A time map

```
% _____
% is_before_or_coincident / 2 succeeds exactly when the constraints in the
% database guarantee that T1 is no later than T2.
% Arguments: T1 (+), T2 (+)
% _____
```

```
is_before_or_coincident( _, infinity ) :- !.
is_before_or_coincident( T1, T2 ) :- iboc( [ T1 ], [ ], T2 ).


iboc( [ T | _ ], _, T ) :- !.
iboc( [ T1 | OpenT ], ClosedT, T2 ) :-
  findall( NextT,
          ( ( potential_fact_token( T1, NextT, _ )
             ; precedes(T1, NextT)
             ; coincident_point( NextT, T1 ) ),
           not( member( NextT, [ T1 | OpenT ] ) ),
           not( member( NextT, ClosedT ) ) ),
          TmpT),
  append( TmpT, OpenT, NewOpenT ),
  iboc( NewOpenT, [ T1 | ClosedT ], T2 ).
```

We illustrate the operation of the basic time map manager through the following example. Consider the time map in Figure 8.3; it is implemented by the following database:

```
contradicts( eat( X ), think( X ) ).
potential_fact_token( t1, t2, eat( philosopher1 ) ).
potential_fact_token( t3, t4, think( philosopher1 ) ).
potential_fact_token( t5, t6, eat( philosopher1 ) ).
potential_fact_token( t7, t8, think( philosopher2 ) ).

precedes( t2, t3 ).
precedes( t2, t5 ).
precedes( t1, t7 ).
precedes( t7, t2 ).
```

The following query will succeed on this map:

tm_holds(t1, t7, eat(philosopher1)).

while the following will fail:

tm_holds(t5, t6, eat(philosopher1)).

8.4.2   Abductive queries

The basic time map manager discussed in Section 8.4.1 is conservative; it succeeds only if the property necessarily holds for the interval, given the constraints (but assuming that no tokens are added). The query is therefore a *deductive* one. In this section we consider a complementary *abductive* query; its format is

abductively_tm_holds(t1, t2, fact, NewConstraints)

where t1, t2, and fact are as before (in particular, they are ground); when this query succeeds, it returns in NewConstraints additional temporal constraints that, along with the constraints already in the time map, guarantee that the fact holds over the interval. Consider, for example, the time map, discussed above, of Figure 8.3. As we have seen, the deductive query

| ?- tm_holds(t5, t6, eat(philosopher1)).

fails. In contrast, we have the following abductive execution:

| ?- abductively_tm_holds(t5, t6, eat(philosopher1), C).
C = [coincident(t6,t3)] ;
C = [precedes(t6,t3)] ;
C = [coincident(t4,t5)] ;
C = [precedes(t4,t5)] ;
no
| ?-

Note that as a special case of abductive queries, a query about (t1, t2) may be posed in which t1 and t2 don't appear at all in the current time map! A successful query, however, will return constraints on these new points, relating them to existing points in the time map. abductively_tm_holds / 4 is defined as follows.

```
% _____
% abductively_tm_holds / 4 determines a list of constraints needed to
% guarantee that a given fact holds over the interval (Start, End), under the
% assumption that precedes( Start, End ) is consistent with the database.
% Arguments: Start (+), End (+), Fact (+), Constraints (−)
% _____


abductively_tm_holds( Start, End, Fact, Constraints ) :-
    setof( ( T3, T4 ),
           potential_fact_token( T3, T4, Fact ),
           FactIntervals ),
    setof0( ( T3, T4 ),
            ( contradiction( Fact, Cont ),
              potential_fact_token( T3, T4, Cont ) ),
            Forbidden ), !,
    find_constraints( Start, End, FactIntervals, Forbidden, Constraints ).
```

```
%
% find_constraints / 5 determines a list of constraints ensuring that
% the interval (Start, End) is supported by some interval in the list FactIntervals
% and is allowed by every interval in the list ForbiddenIntervals.
% Arguments: Start (+), End (+), FactIntervals (+), ForbiddenIntervals (+),
%            Constraints (–)
%
find_constraints( Start, End, FactIntervals, ForbiddenIntervals, Constraints ) :-
  member( ( SupStart, SupEnd ), FactIntervals ),
  subrange( Start, End, SupStart, SupEnd, [ precedes( Start, End ) ], Supports ),
  counter_constraints( Start, End, SupStart, ForbiddenIntervals,
                       Supports, Support_and_Allow ),
  % Do not return the constraint implicit in the input.
  setof0( Constraint,
          ( member( Constraint, Support_and_Allow ),
            Constraint \== precedes( Start, End ) ),
          Constraints ).
%
% subrange / 6 returns a list of new constraints that, taken with those
% in the database and in a given list, guarantee the interval (Start, End) is
% contained in the support interval (SupStart, SupEnd).
% Arguments: Start (+), End (+), SupStart (+), SupEnd (+), Givens (+),
%            NewConstraints (–)
%
subrange( Start, End, SupStart, SupEnd, Givens, NewConstraints ) :-
  clip( SupStart, Start, Givens, Con1 ),
  append( Givens, Con1, Con2 ),
  clip( End, SupEnd, Con2, Con3 ),
  append( Con2, Con3, NewConstraints ).


%
% counter_constraints / 6 returns a list of constraints that, taken with
% those in the database and those given, guarantee that the support starting
% at SupStart for the interval (Start, End) is not clipped by the contradictory
% intervals in the list ForbiddenIntervals.
% Arguments: Start (+), End (+), SupStart (+), ForbiddenIntervals (+),
%            Givens (+), Constraints (–)
%
```

counter_constraints(_, _, _, [ ], Constraints, Constraints).
counter_constraints(Start, End, SupStart, [(T1, T2) | More], Givens, Constraints) :-
   % *Make sure interval* (T1, T2) *stays out of the way. To do this,*
   % *we not only need to make sure that* (T1, T2) *either starts after*
   % (Start, End) *or ends before it, but in the latter case, we must*
   % *make sure that we retain support for* (Start, End), *i.e., that*
   % (T1, T2) *doesn't clip the supporting interval.*
   (clip(End, T1, Givens, NConstraints)
   ; clip(T2, Start, Givens, NoContConstraints),
    append(Givens, NoContConstraints, TmpGivens),
    strict_clip(T1, SupStart, TmpGivens, NoClipConstraints),
    append(TmpGivens, NoClipConstraints, NConstraints)),
   append(Givens, NConstraints, NewGivens),
   counter_constraints(Start, End, SupStart, More, NewGivens, Constraints).

% _____
% clip / 4 *returns* Constraint, *a list of zero or one constraints that, with those in*
% *the database and the list* Givens, *ensures that* T1 *is not after* T2. *Of course*
% *if the database and given constraints imply that* T2 *precedes* T1, clip / 4 *fails.*
% *Arguments:* T1 (+), T2 (+), Givens (+), Constraint (–)
% _____

clip(T1, T2, Givens, Constraint) :-
  relation(T1, T2, Givens, Relation),
  (Relation = before, Constraint = [ ]
  ; Relation = coincident, Constraint = [ ]
  ; Relation = unknown,
   (Constraint = [coincident(T1, T2)]
   ; Constraint = [precedes(T1, T2)])).

% _____
% strict_clip / 4 *returns* Constraint, *a list of zero or one constraints that, taken with*
% *those in the database and the list* Givens, *ensures that* T1 *precedes* T2. *Of*
% *course if the database and given constraints imply otherwise,* strict_clip / 4 *fails.*
% *Arguments:* T1 (+), T2 (+), Givens (+), Constraint (–)
% _____

```
strict_clip( T1, T2, Givens, Constraint ) :-
  relation( T1, T2, Givens, Relation ),
  ( Relation = before, Constraint = [ ]
  ; Relation = unknown, Constraint = [ precedes( T1, T2 ) ] ).
```

```
% _____
% relation / 4 returns Relation, a description of the relationship between T1 and T2
% as implied by the database constraints and the constraint list Givens.
% Arguments: T1 (+), T2 (+), Givens (+), Relation (−)
% _____
```

```
relation( T1, T2, Givens, before ) :- ab_is_before( T1, T2, Givens ), !.
relation( T1, T2, Givens, after ) :- ab_is_before( T2, T1, Givens ), !.
relation( T1, T2, Givens, coincident) :- ab_is_coincident( T1, T2, Givens ), !.
relation( _, _, _, unknown).
```

```
% _____
% ab_is_coincident / 3 succeeds exactly when the database constraints along with
% those in the constraint list Givens imply that T1 and T2 are coincident.
% Arguments: T1 (+), T2 (+), Givens (+)
% _____
```

```
ab_is_coincident( infinity, _, _ ) :- !, fail.
ab_is_coincident( _, infinity, _ ) :- !, fail.
ab_is_coincident( T1, T2, Givens ) :- ic( [ T1 ], [ ], T2, Givens ).
```

```
% _____
% ic / 4 implements depth-first search on the symmetric closure of the set of
% database and given "coincident" arcs. The search proceeds from the nodes in
% OpenT to the node Dest, avoiding nodes appearing in ClosedT. ic / 4 succeeds
% exactly when Dest is reached in such a search. Givens is the list of
% constraints to consider in addition to database constraints.
% Arguments: OpenT (+), ClosedT (+), Dest (+), Givens (+)
% _____
```

```
ic( [ T | _ ], _, T, _ ) :- !.
```

```
ic( [ T1 | OpenT ], ClosedT, T2, Givens ) :-
                setof0( NextT,
                        ( ( coincident_point( T1, NextT )
                          ; member( coincident( T1, NextT ), Givens )
                          ; member( coincident( NextT, T1 ), Givens ) ),
                          not( member( NextT, [ T1 | OpenT ] ) ),
                          not( member( NextT, ClosedT ) ) ),
                        TmpT ),
                append( TmpT, OpenT, NewOpenT ),
                ic( NewOpenT, [ T1 | ClosedT ], T2, Givens ).
```

```
% _____
% ib / 5 embodies a modified depth-first search from the set of nodes in OpenT to
% the node Dest. Arcs in the search are those implying coincidence and strict
% precedence; the search deviates from simple depth-first in that when
% UsedStrict is false, we insist that Dest be reached along a path containing at
% least one arc implying strict precedence. Our assumption of consistency of the
% database with the constraints in Givens guarantees that if there is a path from
% one node to another using at least one strict precedence arc, all paths between
% the same two nodes use at least one such arc. No point in time can be both
% coincident with another point and before it. ClosedT is a list of nodes that
% may not be visited during the search.
% Arguments: OpenT (+), ClosedT (+), Dest (+), Givens (+), UsedStrict (+)
% _____
```

```
ib( [ T | _ ], _, T, _, true ) :- !.
ib( [ T1 | OpenT ], ClosedT, T2, Givens, UsedStrict ) :-
  findall( ( NextT, US ),
          ( ( potential_fact_token( T1, NextT, _ ), US = true
            ; precedes( T1, NextT ), US = true
            ; member( precedes( T1, NextT ), Givens ), US = true
            ; coincident_point( T1, NextT ), US = false
            ; member( coincident( T1, NextT ), Givens ), US = false
            ; member( coincident( NextT, T1 ), Givens ), US = false ),
            not( member( NextT, [ T1 | OpenT ] ) ),
            not( member( NextT, ClosedT ) ) ),
          Pairs ),
  ( member( ( _, true ), Pairs ), US = true; US = false ),
```

```
setof0( NextT, member( ( NextT, _ ), Pairs ), TmpT ),
append( TmpT, OpenT, NewOpenT ),
( UsedStrict , NewUS = true; NewUS = US ), !,
ib( NewOpenT, [ T1 | ClosedT ], T2, Givens, NewUS ).
```

```
%  _____
% ab_is_before / 3 succeeds exactly when the database constraints along with those
% in the constraint list Givens imply that T1 is before T2.
% Arguments: T1 (+), T2 (+), Givens (+)
%  _____
ab_is_before( infinity, _, _ ) :- !, fail.
ab_is_before( _, infinity, _ ) :- !.
ab_is_before( T1, T2, Givens ) :- ib( [ T1 ], [ ], T2, Givens, false ).
```

8.4.3   Causal time maps

In the time maps discussed so far, all fact tokens were simply given by the user in advance. Unlike temporal constraints, no new fact tokens were generated through reasoning. We conclude the discussion of time map management with a more elaborate form of time maps, one in which new tokens in addition to the given ones are implied.

The version of time maps describes in this section integrates elements of action with elements of time. We are already familiar with the notion of a fact holding; in this version, we add the notion of an *event* occurring. We will represent events, too, by ground Prolog terms. Time maps will contain event tokens in addition to fact tokens; in this version of time maps, events are instantaneous and are represented in the form event_token(t, event).

Event tokens are explicitly specified by the user and do not change through reasoning. Even so, these event tokens give rise to new fact tokens through *causal rules,* whose spirit is close to that of STRIPS rules encountered earlier. A causal rule has the form

causes(preconditions, trigger_event, resulting_fact)

The intuitive meaning of this rule is that if *preconditions* hold at a certain time point, and at that time *trigger_event* occurs, then following the event the *resulting_fact* holds and will persist subject to the usual persistence rules. An example of a causal rule might be causes([have_soap], mop_floor, clean_floor)

Notice the similarity to STRIPS rules, discussed earlier in this chapter. The main difference between STRIPS rules and causal rules is that in the latter there is no 'delete-list'; potential fact tokens are automatically clipped when contradictory facts come into being, and there is no need to 'delete' them explicitly.

Causal time maps thus consist of four components:

- a collection of (explicitly given) potential fact tokens

- a collection of event tokens

- a total ordering on time points, in the form time_list([t1, t2, t3, . . .])

- a collection of causal rules

The basic functionality we will expect from the time map is to support the same tm_holds / 3 predicate as in Section 8.4.1. The complication arises because some facts are only implicit in the existing fact and event tokens. In this section we will therefore aim to make these implicit facts explicit, that is, to discover them and add them to the database as potential fact tokens; once we have achieved this, we will be able to use tm_holds / 3 with no change other than considerable simplification of the predicate is_before_or_coincident to take advantage of the total ordering on time points.

In pursuit of this goal, we will support four operations: adding or deleting an event token, and adding or deleting a fact token. As a result of each such addition or deletion, other fact tokens may be automatically added or deleted. It turns out that allowing partially ordered events and facts results in very complicated and, in general, inefficient algorithms. We will therefore limit the discussion here to causal time maps in which all time points are totally ordered. The implicit origins of deduced facts that we add to the database will have to be noted somehow so we can retract such a fact when an event that causes it is deleted. To achieve this, we will increase the arity of our fact representation by one, so that a potential fact token is now of the form

potential_fact_token(t1, t2, fact, ImpliedOrGiven)

where ImpliedOrGiven takes on one of the two values {implied, given}. The following predicate will allow us to use tm_holds unchanged:

potential_fact_token(T1, T2, Fact) :- potential_fact_token(T1, T2, Fact, _).

Given a total ordering on time, the set of potential fact tokens can be computed simulation style. First, the database is modified as specified: a fact or an event token is added or deleted. Then, the ramifications of that change are computed. Since the past cannot be affected by the change, nor can future event tokens be affected, we need only determine the fact tokens starting later than the point of modification. We achieve this by simulating the event tokens in order of occurrence. In the following procedure, let t be the time of the event token being added or deleted, or the start time of the fact token being added or deleted.

PROCEDURE SIMULATE-EVENTS (t: a time point)
$EventQ \leftarrow$ all event tokens whose time is $> t$
while $EventQ$ is not empty do
    $e \leftarrow$ earliest event token in $EventQ$
    remove e from $EventQ$
    (e must have the form event_token(t,e))
    for all causal rules causes($Prec$, e, $fact$) do
        if all facts in $Prec$ hold at time t,
           then add to the database a fact token potential_fact_token(t, infinity, $fact$).

Note that the inner loop can determine whether or not the preconditions hold, since further processing can only affect the future.

The following Prolog program implements deletion and addition of facts and events from and to the time map database:

```
% _____
% del_token / 1 removes Token from the database and updates the
% list of implied potential fact tokens appropriately.
% Arguments: Token (+)
% _____
del_token( Token ) :-
    ( Token = event_token( Change_Time, _ ), retract( Token )
    ; Token = potential_fact_token( Change_Time, End_Time, Fact ),
      retract( potential_fact_token( Change_Time, End_Time, Fact, given ) ) ),
    get_time_order( Change_Time, Later_Times ),
    retract_implied_facts( Later_Times ),
    simulate_events( Later_Times ),
    show_time_map.
```

```
% _____
% add_token / 2 adds Token, a potential fact token or event token, to the
% database and ensures that the resulting implied fact tokens are made explicit.
% NextTime is a list of time points used to locate the time(s) mentioned in
% Token in the database time order. If all the times mentioned in Token are
% present in the database, NextTime is ignored (the value of empty list
% is supplied by convention). Otherwise, NextTime's first element is taken to
% be the time point that should immediately follow the first new time
% ("new" means not already present in the database) mentioned in Token, and
% NextTime's second element (if any) is taken correspondingly for the second
% new time mentioned in Token (if any).
% Arguments: Token (+), NextTime (+)
% _____


add_token( Token, NextTime ) :-
    time_list( Time ),
    ( Token = event_token( ChangeTime, _ ),
      assert( Token ),
      LocTime = NextTime
    ; Token = potential_fact_token( ChangeTime, EndTime, Fact ),
      assert( potential_fact_token( ChangeTime, EndTime, Fact, given ) ),
      ( member( EndTime, Time ), LocTime = NextTime
      ; ( NextTime = [ ], End_NextTime = [ ], LocTime = [ EndTime ]
        ; NextTime = [ Loc | End_NextTime ], LocTime = [ Loc ] ),
        insert_in_time_list( EndTime, End_NextTime ) ) ),
    ( member( ChangeTime, Time )
    ; insert_in_time_list( ChangeTime, LocTime ) ),
    get_time_order( ChangeTime, LaterTimes ),
    retract_implied_facts( LaterTimes ),
    simulate_events( LaterTimes ),
    show_time_map.
    % show_time_map / 0 is assumed to print the time map and implied facts in some
    % convenient form.
```

```
% _____
% potential_fact_token / 3 is a predicate designed to replace the
% ground terms used previously in tm_holds.
% Arguments: T1 (?), T2 (?), Fact (?)
% _____


potential_fact_token( T1, T2, Fact ) :-
    potential_fact_token( T1, T2, Fact, _ ).


% _____
% insert_in_time_list / 2 puts NewTime in the time list before Where.
% If Where is empty, NewTime is inserted at the end.
% Arguments: NewTime (+), Where (+)
% _____


insert_in_time_list( NewTime, Where ) :-
  retract( time_list( Times ) ),
  list_insert( NewTime, Where, Times, NewTimes ),
  assert( time_list( NewTimes ) ).


% _____
% list_insert / 4 scans the given list searching for Where, and inserts T into the
% list just before Where. If Where is the empty list, we insert T at the end
% of the given list.
% Arguments: T (+), Where (+), GivenList (+), NewList (−)
% _____


list_insert( T, [ ], Times, NewTimes ) :-
  append( Times, [ T ], NewTimes ).
list_insert( T, [ Where ], [ Where | Times ], [ T, Where | Times ] ).
list_insert( T, [ Where ], [ Past | Times ], [ Past | NewTimes ] ) :-
  list_insert( T, [ Where ], Times, NewTimes ).
```

```
% _____
% get_time_order gets the list of times including and after Now
% and returns it in Hence.
% Arguments: Now (+), Hence (−)
% _____
get_time_order( Now, Hence ) :-
   time_list( Times ),
   gto( Now, Times, Hence ).
gto( Now, [ Now | Hence ], [ Now | Hence ] ).
gto( Now, [ _ | Thence ], Hence ) :-
   gto( Now, Thence, Hence ).


% _____
% retract_implied_facts / 1 retracts all implied potential fact tokens
% beginning at times in TimeList.
% Arguments: TimeList (+)
% _____

retract_implied_facts( [ ] ).
retract_implied_facts( [ T | Rest ] ) :-
   ( retractall( potential_fact_token( T, _, _, implied ) ) ; true ),
   retract_implied_facts( Rest ).


% _____
% all_hold succeeds when all the facts in FactList necessarily hold at time T.
% Arguments: T (+), FactList (+)
% _____

all_hold( _, [ ] ) :- !.
all_hold( Time, [ Fact | Rest ] ) :-
   tm_holds( Time, Time, Fact ),
   all_hold( Time, Rest ), !.
```

```
% _____
% is_before / 2 serves the same purpose as before, but is simplified here to take
% advantage of the total order on time points.
% Arguments: T1 (+), T2 (+)
% _____
```

```
is_before( Time, infinity ) :- Time = infinity, !.
is_before( T1, T2 ) :- get_time_order( T1, [ T1 | Time ] ), member( T2, Time ).
```

```
% _____
% is_before_or_coincident / 2 serves the same purpose as before, but is simplified here
% to take advantage of the total order on time points.
% Arguments: T1 (+), T2 (+)
% _____
```

```
is_before_or_coincident( _, infinity ) :- !.
is_before_or_coincident( T1, T2 ) :- get_time_order( T1, Time ), member( T2, Time ).
```

```
% _____
% simulate_events / 1 is the main simulation routine outlined in the text.
% Events occurring simultaneously are assumed to be independent.
% Arguments: TimeList (+)
% _____
```

```
simulate_events( [ ] ).
simulate_events( [ Time | Times ] ) :-
  findall( ( Time, Fact ),
         ( event_token( Time, Event ),
           causes( Prec, Event, Fact ),
           all_hold( Time, Prec ) ),
         ImpliedFacts ),
       assert_facts( ImpliedFacts ),
       simulate_events( Times ).
```

```
%
% assert_facts / 1 asserts the facts collected in the list ImpliedFacts.
% Arguments: ImpliedFacts (+)
%
assert_facts( [ ] ).
assert_facts( [ ( Time, Fact ) | Facts ] ) :-
    assert( potential_fact_token( Time, infinity, Fact, implied ) ),
    assert_facts( Facts ).
```

We use the following causal rules to demonstrate the use of events:

```
causes( [ think(X) ], see_Plato(X), eat(X) ).
causes( [ eat(X) ], see_Socrates(X), think(X) ).
```

Beginning with an empty time list and no fact or event tokens in the time map, we have the following sample execution:

```
| ?- show_time_map.
time_list([ ]).
yes
| ?- add_token(potential_fact_token(t1,t2,eat(philosopher1)),[ ]).
time_list([t1,t2]).
potential_fact_token(t1,t2,eat(philosopher1),given).
yes
| ?- add_token(potential_fact_token(t3,t4,think(philosopher1)),[ ]).
time_list([t1,t2,t3,t4]).
potential_fact_token(t1,t2,eat(philosopher1),given).
potential_fact_token(t3,t4,think(philosopher1),given).
yes
| ?- add_token(event_token(t5,see_Plato(philosopher1)),[t4]).
time_list([t1,t2,t3,t5,t4]).
potential_fact_token(t1,t2,eat(philosopher1),given).
potential_fact_token(t3,t4,think(philosopher1),given).
potential_fact_token(t5,infinity,eat(philosopher1),implied).
event_token(t5,see_Plato(philosopher1)).
yes
| ?- tm_holds(t5,infinity,eat(philosopher1)).
yes
| ?- add_token(event_token(t6,see_Socrates(philosopher1)),[t2]).
```

```
time_list([t1,t6,t2,t3,t5,t4]).
potential_fact_token(t1,t2,eat(philosopher1),given).
potential_fact_token(t3,t4,think(philosopher1),given).
potential_fact_token(t6,infinity,think(philosopher1),implied).
potential_fact_token(t5,infinity,eat(philosopher1),implied).
event_token(t5,see_Plato(philosopher1)).
event_token(t6,see_Socrates(philosopher1)).
yes
| ?- tm_holds(t3,t5,think(philosopher1)).
yes
| ?- tm_holds(t6,t5,think(philosopher1)).
yes
| ?- tm_holds(t6,infinity,think(philosopher1)).
no
| ?- tm_holds(t5,infinity,eat(philosopher1)).
yes
| ?-
```

8.5 Further reading

For an initial introduction to representation of time and action in AI, see Shoham and Goyal [76]. For an initial review of automated planning, see Georgeff [27]. The collection edited by Allen et al. [3] contains many of the important papers on planning and temporal reasoning.

Moving on to more specific work, The GPS planner was described in Newell and Simon [57], and the STRIPS planner in Fikes and Nilsson [21]. RSTRIPS was presented in Nilsson [60] as a rational reconstruction of previous planners based on goal regression. The earliest nonlinear planner in the literature was Sacerdoti's NOAH [70], followed by Tate's NONLIN [79]. Chapman's TWEAK planner [5] was a rational reconstruction of the ideas on nonlinear planning, and the first to prove completeness of a nonlinear planner. The systematic nonlinear planner presented in this chapter is due to McAllester and Rosenblitt [46]. Minton, Drummond, and colleagues have investigated the extent to which nonlinearity actually speeds up planning [51]. Finally, the notion of 'time maps' is due to Dean [10, 12] and Dean and McDermott [11]. For a related notion, see Kowalski and Sergot's 'event calculus' [39].

8.6   Exercises

Exercise 8.1 Show a solvable planning problem that defeats RSTRIPS.

Exercise 8.2 The implementations of both linear planners presented in the chapter embodied simplistic depth-first search.

(a) Modify the implementation of STRIPS so as to incorporate heuristic search instead. Can you think of good heuristic functions?

(b) Do the same for RSTRIPS.

Exercise 8.3 Research in planning has tried to capitalize on various notions of *abstraction*. Abstractions come in different flavors, one of which consists of associating with each condition in the language (such as handempty and on(a,b) a *criticality level;* intuitively, the lower the level, the easier it is to achieve this condition. When such levels are defined, planning proceeds in stages. At first the planner considers only the conditions with the highest criticality levels, and develops a plan to achieve those. Then the planner considers the next most critical conditions, and adds steps to the plan (so-called *patches*) to achieve those. The process continues until all conditions have been considered.

(a) Implement criticality levels in STRIPS (when you do so, you will have implemented a version of ABSTRIPS [69]).

(b) Implement criticality levels in RSTRIPS.

Exercise 8.4 It is often the case that certain conditions can be assumed to hold, in the absence of information to the contrary. A block-moving robot, for example, may assume that blocks are by and large clean. As a consequence, if an action such as grasp requires the block to be clean as a precondition, the robot may assume this condition to be satisfied by default and need not plan to establish it. This default may be overridden, however, by a previous action (such as grease-joint). When such a violation occurs, the robot can no longer assume the condition and must patch the plan accordingly.

(a) Implement defeasible assumptions in STRIPS.

(b) Do the same, but assuming that in addition to STRIPS rules you may have domain constraints. The domain constraints are of the form "if *list-of-conditions* then *condition*." Note that the conditions in the if-part may themselves include defeasible assumptions. *Hint:* You may find it useful to use a truth maintenance system.

Exercise 8.5 Prove that the nonlinear planner presented, non_lin_plan, is systematic, that is, it eventually generates all plans, and does not generate any plan fragment more than once.

Exercise 8.6 While nice and tidy, non_lin_plan is a highly impractical planner, since it searches the set partial plans in a blatantly blind fashion (albeit systematically; see previous question). For example, it exhausts all possible orders within a given plan before introducing a new causal link. Implement a heuristic version of the planner that allows for more intelligent search of the space. Test your planner with a number of heuristics that seem plausible to you.

Exercise 8.7 The TMM implemented in this chapter allows the representation of contradictions between pairs of facts, as represented by the predicate contradiction / 2. Extend the implementation to allow for arbitrary collections to be designated as contradictory. Use the predicate contradiction / 1, whose argument will be the list of contradictory items; the interpretation will be that the set as a whole is inconsistent, but strict subsets of it (and pairs in particular) are not necessarily so. Modify the TMM accordingly; what is the new persistence-clipping rule?

Exercise 8.8 In the implementation of the TMM, it was assumed that the input precedes / 2 and coincident / 2 statements are consistent. Implement a routine to verify this consistency.

Exercise 8.9 As implemented, the time maps contain only ordinal relationship between time points. Augment the representation so as to allow for the representation of 'real time' (in the format Year/Month/Day/Hour/Month, say), and modify the TMM accordingly.

Exercise 8.10 The tm_holds / 3 predicate was implemented inefficiently in the chapter. What is the source of inefficiency? Improve the implementation accordingly.

Exercise 8.11 The predicate simulate_events / 1 as given is not very efficient; it considers all the time points in the database, and for each time T, checks for events occurring at T. Rewrite it so that it is more efficient in the case when there are many time points but few events. In particular, the runtime used by simulate_events should be linear in the number of event tokens in the database, and sublinear in the number of time points. *Hint:* To achieve sublinearity in the number of time points, you will have to change add_token and modify the representation of the time map slightly.

Chapter 9

Machine Learning

It is widely recognized in AI that, no matter how smart and knowledgeable the machine is made, the machine must on its own become smarter and more knowledgeable over time. The designer of the machine, it is argued, will not be able either to anticipate all the circumstances in which the machine might operate or to explicitly list all those that *are* in principle foreseeable. This is true for any nontrivial domain: A mobile robot that attempts several times during the week to open a door and fails should be able to induce, at least tentatively, that the door is routinely kept locked, and to modify its plans accordingly; a game-playing program should be able to improve its performance on the basis of past game sessions; an object-recognition program should be able to improve its reliability on the basis of its past correct and incorrect classifications; and so on.

Various forms of machine learning exist, as indicated by the multitude of terms such as *inductive inference, concept formation, explanation-based learning, case-based learning, learning by exploration, PAC learning, reinforcement learning, connectionist learning,* and *genetic algorithms.* Indeed, machine learning is a multifaceted and very active area, and we will not exhaust it. Instead, we will discuss some of the issues involved in implementing two main learning techniques: inductive inference, both in general and in the special case of decision trees, and explanation-based learning.

9.1   Inductive inference

Consider a person who knows that the integers are 1, 2, 3, ... and knows the meaning of arithmetic operations, but does not yet know that prime numbers are those integers that are not divisible by any smaller integer greater than 1. In order to understand the concept of 'prime number' the person must be able to characterize the set of prime numbers, using the rules of arithmetic with which he is familiar.

Suppose the concept is revealed to the person gradually through an ever-increasing list of examples and counterexamples of prime numbers. Initially the information might be: "2 is prime, 3 is prime, 11 is prime, 6 is not, 114 is not, 123 is not, 31 is." Strictly speaking, at this point the person is not in a position to decide whether integers other than those presented are prime; for example, he has no information about whether 4 is prime.

In practice, however, one jumps to conclusions. For example, since no even integers other than 2 were presented as prime, the person may induce that no even integers other than 2 are prime; this is an example of a correct generalization. Since two presented primes ended with a 1 and no nonprimes did, the person may induce that *all* integers ending with 1 are prime; this is an example of overgeneralization. The person may similarly induce on the basis of the list presented so far that no primes are greater than 100; this is an example of undergeneralization.

Both over- and undergeneralization are corrected on the basis of further data. In our example, if the list continues "21 is not prime, 109 is" then both wrong generalizations will have to be relaxed or discarded. This process of repeatedly modifying and refining previous hypotheses of the concept on the basis of examples and counterexamples is called *inductive inference*. The goal of inductive inference is to converge on the correct answer given sufficient data. The heart of an inductive inference process is an *update procedure*, which takes as input (a) a new example or a counterexample, (b) the previous examples and counterexamples, and (c) the most recent hypothesis, and outputs a new hypothesis.

9.1.1   Concept hierarchies

In the previous section we discussed inductive inference at the intuitive level. In order to present precise algorithms we need first to make the problem more concrete. We will be a bit simplistic here; more complete mathematical definitions of inductive inference may be found in the references at the end of the chapter.

The basis for inductive inference is a collection of concepts that constitute the possible hypotheses. Each concept represents a set of *instances;* instances are special concepts that represent themselves. In our previous example, the instances were integers and each concept represented a subset of the integers.

Given this, one can define a natural partial order on these concepts, or a *hierarchy.* This hierarchy denotes specificity: Since each concept stands for a set of instances, concept A is considered more specific than concept B if the set for which A stands is a strict subset of the set for which B stands. In such cases we say that A is lower in the hierarchy than B. Usually the concept names are used without explicit enumeration of the sets for which they stand.

The notion of a concept hierarchy is very general, and it is further specialized by considering the actual representation employed. The primary distinction is between hierarchies represented explicitly and those that are only implicit in the form of the concepts. We discuss one example of the former and two of the latter below.

Explicit hierarchies

A concept hierarchy can be represented explicitly as a directed acyclic graph (DAG). Consider, for example, the hierarchy in Figure 9.1: According to this hierarchy, odd primes are more specific than odd integers, odd integers more specific than integers, the set $\{2,36,214\}$ is more specific than the even integers, and even integers are neither more specific nor less specific than primes.

Often one wants to talk of complex concepts, such as *conjunctive* concepts and *disjunctive* concepts. An example of a conjunctive concept is 'odd prime'; this is an integer that is both odd and prime. Another example of a conjunctive concept is 'an even integer smaller than 100.' An example of disjunctive concepts is 'an integer that is either even or prime.' When one wishes to include these concepts in an explicit hierarchy, these concepts must of course be included in advance as nodes in the graph. Figure 9.2 depicts a concept hierarchy that augments the hierarchy of Figure 9.1.

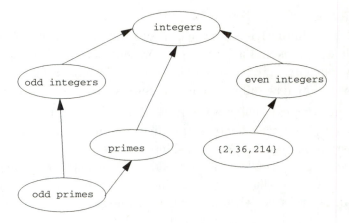

Figure 9.1: A hierarchy of numerical concepts

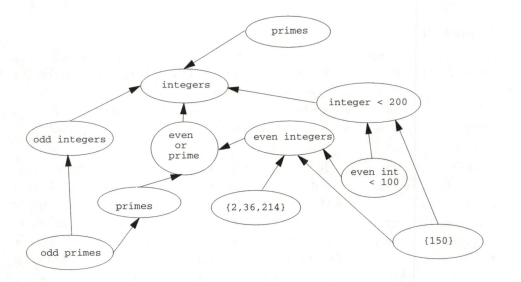

Figure 9.2: An augmented hierarchy of numerical concepts

Pattern hierarchies

While some concept hierarchies may be explicitly represented, most are too large for this purpose. In such cases the means for creating the relevant parts of the hierarchy when the need arises are supplied. More specifically, the representation of concepts is designed so that one can compute the concepts immediately more general than any given concept, as well as those immediately more specific.

A common special case involves concepts that are each defined by a *pattern*. A pattern is an unordered collection of a fixed number of *features*. A feature is a sequence of a fixed number of *aspects;* this sequence is ordered. An aspect is either a ground term or the symbol '?.'

For example, the pattern

$$\{ \text{(large,red,circle)} , \text{(large,?,?)} \}$$

consists of two features, each with three aspects; the concept represents all pairs of large objects, one of which is a red circle (the examples in this section and the next are adapted from examples due to T. Mitchell).

This form of concept implies a specificity ordering as follows. Ground terms are more specific than variables. One feature is more specific than another if each aspect of the first feature is either identical to the corresponding aspect in the second feature or more specific than it, and at least one aspect in the first feature is strictly more specific than the corresponding aspect in the second feature. One pattern (or concept) is more specific than another pattern if the features in the two patterns can be put in a 1-1 correspondence with each other such that each feature of the first pattern is either identical to the corresponding feature in the second pattern or more specific than it, and at least one feature in the first pattern is strictly more specific than the corresponding feature in the second pattern. Figure 9.3 shows a small part of a pattern hierarchy.

Conjunctive hierarchies

Patterns are a limited way in which to describe features, since they require one to specify in advance what all the features are. Furthermore, only features present in the concept, not features absent from it, can be specified.

Conjunctive hierarchies generalize pattern hierarchies in a number of respects, including the two just discussed. In this framework each concept is represented by a *conjunction;* a conjunction is a list of any length:

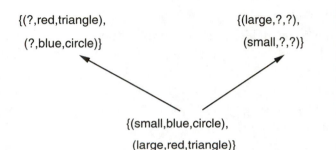

Figure 9.3: A fraction of a pattern hierarchy

$$[C_1, C_2, \ldots , C_n]$$

Each C_i, called a *conjunct*, is of the form

$$[\neg]P_i(Arg_{i_1}, \ldots , Arg_{i_m})$$

where P_i is a predicate symbol, the Arg_{i_j}'s are the lists of arguments to P_i, $\neg$ is the negation sign, and $[\neg]$ means that the negation sign is optional (if the negation sign is present the conjunct is called *negative;* otherwise it is *positive*).

Consider, for example, the following four concepts, which are based loosely on an example due to P. Winston.

Concept 1: [on(Z,X),on(Z,Y),box324(Y),wedge(Z)]
Concept 2: [on(Z,X),on(Z,Y),¬touch(X,Y)]
Concept 3: [on(Z,X),on(Z,Y),centered_on(Z,Y)]
Concept 4: [on(Z,X),on(Z,Y)]

The first concept refers to structures in which a wedge rests on a particular box, box324, and on any other object. The second concept refers to structures in which any object rests on any two nontouching objects. The third concept refers to structures in which any object is on any two objects, and is furthermore centered on one of them. The fourth concept refers to structures in which any object rests on any two objects.

Intuitively, it is clear that the first, second, and third concepts are all more specific than the fourth one, and that the first, second, and third are neither more nor less specific than one another. Formally, we have the following generalization rules:

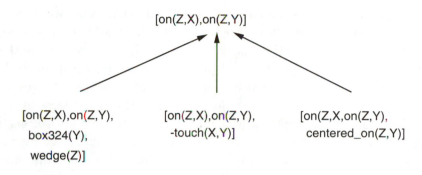

Figure 9.4: A small fragment of a conjunctive hierarchy

1. Replace a positive conjunct c_1 by the positive conjunct c_2, if it is known that c_1 implies c_2.

2. Replace a negative conjunct $\neg c_1$ by the negative conjunct $\neg c_2$, if it is known that c_2 implies c_1.

3. Remove a conjunct c_i (this is a special case of Rule 1 as well as of Rule 2).

4. Replace one occurrence of a multi-occurring variable by a new variable (for example, change [on(Z,X),on(Z,Y)] to [on(Z,X),on(W,Y)]). This is a special case of Rule 3, since, for example, [on(Z,X),on(Z,Y)] is shorthand for [on(Z,X),on(W,Y),W=Z].

Given these rules, and assuming that being 'centered on' implies being 'on,' one can indeed verify the fragment of the conjunctive hierarchy, shown in Figure 9.4, which captures the intuition about the four arch-like concepts.

9.1.2   Prolog representation of concept hierarchies

In the previous section we discussed the general notion of concept hierarchies, including three specific instances. From here on we will continue the discussion at the general level of concept hierarchies. We have not yet defined the inductive inference problem concretely. We will do that in the next section, but first we discuss the Prolog implementation of concept hierarchies.

We will assume that we are given two functions, dgeneralize / 2 and dspecialize / 2, which implement the concept hierarchy. dgeneralize(Concept1,Concept2) accepts Concept1 and returns a concept Concept2 immediately above it in the hierarchy. dspecialize(Concept1,Concept2) accepts Concept1 and returns a concept Concept2 immediately below it in the hierarchy. If there exist more than one more-general or more-specific concept, the rest are returned by Prolog upon backtracking. We intend that dgeneralize / 2 and dspecialize / 2 represent *direct* generalization: If it is the case that dgeneralize(Concept1,Concept2) then there does not exist a Concept3 such that it is the case that both dgeneralize(Concept1,Concept3) and dgeneralize(Concept3,Concept2); similarly for dspecialize / 2. For both functions we assume, as usual, that the output argument may be supplied, and the program will succeed or fail appropriately.

By assuming these functions we have left to the reader a nontrivial task; see Exercise 9.1 in this connection.

Given dgeneralize / 2 and dspecialize / 2, we define other mostly self-explanatory predicates. Notice that generalize / 2 and specialize / 2, the transitive closures of their direct counterparts, operate in a breadth-first fashion:

```
generalize(X,Y) :- gen([X],Y).
gen([X|_],Y) :- dgeneralize(X,Y).
gen([X|Y],Z) :- findall(U,dgeneralize(X,U),L), append(Y,L,W), gen(W,Z).

specialize(X,Y):- spec([X],Y).
spec([X|_],Y) :- dspecialize(X,Y).
spec([X|Y],Z) :- findall(U,dspecialize(X,U),L), append(Y,L,W), spec(W,Z).

as_general(C,C).
as_general(C1,C2) :- generalize(C1,C2).

as_specific(C,C).
as_specific(C1,C2) :- specialize(C1,C2).
```

9.1.3 Inductive inference algorithms

Having discussed at length the notion of concept hierarchies and their Prolog implementation, we are now in a position to define the inductive inference problem. In fact, as we shall see, there are slightly different versions of the definition. Here we give the simplest one.

The input to the problem consists of the sequence of positive and negative examples, and the output is a hypothesis. In most formulations all examples or counterexamples are assumed to be maximally specific concepts, that is, instances (for example, 'the number 150' in our running example). However, we will allow all concepts as examples, but we must be careful about the meaning of such examples. Positive examples pose no particular problem; if 'primes' is presented as a positive example, the implication is that all primes are in the target concept. By contrast, if 'primes' is presented as a negative example, the interpretation will not be that no prime number is in the target concept but rather that at least one is not (see Exercise 9.2 in this connection). The output hypothesis is a concept that is as general as all examples and not as general as any counterexample.

Given the hierarchy of concepts, there exist two natural heuristics when hypothesizing concepts: Pick the most specific concept that includes the currently known examples, and pick the most general concept that excludes the currently known counterexamples. There are two well-known uses in AI of these heuristics, which we introduce in the remainder of this section.

The best-guess approach

In this version of inductive inference, at each execution point there is a single hypothesis about the concept, assessed to best match the examples and counterexamples examined thus far. As each new datum is examined, the previous hypothesis is minimally perturbed to accommodate a new datum. However, since there might be several ways in which to minimally perturb a concept, unlucky choices will lead to backtracking later on.

The notion of 'minimal perturbation' may be interpreted in many ways. In the following we roughly follow a procedure due to P. Winston.

1. *Given a new example:* Minimally generalize the previous hypothesis so as to cover the new example without covering any of the previous negative examples. If no such concept exists then backtrack to a previous choice point and reprocess the examples and counterexamples processed since that point. If no such choice point exists then fail.

2. *Given a new counterexample:* Verify that the current hypothesis does not cover the new example. If it does then backtrack to a previous choice point and reprocess the examples and counterexamples processed since that point. If no such choice point exists then fail.

It is worth pointing out that although this procedure is conservative in the generalizations it makes, it does not always find the most specific legal hypothesis; see Exercise 9.3.

In the following Prolog implementation, we assume that positive examples have the form +content and negative examples the form –content. For convenience, we assume that the list is nonempty and starts with a positive example.

```
% _____
% best_guess / 2 accepts a nonempty list of (positive and negative) examples,
% the first of which is positive, and returns a concept from the concept hierarchy.
% _____

best_guess( [+Ex | MoreEx], Hyp ) :-
    write( 'First example and hypothesis: ' ), write( +Ex ), nl,
    bg( MoreEx, Ex, [+Ex], Hyp ).


% _____
% The arguments of bg / 4, the main subroutine, are as follows:
% list of positive and negative examples (+), current hypothesis (+),
% list of previous (positive and negative) examples (+), new hypothesis (–)
% _____

bg( [ ], Hyp, _, Hyp ).
bg( [+Ex | MoreEx], OldHyp, OldEx, NewHyp ) :-
    write( 'Next example (positive): ' ), write( +Ex ), nl,
    find_some_minimal_generalization( OldHyp, Ex, TmpHyp ),
    not(( member( –Concept, OldEx ),
          generalize( Concept, TmpHyp ) )),
    write( 'New hypothesis: ' ), write( TmpHyp ), nl,
    bg( MoreEx, TmpHyp, [+Ex | OldEx], NewHyp ).
bg( [–Ex | MoreEx], OldHyp, OldEx, NewHyp ) :-
    write('Next example (negative): '), write(–Ex), nl,
    (not( as_general( Ex, OldHyp ) )
    ->
    write( 'the example does not violate current hypothesis' )
    ;
    write( '>> example violates current hypothesis; backtracking ...' ),
    nl, fail ),
    bg( MoreEx, OldHyp, [–Ex | OldEx], NewHyp ).
```

```
% _____
% Only one of the following two subroutines is needed here, but both will be needed
% in the next program. find_some_minimal_generalization / 3 returns in the third
% (output) argument a concept which is the result of minimally generalizing the
% concept given as the first (input) argument so that it is as general as the concept
% given as the second argument. Similarly, find_some_minimal_generalization / 3
% minimally specializes the first concept so that it is not as general as the
% second concept. Note that in both cases there might be more than one such
% minimal perturbation.
% _____
```

```
find_some_minimal_generalization( Con1, Con2, Con3 ) :-
    as_general( Con2, Con1 ), !, Con3 = Con1.


find_some_minimal_generalization( Con1, Con2, Con3 ) :-
    generalize( Con1, Con4 ), % recall the breadth-first search ...
    find_some_minimal_generalization( Con4, Con2, Con3 ).


find_some_minimal_specialization( Con1, Con2, Con3 ) :-
    not( as_general( Con2, Con1 ) ), !, Con3 = Con1.


find_some_minimal_specialization( Con1, Con2, Con3 ) :-
    dspecialize( Con1, Con4 ),
    find_some_minimal_specialization( Con4, Con2, Con3 ).
```

Consider, for example, an encoding of the concept hierarchy from Figure 9.2:

```
dgeneralize(number_150,evens).
dgeneralize(number_150,integers_less_than_200).
dgeneralize(oddprimes,primes).
dgeneralize(oddprimes,odds).
dgeneralize(primes,even_or_primes).
dgeneralize(odds,integers).
dgeneralize(even_or_primes,integers).
dgeneralize(set_2_36_214,evens).
dgeneralize(evens,even_or_primes).
dgeneralize(evens_less_than_100,evens).
dgeneralize(evens_less_than_100,integers_less_than_200).
dgeneralize(integers_less_than_200,integers).
```

Here are two sample queries:

```
| ?- best_guess( [+set_2_36_214, +oddprimes, +number_150,
                  -integers_less_than_200], H ).
```

First example and hypothesis: +set_2_36_214
Next example (positive): +oddprimes
New hypothesis: even_or_primes
Next example (positive): +number_150
New hypothesis: even_or_primes
Next example (negative): -integers_less_than_200
the example does not violate current hypothesis
Final hypothesis: even_or_primes

H = even_or_primes
yes
```
| ?- best_guess([+evens_less_than_100,+number_150,-set_2_36_214], H ).
```
First example and hypothesis: +evens_less_than_100
Next example (positive): +number_150
New hypothesis: evens
Next example (negative): -set_2_36_214
>> example violates current hypothesis; backtracking ...
New hypothesis: integers_less_than_200
Next example (negative): -set_2_36_214
the example does not violate current hypothesis
Final hypotesis: integers_less_than_200

H = integers_less_than_200
yes
| ?-

The least-commitment approach

As we have seen, the best-guess approach necessitated backtracking at times. In contrast, the least-commitment approach acknowledges the fact that usually there is not enough information to commit to a single hypothesis. Instead, it maintains at all times *bounds* on the possible concepts, keeping those bounds as far apart as possible. The output hypothesis is therefore not a single concept, but rather the bounds on possible concepts.

The best-known example of least-commitment in inductive inference is T. Mitchell's notion of *version space,* which we follow here. In this framework two sets of concepts are maintained at all times, a set of upper-bounding concepts and a set of lower-bounding concepts; the actual concept is at least as specific as one of the upper-bounding concepts and at least as general as one of the lower-bounding concepts.

The initial upper and lower bounds are, respectively, the most general and most specific concepts in the hierarchy. Then, as new examples and counterexamples are processed, the lower bound is raised and the upper bound lowered; the cardinality of each might either shrink or increase as a result. If at some point the two bounds each consist of the same single concept, that is the target concept. Figure 9.5 depicts the process pictorially. The precise procedure for updating the upper and lower bounds, U and L respectively, is as follows.

1. *Given a new example:*

    - Remove from U all concepts not as general as the example.
    - Minimally generalize each concept in L so as to be as general as the new example.
    - Discard from L all concepts that are not more specific than some element in U.
    - Now discard from L any concept that is more general than some other concept in L.

2. *Given a new counterexample:*

    - Remove from L all concepts that are as general as the counterexample.
    - Maximally specialize each concept in U so as to not be as general as the new counterexample.
    - Discard from U all concepts that are not more general than some element in L.
    - Now discard from U any concept that is more specific than some other concept in U.

This procedure can be implemented with various degrees of efficiency; the following implementation is fairly efficient, but see Exercise 9.4 for improvements.

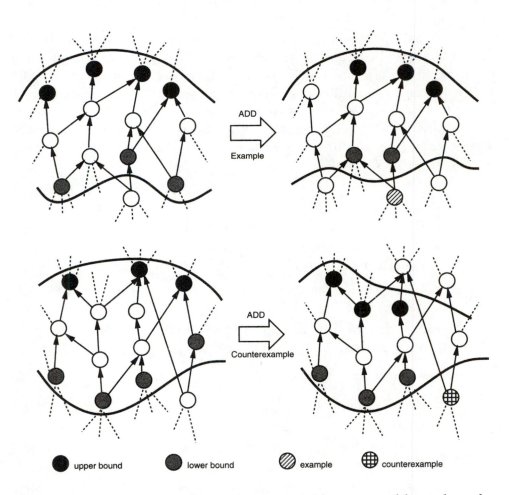

Figure 9.5: A fragment of a version space with upper and lower bounds

```
% _____
% version_space / 3 accepts as input a list of positive and negative examples, and
% returns two lists – the upper-bounding concepts, and the lower-bounding ones.
% _____

version_space( Examples, Up, Low ) :-
    most_general( InitialUp ), most_specific( InitialLow ),
    write( 'Initial upper bound: ' ), write( InitialUp ), nl,
    write( 'Initial lower bound: ' ), write( InitialLow ), nl,
    vs( Examples, InitialUp, InitialLow, Up, Low ).


% _____
% vs / 5, the main subroutine, has the following arguments:
% list of examples (+), previous upper-bounding concepts (+), previous
% lower-bounding concepts (+), new upper bound (–), new lower bound (–).
% _____

vs( [ ], Up, Low, Up, Low ).

vs( [+Ex | More], OldUp, OldLow, NewUp, NewLow ) :-
    write( 'Next example: ' ), write( +Ex ), nl,
    filter_upper_bound( Ex, OldUp, TmpUp ),
    minimally_generalize_lower_bound( OldLow, Ex, TmpLow1 ),
    discard_uncovered_low( TmpLow1, TmpUp, TmpLow2 ),
    discard_non_minimal( TmpLow2, TmpLow ),
    write( 'New upper bound: ' ), write( TmpUp ), nl,
    write( 'New lower bound: ' ), write( TmpLow ), nl,
    vs( More, TmpUp, TmpLow, NewUp, NewLow ).

vs( [–Ex | More], OldUp, OldLow, NewUp, NewLow ) :-
    write( 'Next example: ' ), write( –Ex), nl,
    filter_lower_bound( Ex, OldUp, OldLow, TmpLow ),
    minimally_specialize_upper_bound( OldUp, Ex, TmpUp1 ),
    discard_noncovering_up( TmpUp1, TmpLow, TmpUp2 ),
    discard_non_minimal( TmpUp2, TmpUp ),
    write( 'New upper bound: ' ), write( TmpUp ), nl,
    write( 'New lower bound: ' ), write( TmpLow ), nl,
    vs( More, TmpUp, TmpLow, NewUp, NewLow ).
```

```
% _____
% filter_upper_bound / 3 accepts a single positive example and a previous upper
% bound as input, and outputs a new upper bound, the result of removing from the
% old upper bound all concepts that are not as general as the new positive example.
% It does so rather naively, by moving upward from the concept in a breadth-first
% fashion along dgeneralize links, and examining each concept along the way for
% membership in the previous upper bound. filter_lower_bound / 3 operates in a
% similar fashion, accepting a negative example and a previous lower bound, and
% outputting a new lower bound which is the result of omitting from the previous
% lower bound all those which are as general as the negative example. Note the
% asymmetry in the implementation: In the upper-bound filtering one starts with
% the empty upper bound and adds to it incrementally, whereas in the lower-
% bound filtering one starts with the previous lower bound and deletes from it
% incrementally.
% _____

filter_upper_bound( Ex, OldUp, TmpUp ) :-
   fub( [Ex], OldUp, [ ], TmpUp ),
   ( TmpUp = [_ | _]
     -> true
     ; write( 'failed to filter upper bound' ), nl, fail ).


fub( [ ], _, GoodUp, GoodUp ).


fub( [Concept | More], OldUp, GoodUp, NewUp ) :-
   member( Concept, OldUp ), !,
   ( member( Concept, GoodUp)
     -> fub( More, OldUp, GoodUp, NewUp )
     ; fub( More, OldUp, [Concept | GoodUp], NewUp ) ).


fub( [Concept | More], OldUp, GoodUp, NewUp ) :-
   findall( Concept1, dgeneralize( Concept, Concept1 ), ConList ),
   append( More, ConList, NewConList),
   fub( NewConList, OldUp, GoodUp, NewUp ).
```

```
filter_lower_bound( Ex, OldUp, OldLow, TmpLow ) :-
   flb( [Ex], OldUp, OldLow, OldLow, TmpLow ),
   ( TmpLow = [_ | _]
     -> true
     ; write('failed to filter lower bound'), nl, fail ).


flb( [ ], _, _, GoodLow, GoodLow ).
flb( [Concept | More], OldUp, OldLow, GoodLow, NewLow ) :-
   member( Concept, OldLow ), !,
   (remove( Concept, GoodLow, TmpLow ) -> true ; TmpLow = GoodLow ),
   flb( More, OldUp, OldLow, TmpLow, NewLow ).


flb( [Concept | More], OldUp, OldLow, GoodLow, NewLow ) :-
   member( Concept, OldUp ), !,
   flb( More, OldUp, OldLow, GoodLow, NewLow ).


flb( [Concept | More], OldUp, OldLow, GoodLow, NewLow ) :-
   findall( Concept1, dgeneralize( Concept, Concept1 ), ConList ),
   append( More, ConList, NewConList),
   flb( NewConList, OldUp, OldLow, GoodLow, NewLow ).
```

```
% _____
% The following programs perform the same minimal generalization and
% specialization as in the best-guess approach, but (1) they apply the minimal
% perturbation to all concepts in the (upper or lower) bound, and (2) for each
% such concept, they compute all the possible minimal perturbations.
% _____
```

```
minimally_generalize_lower_bound( Low1, Ex, Low2) :-
   setof( Concept,
          Concept1^
          ( member( Concept1, Low1 ),
            find_some_minimal_generalization( Concept1, Ex, Concept ) ),
          Low2 )
   -> true
   ; write( 'cannot generalize lower bound to cover example' ), nl, fail.
```

```
minimally_specialize_upper_bound( Up1, Ex, Up2) :-
    setof( Concept,
           Concept1^
           ( member( Concept1, Up1 ),
             find_some_minimal_specialization( Concept1, Ex, Concept ) ),
           Up2 )
    -> true
    ; write( 'cannot specialize upper bound so as to not cover example' ), nl, fail.
```

```
%  _____
```
% discard_uncovered_low / 2 *takes a lower bound and an upper bound as input, and*
% *outputs a new lower bound, the result of removing from the lower bound all*
% *concepts in the previous lower bound that do not generalize to some concept in*
% *the upper bound.* discard_noncovering_up / 3 *performs the symmetric filtering on*
% *an upper bound.*
```
%  _____
```

```
discard_uncovered_low( Low1, Up, Low2 ) :-
    setof( Concept,
           ( member( Concept, Low1),
             generalize(Concept,Concept1),
             member(Concept1,Up) ),
           Low2)
    -> true
    ; write( 'no generalization of lower bound is covered by upper bound'), nl, fail.
```

```
discard_noncovering_up( Up1, Low, Up2 ) :-
    setof( Concept,
           ( member( Concept, Up1),
             as_general( Concept1, Concept ),
             member( Concept1, Low ) ),
           Up2)
    -> true
    ; write( 'no specialization of upper bound covers lower bound' ),
      nl, fail.
```

```
% _____
% discard_non_minimal / 2 accepts a set of concepts as input, and removes from
% the set the concepts that are more general than some other concept in the set.
% _____
```

```
discard_non_minimal( Set1, Set2 ) :-
   setof( Concept,
         ( member(Concept, Set1),
           not(( member(Concept1, Set1), dgeneralize(Concept1, Concept) ))),
         Set2 ).
```

Finally, we use the following programs to compute the initial bounds:

```
most_general( U ) :- setof( X, Y^ ( dgeneralize(Y,X), not(dgeneralize(X,_)) ), U ).
most_specific( L ) :- setof( X, Y^ ( dgeneralize(X,Y), not(dgeneralize(_,X)) ), L ).
```

Here is a sample run of the program:

```
| ?- version_space([+set_2_36_214, +primes, -odds], U,L).

Initial upper bound: [integers]
Initial lower bound: [evens_less_than_100,nonprimes,
                        number_150,oddprimes,set_2_36_214]
Next example: +set_2_36_214
New upper bound: [integers]
New lower bound: [set_2_36_214]
Next example: +primes
New upper bound: [integers]
New lower bound: [even_or_primes]
Next example: -odds
New upper bound: [even_or_primes]
New lower bound: [even_or_primes]

yes
| ?-
```

9.2   Induction of decision trees (ID3)

This section is still concerned with inductive inference, but of a special kind: induction of decision trees. A decision tree is used to categorize data into classes in the following way. Each leaf of the tree is labeled with a name of a class, and each internal node is labeled with a test. An internal node whose associated test has n possible outcomes has exactly n arcs, one for each outcome; each arc is labeled with that outcome. For example, if the test is a yes/no (or binary) test, then it has two arcs (and thus two children) below it in the tree; one arc is labeled 'yes' and the other 'no.'

Given a decision tree, the process of categorization is straightforward. A datum to be categorized is first subjected to the test in the root. Depending on the outcome it is passed down the appropriate arc, subjected to the test in the node at the end of that arc, and so on until it finally reaches a leaf node; it is then categorized as belonging to the class associated with that leaf.

In the context of ID3, the data and the tests have particular forms. We start by fixing some finite set of attributes and associating a set of possible values with each attribute. (Although ID3 can be applied to the case in which the sets of possible values are infinite and even continuous, for simplicity we will consider only the case in which the sets of possible values are all finite.) We also decide on a set of categories into which the data must fall; we will concentrate on the binary case, with only two possible categories.

Given this structure, the data and tests have the following forms. Each datum is a pair (*category, feature vector*), where a feature vector is a collection of attribute values (one value for each attribute). The test in each internal node will consist of examining exactly one of the attributes; the arcs below it will be labeled with the possible values of that attribute.

Consider, as an example, the criteria for accepting candidates to the Ph.D. program at the mythical University of St. Nordaf. Each candidate is evaluated according to four attributes: The grade point average (GPA), the quality of the undergraduate university attended, the publication record, and the strength of the recommendation letters. To simplify our example, let us discretize and limit the possible values of each attribute: Possible GPA scores are 4.0, 3.7, and 3.5; universities are categorized as top_10, top_20, and top_30 (by top_20 we mean places 11–20, and by top_30 we mean 21–30); publication record is a binary attribute – either the applicant has published

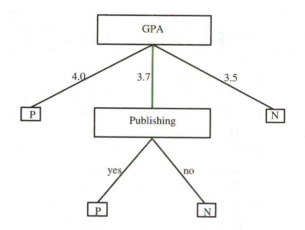

Figure 9.6: A simple decision tree

previously or not; and recommendation letters are similarly binary, they are either good or normal. Finally, the candidates are classified into two classes: accepted, or P (for 'positive'), and rejected, or N (for 'negative'). Figure 9.6 shows one possible decision tree determining acceptance.

The problem we consider is this. We are given a collection of data and their categorizations into one of two classes, and we wish to find a decision tree that classifies them correctly. Returning to our academic example, Figure 9.2 shows sample data concerning a number of applications and their outcomes. We would like our algorithm to return a decision tree that correctly classifies all these data; one such tree is the one from Figure 9.6, mentioned earlier.

The ID3 algorithm, due to R. Quinlan, constructs the tree in a recursive fashion. The data start out as one big equivalence class; if all the data happen to be classified identically, the procedure terminates, and the tree consists of a single node. Otherwise, ID3 picks one attribute, and splits the data according to the different values of that attribute (that is, all the data with the same value for that attribute form a new equivalence class). Each equivalence class is now repeatedly split in a similar fashion, until the data in each equivalence class are classified identically.

The only nonobvious step in ID3 is the choice of attribute on which to split at each node. This choice is critical, as different choices may yield radically different trees. For example, a different choice in our example would

No.	Attributes				Class
	GPA	University	Published	Recommendation	
1	4.0	top_10	yes	good	P
2	4.0	top_10	no	good	P
3	4.0	top_20	no	normal	P
4	3.7	top_10	yes	good	P
5	3.7	top_20	no	good	N
6	3.7	top_30	yes	good	P
7	3.7	top_30	no	good	N
8	3.7	top_10	no	good	N
9	3.5	top_20	yes	normal	N
10	3.5	top_10	no	normal	N
11	3.5	top_30	yes	normal	N
12	3.5	top_30	no	good	N

Figure 9.7: Sample data of admission applications and decisions

yield the tree shown in Figure 9.8; clearly, it is vastly more complicated than the earlier tree from Figure 9.6.

Intuitively, we would like to make the choices that lead to a simplest possible tree; ID3 captures this intuition by appealing to the formal notion of *entropy* from information theory. We will not aim for deep understanding of the notion here, but in order to understand ID3 we will need a few basic definitions.

For simplicity, we will continue to consider only binary categorizations, that is, categorization into one of two possible values (P and N, in our notation); see Exercise 9.5 for possible extensions. We start by defining the amount of information present in a given collection of (categorized) data. Intuitively, the more uniform the data, the higher the information content of the collection. For example, if all the data are categorized identically, the information content is highest; if half the data are categorized P and half N, the information content is lowest.

Actually, rather than measure directly the information content, it is usual to measure instead information absence (that is, the inverse of information content), called *entropy*. Let us denote by $p(P)$ the fraction of the data in the collection categorized as P, and by $p(N)$ the fraction of data categorized

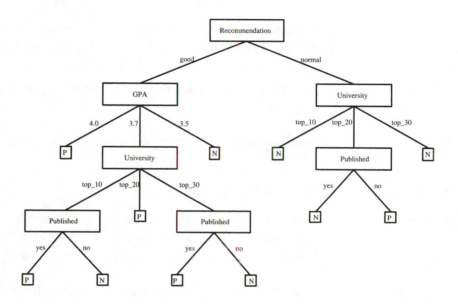

Figure 9.8: A complex decision tree

as N (obviously, $p(P) + p(N) = 1$). The entropy of the collection, $H(C)$, is then defined by the formula

$$H(C) = -(p(P)\log p(P) + p(N)\log p(N))^1$$

The definition of entropy extends easily to a collection of disjoint collections of data; the total entropy of a 'collection of collections' is simply the sum of the entropies of each collection.

Now let us return to ID3 and the choice of attribute on which to split a given node. At this point in the execution of ID3, several of the input data end up at that node (and obviously some are labeled P and some N, or else we would not have to split the node). Suppose we pick any particular attribute. When we split the node on that attribute, we create several new children nodes, and the data previously associated with the node are now distributed uniquely among the children nodes (if the parent is marked *attr*, a child at the end of an arc marked v gets all the data, previously associated with the parent, that have the value v for attribute *attr*). The collections associated with the new children will each have a particular entropy, and the total entropy of the children will be the sum of their individual entropies.

---

[1]The reader may verify that the values $p(P) = 0$ and $p(P) = 1$ yield the lowest possible entropy, 0, whereas the value $p(P) = 0.5$ yields the highest possible entropy.

So, on which attribute does ID3 split a given node? The answer is now simple: It selects the attribute that results in the lowest total entropy (and thus maximal total information) in the resulting children nodes.

The full ID3 algorithm takes into account a number of different phenomena, including the following:

- The data might spread across any number of classes, not necessarily two.

- Some data may be missing the values of some attributes.

- The training data might be noisy in at least two ways: Some of the attributes may be corrupted (as opposed to merely missing, as in the previous case), and some of the classifications may be wrong too.

However, the implementation below allows none of that: It assumes that only two types of class, P and N, exist; that all the data have all the attributes; and that the training set is correct (but see Exercise 9.5).

In the following Prolog implementation, the input consists of a list of *(category,datum)*-pairs, where *category* is one of the possible categorizations (in our case, P or N), and *datum* is a list of *(attribute,value)* pairs. The output is a decision tree, which is represented in the embedded-list notation. For clarity, internal nodes are labeled as internal(*attribute*), and leaf nodes as leaf(*category*). Furthermore, with each child we associate the label of the arc leading to it from the parent; for example, if *attribute* has possible values yes and no, the subtree below *attribute* will have the form ... (internal(*attribute*), [yes–*subtree1*, no–*subtree2*]).

```
% _____
% Arguments to id3 / 3:
% attribute list (list of (attribute-name, list-of-possible-values) pairs) (+),
% input data (list of (category, feature-vector) pairs) (+), decision tree (-).
% _____


id3( _, Data, Tree ) :-
  all_same_category( Data, Categ ), !,
  Tree = leaf( Categ ).


id3( AttrList, Data, Tree ) :-
  select_and_split( AttrList, Data, BestAttr, BestDataPartition ),
  generate_children_trees( AttrList, BestDataPartition, ChildrenTrees ),
  Tree = tree( internal( BestAttr ), ChildrenTrees ).


% _____
% all_same_category / 2 accepts a list of categorized data as input, succeeds only if
% they are all categorized identically, and if so outputs that category
% _____


all_same_category( [ ], _ ).
all_same_category( [ ( Categ, _ ) | MoreData ], Categ ) :-
  all_same_category( MoreData, Categ ).


% _____
% select_and_split / 4 finds all the partitions of the input data, one for each
% attribute. It computes the entropy of each partition, and selects the partition
% with the lowest entropy.
% Arguments: attribute list (+), data (+), the attribute partitioning on which
% yields the lowest entropy (-), the corresponding partition (-)
% _____


select_and_split( AttrList, Data, BestAttr, BestPartition ) :-
  findall( ( Attr, Partition, Entropy ),
          ( member( ( Attr, PosAttrValues ), AttrList ),
            partition( Data, Attr, PosAttrValues, Partition, Entropy ) ),
          AllPartitions ),
  select_minimal_entropy( AllPartitions, BestAttr, BestPartition ).
```

```
% _____
% partition / 5 partitions the input data according to the values they have fpr
% a given attribute.
% Arguments: list of categorized data (+), the attribute (+), all possible values
% for that attribute (+), the resulting partition (−), its entropy (−)
% _____


partition( _, _, [ ] , [ ], 0 ).
partition( Data, Attr, [ OnePosAttrValue | RestValues ] , Partition, Entropy ) :-
  select_by_attr_value( Data, Attr, OnePosAttrValue, SubData ),
  ( SubData = [ ]
    -> partition( Data, Attr, RestValues, Partition, Entropy )
    ;
    compute_set_entropy( SubData, SubEntropy ),
    partition( Data, Attr, RestValues, RestPartition, RestEntropy ),
    Partition = [ OnePosAttrValue−SubData | RestPartition ],
    Entropy is SubEntropy + RestEntropy ).


select_by_attr_value( [ ], _, _, [ ] ).
select_by_attr_value( [ (V,Datum) | MoreData ], Attr, AttrValue, SubData ) :-
  member( (Attr,AttrValue), Datum )
  -> select_by_attr_value( MoreData, Attr, AttrValue, MoreSubData ),
      SubData = [ (V,Datum) | MoreSubData ]
  ; select_by_attr_value( MoreData, Attr, AttrValue, SubData ).


compute_set_entropy( Data, Entropy ) :-
  count_positive( Data, Pnum ),
  length( Data, Dnum ),
  Pp is Pnum / Dnum,
  Pn is 1 − Pp,
  xlogx( Pp, PpLogPp ),
  xlogx( Pn, PnLogPn ),
  Entropy is − ( PpLogPp + PnLogPn ).


count_positive( [ ], 0 ).
count_positive( [ ( p, _ ) | More ], Pnum ) :- !,
  count_positive( More, Pnum1 ), Pnum is Pnum1 + 1.
count_positive( [ ( n, _ ) | More ], Pnum ) :- count_positive( More, Pnum ).
```

```
xlogx( X, N ) :- X is 0.0E+00, !, N = 0.
xlogx( X, N ) :- log( X, LogX ), N is X * LogX.
```

```
% _____
% select_minimal_entropy / 3 accepts a list of (attribute, partition-induced-by-that
% -attribute, resulting-entropy) triples and outputs the attribute yielding the
% partition of lowest entropy as well as the partition itself.
% _____
select_minimal_entropy( [ (Attr, Partition, Entropy ) | MorePartitions ],
                        BestAttr, BestPartition ) :-
   select_minimal_entropy_aux( MorePartitions, (Attr, Partition, Entropy),
                               BestAttr, BestPartition ).


select_minimal_entropy_aux( [ ], ( Attr, Partition, _ ), Attr, Partition ).
select_minimal_entropy_aux( [ (Attr1, Partition1, Entropy1) | MorePartitions ],
                            ( _, _, Entropy), BestAttr, BestPartition ) :-
   Entropy1 < Entropy , !,
   select_minimal_entropy_aux( MorePartitions, (Attr1, Partition1, Entropy1),
                               BestAttr, BestPartition ).
select_minimal_entropy_aux( [ _ | MorePartitions ], (Attr, Partition, Entropy),
                            BestAttr, BestPartition ) :-
   select_minimal_entropy_aux( MorePartitions, (Attr, Partition, Entropy),
                               BestAttr, BestPartition ).
```

```
% _____
% generate_children_trees / 3 generates a list of decision trees, one for each of the
% subdata, associating with each tree the name of the arc (i.e., the attribute value)
% leading to it.
% Arguments: attribute list (+), list of (attribute-value, subdata) pairs (+),
% list of trees (–)
% _____
```

```
generate_children_trees( _, [ ], [ ] ).
generate_children_trees( AttrList, [ Value–SubData | MoreData ], ChildrenTrees ) :-
   id3( AttrList, SubData, ChildTree ),
   generate_children_trees( AttrList, MoreData, MoreTrees ),
   ChildrenTrees = [ Value–ChildTree | MoreTrees ].
```

Finally, here is a sample run of the program on the example given earlier; note that it ends up constructing the simple decision tree shown earlier in Figure 9.6.

```
| ?- id3( [ ( gpa, [4.0,3.7,3.5] ),
            ( univ, [top_10,top_20,top_30] ),
            ( publ, [yes,no] ),
            ( rec, [good,normal] )
          ],
          [ ( p, [(gpa,4.0),(univ,top_10),(publ,yes),(rec,good)] ),
            ( p, [(gpa,4.0),(univ,top_10),(publ,no),(rec,good)] ),
            ( p, [(gpa,4.0),(univ,top_20),(publ,no),(rec,normal)] ),
            ( p, [(gpa,3.7),(univ,top_10),(publ,yes),(rec,good)] ),
            ( n, [(gpa,3.7),(univ,top_20),(publ,no ),(rec, good)] ),
            ( p, [(gpa,3.7),(univ,top_30),(publ,yes),(rec,good )] ),
            ( n, [(gpa,3.7),(univ,top_30),(publ,no),(rec,good)] ),
            ( n, [(gpa,3.7),(univ,top_10),(publ,no),(rec,good)] ),
            ( n, [(gpa,3.5),(univ,top_20),(publ,yes),(rec,normal)] ),
            ( n, [(gpa,3.5),(univ,top_10),(publ,no),(rec,normal)] ),
            ( n, [(gpa,3.5),(univ,top_30),(publ,yes),(rec,normal)] ),
            ( n, [(gpa,3.5),(univ,top_30),(publ,no),(rec,good )] )
          ] ,
          Tree ).


Tree = tree( internal(gpa),
             [ 4.0E+00 - leaf(p),
               3.7E+00 - tree( internal(publ),
                               [ yes - leaf(p),
                                 no - leaf(n) ] ),
               3.5E+00 - leaf(n) ] )
| ?-
```

9.3 Explanation-based learning

Underlying a variety of learning methods that come under the general heading 'explanation-based' is the intuition that there are more aspects of experience on which to base learning than mere examples and counterexamples. In particular, it is observed that when we reach a conclusion, we have *reasons* for reaching that conclusion. These reasons can play a double role in learning.

First, if the conclusion turns out to be right, by tracing the reasoning process we may be able to identify the parts of the context that actually contributed to the correct conclusion (the so-called *credit assignment* problem). We may then generalize the conclusion by ignoring the other aspects of the context; this explanation-based learning is also called *explanation-based generalization*. Second, if the conclusion turns out to be wrong, the reasoning may provide a clue as to where the problem lies (*blame assignment*) and how to correct it. This method is sometimes called *failure-based learning*.

Since many forms of reasoning exist, it follows that there are at least as many explanation-based learning methods. In this section we will concentrate on backward chaining as the reasoning mechanism, and explore two forms of explanation-based learning.

9.3.1 Generalizing correct reasoning

Recall the explanatory meta-interpreter from Chapter 3, which upon successful computation also supplied the proof tree by way of explanation:

```
meta_exp( ( A, B ), Proof ) ) :- !,
    meta_exp( A, AProof ), meta_exp( B, BProof ),
    append_proofs( AProof, BProof, Proof ).
meta_exp( A, A ) :- clause( A, B ), system( B ), B.
meta_exp( A, tree(A,Proof) ) :-
    clause( A, B ), meta_exp( B, BProof ), attach_proof( BProof, Proof ).

append_proofs( AProof, [BProof | More], Proof ) :- !, Proof = [AProof, BProof | More].
append_proofs( AProof, BProof, [AProof, BProof] ).
attach_proof( [BProof | More], Proof ) :- !, Proof = [BProof | More].
attach_proof( BProof, [BProof] ).
```

We now use this explanation mechanism to generalize the answer. The idea behind the following program, adapted from a program due to Kedar-Cabelli and McCarty, is this: Instead of supplying a single argument as above, one supplies two arguments to the meta-interpreter, a goal and a generalized form of the goal, one in which variables replace some constants. Until the specific goal is explicitly encountered in the database, the program uses clauses based on the general goal, while making sure the heads of the clauses selected unify with the specific goal as well (the third clause). When the specific goal is encountered in the database the computation succeeds without the general goal being further instantiated (the second clause).

```
ebg( (A,B), (GenA,GenB), Proof, GenProof ) :- !,
    ebg( A, GenA, AProof, GenAProof ),
    ebg( B, GenB, BProof, GenBProof ),
    append_proofs( AProof, BProof, Proof ),
    append_proofs( GenAProof, GenBProof, GenProof ).
ebg( A, GenA, A, GenA ) :- clause(A,B), system(B), B.
ebg( A, GenA, tree(A, Proof), tree(GenA, GenProof) ) :-
    clause( GenA, GenB ),
    copy_term( (GenA,GenB), (A,B) ),
    ebg( B, GenB, BProof, GenBProof ),
    attach_proof( BProof, Proof ),
    attach_proof( GenBProof, GenProof ).
% append_proofs, attach_proof as above
```

Consider the following program, also due to Kedar-Cabelli and McCarty:

```
kill(A, B) :- hate( A, B), possess(A, C), weapon(C).
hate(A, A) :- depressed(A).
possess(A, C) :- buy(A, C).
weapon(C) :- gun(C).

depressed(john).
buy(john,gun17).
gun(gun17).
```

and the following sample run (friendly formatting added):

| ?- ebg(kill(john,john), kill(X,X), Exp, GenExp).

X = _9171,

Exp = tree(kill(john,john),
         [tree(hate(john,john),
            [depressed(john)]),
        tree(possess(john,gun17),
            [buy(john,gun17)]),
        tree(weapon(gun17),
            [gun(gun17)])
        ]),

GenExp = tree(kill(X,X),
          [tree(hate(X,X),
             [depressed(X)]),
         tree(possess(X,_9171),
            [buy(X,_9171)]),
         tree(weapon(_9171),
            [gun(_9171)])
         ])

As can be seen from the example, explanation-based generalization does not result in any knowledge that was not already implicit in the database. What the procedure does is index that general and, presumably, vast knowledge on the basis of particular cases. We now turn to learning from failed reasoning.

9.3.2   Learning from failed reasoning

Section 9.3.1 demonstrated the utility of tracing correct reasoning. As was mentioned at the beginning of Section 9.3, tracing incorrect reasoning can be no less instructive. In this section we consider a program that traces incorrect backward-chaining reasoning and attempts to find the component responsible for the error. This section is based on the work of E. Shapiro; the interested reader is referred to the sources at the end of the chapter for more details.

We consider two programs: one that diagnoses reasoning that incorrectly succeeded and another that diagnoses reasoning that incorrectly failed.

Finding overly strong rules

The following program accepts as input a goal that incorrectly succeeds and, using advice from the user, identifies a rule instance that is the cause of the problem. (Recall that writel / 1 writes all members of the input list.)

```
% _____
% To find the culprit clause in a conjunction, look for it first in the first conjunct,
% and if it is not found then look in the remaining conjuncts. System predicates
% are safe. For other single goals, examine the body of a clause for the culprit.
% _____
```

```
too_strong( (A,B), Culprit ) :- !,
  too_strong( A, ACulprit ),
  conj_culprit( ACulprit, B, Culprit ).
too_strong( A, Culprit ) :- system( A ), !, A, Culprit = ok.
too_strong( A, Culprit ) :-
  clause( A, B ),
  too_strong( B, BCulprit ),
  clause_culprit( A, B, BCulprit, Culprit ).

conj_culprit( ok, B, Culprit1 ) :- !, too_strong( B, Culprit2 ), Culprit2 = Culprit1.
conj_culprit( ACulprit, _, ACulprit ).
```

```
% _____
% Query the user whether the head A should succeed. If both A and the body B
% should succeed, then the clause is safe. If B should succeed and A not, the
% clause A:-B is the culprit. Otherwise, the culprit lies with B.
% _____
```

```
clause_culprit( A, _, ok, Culprit ) :- should_succeed( A ), !, Culprit = ok.
clause_culprit( A, B, ok, Culprit ) :- !, Culprit = ( A :- B ).
clause_culprit( _, _, BCulprit, BCulprit ).

should_succeed(A) :- nl, writel(['Should ',A,' succeed? ']), read(yes).
```

Consider the following example:

```
fly(X) :- bird(X).        bird(X) :- penguin(X).        penguin(tweety).
```

These overly strong rules allow us to infer that 'Penguins can fly.' To find the culprit rule, we use the following query:

```
| ?- too_strong(fly(tweety),Culprit).
Should penguin(tweety) succeed? yes.
Should bird(tweety) succeed? yes.
Should fly(tweety) succeed? no.

Culprit = (fly(tweety):-bird(tweety))

| ?-
```

Finding missing rules

The following program accepts as input a goal that incorrectly fails and, using advice from the user, locates the culprit 'uncovered' goal.

```
% _____
% To find the culprit clause in a conjunction, run the first conjunct. If it succeeds,
% the culprit must lie with the remaining conjuncts. For uncovered single goals,
% examine the clauses for the goal. If there exists one whose body should succeed,
% the problem lies with that body. Otherwise the single goal itself is the culprit.
% _____

too_weak( (A,B), BCulprit ) :- A, too_weak( B, BCulprit ).
too_weak( (A,_), ACulprit ) :- too_weak( A, ACulprit ).

too_weak( A, BCulprit ) :-
   clause( A, B ),
   should_succeed( B ),!,
   too_weak( B, BCulprit ).
too_weak( A, A ) :-
   (ground(A), not(A), ! ; nl, writel(['Which instance of ',A,' ? ']), read(A)).
```

Consider the following example:

```
migrates(X) :- bird(X), habitat(X,Y), northern(Y).
bird(X) :- dove(X).
dove(chirpy).
```

Now, we want to find out why we cannot determine a migrating individual; as a bonus we discover such an individual:

| ?- too_weak(migrates(X),Culprit).
Should bird(_3190),habitat(_3190,_3381),northern(_3381) succeed? yes.
Which instance of habitat(chirpy,_3381) ? habitat(chirpy,alaska).

X = chirpy,
Culprit = habitat(chirpy,alaska)

| ?-

From diagnosis to learning

Both error-tracing programs discussed above merely identified either a missing rule or an overly strong rule. We have not discussed the automatic modification of the program as a result of this diagnosis. If a rule instance is discovered to be too strong, should the rule be discarded? Should it only be instantiated, perhaps partially? Similarly, if an uncovered goal is found, should it simply be added to the database as a fact? If many uncovered goals are found that have the same predicate but different arguments, should all instances be added or perhaps instead a rule with variables that will cover all instances?

Clearly, once the culprit is identified, the problem is no different from (and thus no easier than) the general problem of hypothesis update in inductive inference. We will therefore not address it further here. To pursue this in more detail, the reader should consult the appropriate source mentioned in the next section; see also Exercise 9.7.

9.4   Further reading

The literature on machine learning is vast. Several annual conferences on learning are held, and their proceedings are a good source on current ideas. Dietterich [16] is a clear summary of work in the field, and Dietterich and Shavlik [74] contains many of the important papers in this area. The *Journal of Machine Learning* is another important reference, as are the edited collections [49, 50, 36]. Angluin and Smith [4] is a good survey of induc-

tive inference. Winston [82] and Mitchell [52] are AI 'classics' on inductive
inference. DeJong [15] surveys explanation-based learning. Shapiro's work
on automated debugging of logic programs is documented in [73]. Kedar-
Cabelli and McCarty's program for explanation-based learning is described
in [35]. Finally, recent years have seen important advances in inductive synthesis of logic programs; Lavrac and Dzeroski [41] is a collection of recent
articles; Muggleton's GOLEM program [53] and Quinlan's FOIL [66] have
been particularly influential.

9.5   Exercises

Exercise 9.1 When discussing inductive inference, we assumed a predicate dgeneralize, which, given a concept, returned all concepts directly above it in the hierarchy. If the hierarchy is explicit then the implementation is of course straightforward, but otherwise it is not.

(a) Implement the predicate for pattern hierarchies.

(b) Implement the predicate for conjunctive hierarchies.

Exercise 9.2 In Section 9.1.3 we allowed arbitrary classes as examples (that is, not necessarily instances). However, when doing so we assumed a particular interpretation of negative examples (or counterexamples); if X was a negative example, this meant that at least one member of the class X was not in the target concept. This is sometimes called *weak negation*. Now consider the alternative interpretation, namely that *no* member of X is in the target concept; this is sometimes called *strong negation*.

(a) Modify the best-guess implementation to accommodate the strong-negation interpretation.

(b) Do the same for the least-commitment implementation.

Exercise 9.3

(a) Show that the best-guess algorithm given does not always return a most specific concept consistent with the examples.

(b) Modify the algorithm and its implementation so that it does.

Exercise 9.4 The inductive inference algorithms, both best-guess and least-commitment, rely on searching the concept hierarchy. The efficiency of their implementation depends on the efficiency of this search. In particular, two operations that are used heavily are finding one of (or all) the least upper bounds of two given concepts, and finding one of (or all) their greatest lower bounds.

Can you improve on the implementation? What is the worst-case time complexity of your implementation for a single query? What is it in practice? What is its *amortized* time complexity? *Hint:* Remember that the concept hierarchy is fixed.

Exercise 9.5 The implementation of ID3 given in this chapter handles data that belong to one of two categories (P and N, in our notation). Generalize the implementation of ID3 to allow for data that distribute among *any* (given and fixed) number of categories.

Exercise 9.6 In connection with learning from failed reasoning, this chapter presented two diagnostic programs, too_strong / 2 and too_weak / 2, that detect culprit clauses in faulty programs. These two programs do not fare well when the diagnosed program involves recursion. Eliminating infinite recursion without affecting the diagnosed program is not possible in general, but in practice programmers definitely do have heuristics for identifying situations in which the program is trapped in an infinite loop. Identify such heuristics, and modify the diagnostic programs so as to embody the heuristics.

Exercise 9.7 Shapiro's work, from which the simple diagnostic programs are derived, extends the process of diagnosis to a process of debugging; he presents programs that not only identify culprit clauses but also automatically modify the program so as to eliminate the problems. Your goal here is to create a more limited tool, not an automatic debugger but a 'debugger's assistant.'

Write a program debug_help/1 that accepts a list of n goals, each annotated with + (if it is to succeed) or − (if it is to fail). The program executes the following loop:

(1) $i \leftarrow 0$

(2) $i \leftarrow i + 1$

(3) if the i'th goal succeeds or fails as it should

      then go to (2)

      else run the appropriate of the two diagnostic programs, notify the user of the culprit clause, have the user modify the program on the basis of that (which could consist of eliminating, generalizing, or specializing a given clause, or adding a new clause), and go to (1)

Chapter 10

Natural Language

Natural language processing has always been a very active research area in artificial intelligence. Its applications range from natural-language database queries to voice-activated typewriters to machine translation. Interestingly, the development of Prolog has been linked to the development of new computational linguistic theories with the result that many linguistic notions are easily encoded in Prolog. This chapter presents some of these linguistic notions. We should first review the main levels of natural languages.

- *Phonetics:* Concerned with the sound of human speech and pronunciation, this level provides different symbols, called *phonemes*, that represent each sound.

- *Morphology:* This level concerns the different *inflections* of a word, i.e., the various forms a word can take in a phrase: singular/plural forms for a noun, different tenses for a verb, and so on.

- *Syntax:* This level determines which sequences of words form grammatically correct sentences in the language.

- *Semantics*: This is where the meaning of words, sentences, and larger text fragments is taken into account. Not only do semantics aid in the parsing of sentences, but in fact the main goal of parsing is to derive a semantic representation of the sentence's meaning.

- *Pragmatics:* This level deals with the context and intentions of the conversants.

We cover only some elements of the syntactic and semantic levels here. Section 10.1 shows how to implement and extend context-free grammars with the Prolog built-in formalism called the *Definite Clause Grammar (DCG)*. Section 10.2 illustrates how semantic representations based on modal logics can be directly derived from the syntactic analysis.

It should be emphasized that natural-language processing is an immensely complex task, and here we will only scratch the surface. In particular, we will not address the intricate interplay between syntax and semantics and will not treat text components larger than sentences, such as paragraphs.

10.1   Syntax

The syntax of natural language determines the grammaticality of sentences, that is, it determines which of the many word combinations are to be acceptable as legal sentences. Grammar rules can be used to determine the grammaticality of a given sentence, to break it down into its linguistic constituents, or to generate a grammatical sentence.

10.1.1   Context-free grammars

Computer science has developed a set of efficient algorithms to deal with artificial languages such as programming languages. Most of them are based on the context-free grammar formalism. A context-free grammar has four components:

- an initial nonterminal symbol, (usually s for "sentence" in natural language)

- a set of nonterminal symbols

- a set of terminal symbols

- a set of rules composed of a nonterminal, called the *left-hand side* or *head* of the rule; an arrow; and a sequence of nonterminals and/or terminals separated by a comma, called the *right-hand side* or *tail* of the rule

Linguists have debated at length whether natural language can be modeled by context-free rules. While there has been no decisive final argument, it has become clear that context-free grammars suffice to capture nearly all language constructions. Therefore, parsing of natural language sentences can benefit from techniques developed for the compilation of programming languages. Nevertheless, fundamental differences between artificial and natural languages complicate the situation. In particular, the number of grammar rules for natural languages can be very large, and it is often preferable to augment the power of the context-free formalism by introducing arguments or features that reduce the number of required rules. The grammar then becomes easier to write and to debug, while retaining some advantages of its context-free structure. We will present one of these context-free-based formalisms called the Definite Clause Grammar (DCG).

In natural language, terminals correspond to words and nonterminals correspond to phrase constituents or *phrase structures* for which mnemonic names will be used throughout this chapter. Here are several important names with their corresponding phrase-structure parts.

Name	Phrase structure
s	sentence
np	noun phrase
pn	proper noun
pron	pronoun
vp	verb phrase
iv	intransitive verb
tv	transitive verb
det	determiner
n	noun

A terminal in our notation will be represented by a list, as in

$$n \longrightarrow [apple]$$

in which the terminal *apple* is associated with n. In some cases this terminal list can comprise several words grouped together as a terminal category.

The rule

$$x \longrightarrow v_1, v_2, v_3$$

defines x as the concatenation of the symbols respectively associated with v_1, v_2, and v_3. Each rule tells us how to split a phrase structure into subparts. For example the rule $s \longrightarrow np,\ vp$ means that a sentence s is composed of a noun phrase np followed by a verb phrase vp. The noun phrase and verb phrase themselves are further decomposed into subphrase structures by elimination of the nonterminal symbols.

A set of context-free rules forms a grammar, such as the following:

$$
\begin{array}{lcl}
s & \longrightarrow & np,\ vp. \\
vp & \longrightarrow & tv,\ n. \\
vp & \longrightarrow & iv. \\
np & \longrightarrow & pron. \\
pron & \longrightarrow & [he]. \\
n & \longrightarrow & [apples]. \\
tv & \longrightarrow & [eats]. \\
iv & \longrightarrow & [sleeps].
\end{array}
$$

This grammar accepts the sentences "He eats apples" and "He sleeps" but rejects the sentence "He sleeps apples."

10.1.2   Definite Clause Grammars (DCGs)

In fact, the context-free formalism as presented here is a subset of what is called the *Definite Clause Grammar (DCG)* formalism. However, this DCG formalism extends the context-free one in allowing the use of arguments and procedures embedded in the grammar rules. Furthermore DCG rules can be automatically translated into Prolog clauses by a built-in Prolog mechanism.

Context-free rules in Prolog

Let us start by seeing how to implement context-free rules in Prolog. We have seen in section 10.1.1 how context-free rules break sentences down into their phrase structures. One way to implement this phrase structure decomposition mechanism in Prolog is to augment all nonterminals of the grammar with a variable containing the list of all associated words. For example, in the rule

$$s \longrightarrow np,\ vp$$

the s (resp. np, vp) nonterminal symbol will be associated with a variable S (resp. NP, VP) containing the list of words for the corresponding sentence (resp. noun phrase, verb phrase). The list of words associated with *s* is obtained by concatenating the list of words associated with *np* and *vp* respectively. This phrase decomposition can then be expressed in Prolog as follows:

s(S) :- np(NP), vp(VP), append(NP, VP, S).

The implicit sequencing mechanism of the context-free rules must be made explicit in Prolog by an append/3 predicate. However, many such append/3 predicates will blur the implementation and slow down the execution. The solution to this problem is to use difference lists instead (see discussion of difference lists in Chapter 1). The sublist of words associated with the variable NP, for example, is the difference between the original list S and the VP list:

NP = S\VP.

If the sentence is "he eats apples," the noun phrase is "he," obtained by subtracting the verb phrase "eats apples" from the whole sentence. A second argument associated with every nonterminal implements this difference list. The above example becomes:

s(S,R) :- np(S,VP), vp(VP,R).

The sentence is now represented by the difference of the list S and sublist R. In particular the sentence "he eats apples" can be represented as the list [he,eats,apples] minus the empty list [ ]. This sentence can therefore be accepted, as verified by the following query:

?- s([john, sleeps], [ ]).

Terminal symbols are already expressed as a list and their translation in Prolog as a difference list is straightforward. For example, the rule

n ⟶ [apples]

is translated into

n(S1,S2) :- S1 = [apples | S2].

Similarly, the rule

x ⟶ y, [apples], x

is translated into

x(S0,S3):- y(S0,S1), S1 = [apples | S2], x(S2,S3).

In fact, most Prolog systems recognize the symbol '⟶' (written '-- >') as a delimiter for DCG rules and automatically translate DCG rules into their Prolog equivalent by adding the appropriate arguments. Thus the grammar of the example is automatically translated into the following Prolog rules:

```
s(S,X)              :—   np(S,VP), vp(VP,X).
vp(VP,X)            :—   tv(VP,N), n(N,X).
vp(VP,X)            :—   iv(VP,X).
np(NP, X)           :—   pron(NP,X).
pron([he|X],X).
n([apples|X],X).
tv([eats|X],X).
iv([sleeps|X],X).
```

Extending context-free rules with arguments

When the pronoun "I" is added to the previous grammar, it must be rewritten in order to avoid a sentence like "I eats apples." In order to deal with such person agreement, the rules must be duplicated for the first- and third-person cases. We get:

```
s          ⟶    np1, vp1.
s          ⟶    np3, vp3.
vp1        ⟶    tv1, n.
vp3        ⟶    tv3, n.
np1        ⟶    pron1.
np3        ⟶    pron3.
pron1      ⟶    ['I'].
pron3      ⟶    [he].
tv1        ⟶    [eat].
tv3        ⟶    [eats].
n          ⟶    [apples].
```

However, natural language contains many similar agreement rules, and it will be impossible to significantly extend such rule duplication. The easiest way to overcome this problem is by introducing arguments in the grammar formalism, which is where the DCG formalism differs from context-free grammars. We can easily rewrite the previous grammar as follows:

s	$\longrightarrow$	np(Num), vp(Num).
vp(Num)	$\longrightarrow$	tv(Num), n.
np(Num)	$\longrightarrow$	pron(Num).
pron(1)	$\longrightarrow$	['I'].
pron(3)	$\longrightarrow$	[he].
tv(1)	$\longrightarrow$	[eat].
tv(3)	$\longrightarrow$	[eats].
n	$\longrightarrow$	[apples].

The agreement between the pronoun and the verb is now taken into account by a shared variable. In general, variables allow us to share information between different phrase structures. Section 10.1.4 will give two more-elaborate examples of this agreement technique, while sections 10.1.3 and 10.2 introduce other uses of variables in DCG grammars.

Embedding Prolog calls within DCG rules

The DCG formalism also allows procedures, expressed as Prolog predicate calls, to be included in the grammar rules. However, these Prolog calls do not participate in the phrase structure decomposition, and therefore they have to be left unchanged by the automatic translation process of DCG rules into Prolog clauses. They must be enclosed in braces in the DCG formalism. For example the rule

$$x \longrightarrow y, b(I), \{test(I)\}, x.$$

is translated in Prolog to

$$x(S0,S3) :- y(S0, S1), b(I, S1, S2), test(I), x(S2,S3).$$

Let us give a classic example of the use of embedded Prolog calls in DCG (taken from [65]). It presents an efficient way of implementing different inflections of a word, and more specifically here the singular and plural forms. A table, accessed by a general rule, implements all the inflections of a word. The table of nouns in their singular and plural forms could be implemented as the n/2 predicate in which the arguments correspond to the singular and plural forms. A generic n/1 predicate decodes the lexicon table for nouns.

n(singular)	$\longrightarrow$	[Word], {n(Word, _)}.
n(plural)	$\longrightarrow$	[Word], {n(_, Word)}.

$\vdots$

n(apple,	apples).
n(sheep,	sheep).
n(parenthesis,	parentheses).
n(phenomenon,	phenomena).

$\vdots$

In summary, the DCG formalism consists thus of rules whose left-hand side is separated from the right-hand side by the '$\longrightarrow$' operator. The right-hand side is composed of terms separated by commas, each term being itself either a nonterminal, a terminal represented by a list of words, or a Prolog call in brackets. Both nonterminal symbols and Prolog calls can take arguments. The automatic translation of DCG into Prolog is carried out by adding two arguments to all terms of the DCG rule. Exceptions would be the bracketed terms and all the lists of terminal symbols; the latter are translated to calls to the built-in 'C'/3 predicate.

10.1.3   Parse trees

So far, we have used grammars only to recognize the grammaticality of sentences. The answer to a query such as

?- s([he, eats, apples], [ ]).

will be a frustrating **yes** or **no**, depending on the sentence acceptance or rejection. It would be more informative to get the phrase structure of the sentence, which, besides functioning as an explanation of the answer, might be needed for other tasks such as semantic analysis.

The phrase structure of a sentence can be represented as a *phrase structure tree* or *parse tree*. Figure 10.1 shows the parse tree for the sentence "he eats apples." Each nonterminal node corresponds to a nonterminal symbol of the grammar whose children nodes correspond to the symbols on the right-hand side of the corresponding rule. The root node, for example, corresponds to the s nonterminal and its children nodes to np and vp as given by the rule s $\longrightarrow$ np, vp used during the parsing. The leaves of the tree correspond to the terminal symbols of the grammar. The parse tree can thus

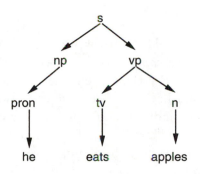

Figure 10.1: Parse tree

be seen as a trace of the parsing process in which each rule used to parse the sentence corresponds to a node. In much the same way as we extended the standard Prolog interpreter to return explanations in Chapter 3, we can derive this parse tree as a side effect of the parsing.

The parsing will now be activated by a query such as

-? s(Tree, [he, eats, apples], [ ]).

which will return the following answer corresponding to the parse tree shown in Figure 10.1:

```
Tree = s( np(pron(he))
          vp( tv(eats)
              n(apples)))
```

A sentence is said to be *ambiguous* when it has more than one associated parse tree. In such a case, only the first parse tree will be returned while backtracking can derive the other ones. Finally, we note that the depth-first, left-to-right parsing order that is inherited by the standard Prolog interpreter is not always the most efficient one, and other orders are possible.

10.1.4   Syntactic extensions

Two examples from the work of Pereira and Shieber [65] illustrate how the DCG formalism can implement complex linguistic phenomena.

Auxiliary Verbs

In this first example we would like to write a grammar capable of dealing with auxiliary verbs such as *could, have,* and *been* in the sentence "He could have been eating apples." For this Pereira and Shieber use a simple analysis of auxiliaries in English: "a verb phrase can always have an auxiliary prefixed to it if a certain condition holds, namely, that the *form* of the verb phrase that follows the auxiliary is the form that the auxiliary *requires.*" This analysis identifies for each verb different forms called *finite, nonfinite, infinitive, present participle,* and *past participle.* The following table gives some examples of these forms:

form	examples
finite	eats, ate, is eating, has been eating
present participle	eating
past participle	eaten, been eating
nonfinite	eat, be eating
infinitive	to eat, to have been eating

Any of these forms could be expressed in the DCG formalism by rules such as the following:

$$\text{tv(Form)} \longrightarrow \text{[TV]}, \{\text{tv(TV, Form)}\}.$$

```
tv(eats,     finite).
tv(eat,      nonfinite).
tv(eating,   present_participle).
tv(eaten,    past_participle).
   ⋮
```

Each auxiliary verb is then associated with a Form/Requires pair specifying the form of the auxiliary (Form) and the required form of the following verb phrase (Requires). For example, the auxiliary *be* requires a following verb phrase in the present participle form while the auxiliary *have* must be followed by a verb phrase in the past participle form. This will lead to auxiliary verb entries in the lexicon such as

$$\text{aux(Form)} \longrightarrow \text{[Aux]}, \{\text{aux(Aux, Form)}\}.$$

```
aux(be,        nonfinite/present_participle).
aux(have,      nonfinite/past_participle).
aux(could,     finite/nonfinite).
aux(has,       finite/past_participle).
aux(been,      past_participle/present_participle).
⋮
```

The verb phrase must now be defined by three rules: the intransitive and transitive verb cases, and the auxiliary verb construction with the Form/Require restriction.

$$vp(Form) \longrightarrow iv(Form).$$
$$vp(Form) \longrightarrow tv(Form), n.$$
$$vp(Form) \longrightarrow aux(Form/Require), vp(Require).$$

The third rule corresponds to a verb phrase with an auxiliary verb of a certain Form form requiring the following verb phrase in the Require form.

This grammar will accept "could have been eating apples" as a verb phrase because "eating" is a present participle transitive verb, hence satisfying the requirement of the auxiliary verb "been." Thus "been eating" is a well-formed verb phrase whose past participle form satisfies the requirement of the "have" auxiliary verb. In the same way "have been eating" is of the nonfinite form satisfying the "could" auxiliary verb requirement.

Long-distance dependencies

A second example of complex linguistic features that can be implemented in the DCG formalism involves long-distance dependencies. Often the phrase structures are not easy to locate; some may be missing or dislocated. Relative clauses, for example, present this problem. In the sentence (taken from [65]) "Terry read every book that Bertrand wrote," the complement of the phrase "Bertrand wrote" is missing from its normal location, but another phrase, occurring before, stands for the missing part. The missing part is called the *gap,* while the phrase standing for this part is called the *filler.* There is a dependence between the gap and the filler: A gap can only occur when a filler has been found. Thus we can say that the filler allows the gap

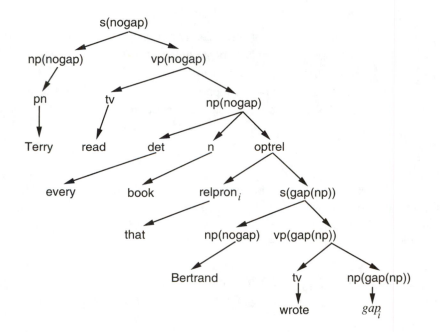

Figure 10.2: Parse tree with filler-gap dependency

to occur. Furthermore, the filler can be associated with a type in such a way that it can only accept gaps of compatible types. These *filler-gap* dependencies are a subclass of what are called *long-distance dependencies*, so called because of the dependency existing between phrase structure elements occurring relatively far from each other. Figure 10.2, for example, shows the parse tree of the sentence "Terry read every book that Bertrand wrote." The gap is represented by a pseudo-terminal gap_i linked to the relative pronoun "that" by the index i on the nonterminal relpron$_i$. These filler-gap dependencies can also be embedded, as in the sentences "Terry read every book that Bertrand told a student to write" and "Terry read every book that Bertand told a student to ask a professor to write."

The now-classic way of handling this filler-gap dependency is to pass an additional argument between the different nonterminals. The top level sentence cannot have a filler preceding it, and therefore the s / 1 nonterminal is called with an argument nogap. However, after a relative pronoun has been found, the next sentence may contain a gap; thus the s / 1 nonterminal is called with an argument gap(np) indicating that a gap of type np is expected.

A noun phrase can be empty when an np gap is allowed. The gap information must be distributed to the correct nonterminals. Here follows the corresponding grammar, taken from [65]:

```
s ⟶ s(nogap).
s(GapInfo) ⟶ np(nogap), vp(GapInfo).

np(_) ⟶ det, n, optrel.
np(nogap) ⟶ pn.
np(gap(np)) ⟶ [ ].

vp(GapInfo) ⟶ tv, np(GapInfo).

optrel ⟶ [ ].
optrel ⟶ relpron, s(gap(np)).

det ⟶ [a].
det ⟶ [every].

pn ⟶ [john].
pn ⟶ [bertrand].

tv ⟶ [read].
tv ⟶ [wrote].

relpron ⟶ [that].
```

In order to allow *subject relative* clauses as well, i.e., clauses in which the entire subject is gapped, as in "Bertrand who wrote the book," the grammar should be further augmented:

```
optrel ⟶ relpron, vp(nogap).

repron ⟶ [who].
```

Indeed the relative pronoun can be a subject filler, in which case the verb phrase cannot have any missing part. Therefore, nogap is passed as argument to the nonterminal vp/1.

Much more could be said about the parsing of natural-language sentences. However, as we explained at the beginning of this chapter, we only begin to explore the topic here. We now move on to the semantics of natural language.

10.2   Semantics

The semantics of natural language deals with the meaning of sentences. In one instance it could be used to further restrict the language accepted by the grammar. For example, the sentence "Erase the first page of the first line" is syntactically correct, but must be rejected on semantic grounds because a "page" cannot be part of a "line." Conversely, the sentence "Erase the first line of the first page" is semantically correct as well as grammatical. Some semantic features can be incorporated into the syntax by additional arguments. In the previous case, for example, the hierarchy of nouns can be modeled by associating a number with every noun:

$$n(3) \longrightarrow [character].$$
$$n(4) \longrightarrow [word].$$
$$n(5) \longrightarrow [line].$$
$$n(6) \longrightarrow [page].$$

The embedded noun phrase must then carry a noun with a higher associated number. This is modeled by the test $\{In < Inn\}$ as shown in the following grammar fragment (taken from [18]):

$$np(In) \longrightarrow det, adj, n(Inn), \{In < Inn\}.$$
$$np(In) \longrightarrow det, adj, n(Inn), \{In < Inn\}, [of], np(Inn).$$

However, semantics is not merely an aid to parsing. In fact, the primary goal of natural-language processing is to *interpret* the text, that is, to determine its meaning. For that purpose a language is needed for representing meaning; and, while not the only candidate, *logic* has been the language most commonly used for representing meaning.

Section 10.2.1 presents some elements of first-order logic, augmented by a few additional ingredients. This section is also concerned with the representation of this logical language in Prolog. Section 10.2.2 explains how natural language expressions can be translated automatically into this semantical language. We illustrate this automatic semantic translation mechanism by two examples, one dealing with quantifiers and one with tensed verbs.

10.2.1 Semantic representation

Semantic representation means here the encoding of the meaning of natural-language expressions in a well-defined and unambiguous language, which can be automatically manipulated by a machine. We will use a very simple language; it is based on first-order modal logic, but, in the spirit of this book, we will simply present it without any substantial discussion of the logic.

Logic-based representation

In this section we will present the formal language and its connection to natural language; in the next section we will discuss the Prolog representation of the formal language.

The language is explained through the following examples:

- Natural Language: John sleeps.
  Logic: *sleeps(john)*

- Natural Language: Every student walks.
  Logic: $\forall x[student(x) \supset walks(x)]$

- Natural Language: Every student likes Mary.
  Logic: $\forall x[student(x) \supset likes(x,mary)]$

- Natural Language: John will always sleep.
  Logic: $[F]sleeps(john)$

- Natural Language: Every student will sleep sometime.
  Logic: $(\forall x)(student(x) \supset \langle F \rangle(sleeps(x)))$

The *lambda (or λ) operator* is used to represent sets and will play an important role in the automatic semantic translation process introduced in section 10.2.2. Consider, for example, the set of U.S. senators, represented formally by

$$\{x \mid x \text{ is a U.S. senator }\}.$$

This is exactly the way in which the λ-expression represents properties; the notation is:

$$\lambda x[\text{ logical formula containing } x\text{ }].$$

For instance in our previous example, the set of students liking Mary is represented by $\lambda x[likes(x, mary)]$. This abstraction from a particular statement (John liking Mary) to a general property (the property of liking Mary) is called λ-*abstraction*. The fact that John likes Mary can be expressed as $\lambda x[likes(x, mary)](john)$. Of course, it can also be represented simply as $likes(john, mary)$, and indeed the two sentences are equivalent (the reduction from the first to the second is called β *reduction*).

Semantic representation in Prolog

We now encode the logical notions in Prolog; each logic operator is encoded in Prolog as shown by the following table, where the $\phi^\star$ is the Prolog equivalent to the ϕ logic formula.

Logical form	Prolog equivalent
$\phi \supset \psi$	$\phi^\star => \psi^\star$
$\phi \wedge \psi$	$\phi^\star, \psi^\star$
$\phi \vee \psi$	$\phi^\star; \psi^\star$
$\forall x \phi$	forall(X, $\phi^\star$)
$\exists x \phi$	exist(X, $\phi^\star$)
$\lambda x \phi$	X^$\phi^\star$
$[F]\,\phi$	all_future($\phi^\star$)
$\langle F \rangle\,\phi$	one_future($\phi^\star$)
$[P]\,\phi$	all_past($\phi^\star$)
$\langle P \rangle\,\phi$	one_past($\phi^\star$)

Thus the logic formula

$$(\forall x)(student(x) \supset \langle F \rangle(sleeps(x)))$$

is translated into the Prolog semantic representation

forall(X, student(X) => one_future(sleeps(X))).

10.2.2 Compositionality principle

Now that a semantic representation language has been introduced, we can turn to the question of its automatic derivation from natural-language expressions. There have been various answers to this question, and most of them rely on the *compositionality principle*, which can be stated as follows:

The meaning of the whole is a function of the meaning of its parts.

For example, the meaning of the sentence "What is the color of Napoleon's hat?" can be derived from the meanings of the words "color," "Napoleon," and "hat"; by determining the set of all (object,color) pairs, the identity of Napoleon, and the set of all (hat,owner) pairs, we can settle the question.

The compositionality principle raises two questions:

1. What are the "parts" of a sentence?

2. How are the meanings associated with those "parts" combined to produce the meaning of the "whole"?

The syntax generally provides the clues about the semantics, as there is a close relationship between syntactic and semantic categories; as syntactic constituents are merged into more general subcategories, the meaning of parts can be grouped together. The details of this semantic composition are specified by associating semantic rules with each syntactic rule and by specifying the way the meaning of the parts must be combined to represent the meaning of the whole.

This semantic translation mechanism is once again implemented in the DCG formalism by adding a new parameter. The DCG rules will look like

$$s(S) \longrightarrow np(NP), vp(VP), \{sem\_rule(VP, NP, S)\}$$

in which S, NP, and VP are the translation arguments associated with, respectively, the s, np, and vp syntactic categories. Related to this rule is the semantic predicate sem_rule / 3, which combines the translation arguments of the right part of the syntactic rule into the translation argument of the left part of the rule. This predicate may be defined by several rules or it can be directly included in the translation parameters of the syntactic rule.

10.2.3   Quantification

Let us give an example of the automatic derivation of semantic representations in the case of quantifiers. The classic Montague treatment of quantifiers is implemented in the DCG formalism following ideas developed by Pereira and Shieber in [65]. Let us start with the semantic representations of two similar sentences:

> "Every student walks" $\equiv$ forall(X, student(X) => walks(X)).
> "Every student sleeps" $\equiv$ forall(X, student(X) => sleeps(X)).

The word "Every" has been translated into the universal quantifier on a variable X that is shared between the predicates associated with "student" and the verb "walks" or "sleeps." The form of the semantic representation of these two phrases is very similar. Only the predicate associated with the verb has changed. We can generalize this by replacing the verb with a variable *V*:

> "Every student *V*" $\stackrel{?}{\equiv}$ forall(X, student(X) => *V*(X)).

However, such a formulation is impossible in first-order logic or in Prolog: A variable cannot be used as a predicate name. Instead we must use the λ-operator:

> "Every student *V*" $\equiv$ V^forall(X, student(X) => V).

One problem remains: The variable X was shared between student(X) and walks(X). This could be solved by making the variable explicit in viewing the semantic representation of the verb itself as a λ-expression:

> v(X^walks(X)) $\longrightarrow$ [walks].
> v(X^sleeps(X)) $\longrightarrow$ [sleeps].

The semantic expression associated with the noun phrase can then unify shared variables:

> "Every student" $\equiv$ (X^V)^forall(X, student(X) => V).

where the variable V will be unified with the verb predicate walks(X) or sleeps(X) with variable X correctly bound to the variable of student(X).

In general, the semantic representation associated with the sentence "Every student V" can be seen as the composition of the semantic representation of the noun phrase "Every student" with the semantic representation associated with verb V. Therefore, the automatic semantic translation can be carried out by the corresponding DCG syntactic rule augmented by a semantic parameter:

$$s(S) => np(V^{\wedge}S), v(V).$$

Here the semantic representation of the sentence is the λ-expression associated with the noun phrase whose variable under the λ-operator has been instantiated with the semantic representation of the verb.

In its turn, the semantic representations of the determiner and of the noun can be composed to derive the corresponding noun-phrase semantic representation. The noun-phrase rule is thus very similar to the sentence rule:

$$np(NP) \longrightarrow det(N^{\wedge}NP), n(N).$$

The lexicon entries for nouns are similar to the verb entries:

$$n(X^{\wedge}student(X)) \longrightarrow [student].$$

The semantic representation associated with the determiner "every" is somewhat more complex and is given by the general formula in which the specific terms referring to the noun or verb have been replaced by λ-expressions:

$$det((X^{\wedge}N)^{\wedge}(X^{\wedge}V)^{\wedge}forall(X, N => V)) \longrightarrow [every].$$

10.2.4   Tensed verbs

Section 10.1.4 demonstrated how to parse auxiliary verbs. Here we will extend the analysis of Section 10.1.4 to include an automatic derivation of the semantic representations corresponding to auxiliary verbs, including the notion of tense. This presentation will, however, be simplified for reasons of clarity. Let us augment the lexicon verb entries with semantic and tense information:

iv(Form, Tense, Sem) ⟶ [IV], {iv(IV, Form, Tense, Sem)}.

iv(walking, present_participle, present, X^walk(X)).
iv(walks, finite,   present, X^walk(X)).
iv(walk,   nonfinite,   present, X^walk(X)).
iv(walking, present_participle, present, X^walk(X)).
iv(walked, past_participle,   past,   X^walk(X)).
⋮

The auxiliary verb entries can be updated in the same way, except that here there is no need for semantic arguments since auxiliary verbs can only change the tense of their associated verbs.

aux(Form, Tense) ⟶[Aux], {aux(Aux, Form, Tense)}.

aux(been,past_participle/present_participle, present).
...
aux(have, nonfinite   /past_participle,   past).
aux(has, finite   /past_participle,   past).
aux(will, finite   /nonfinite,   future).
⋮

The verb-phrase rules now take these new arguments into account. The verb carries the tense information except when an auxiliary verb is used:

vp(Form, Tense, Sem)   ⟶   iv(Form, Tense, Sem).
vp(Form, Tense, Sem)   ⟶   aux(Form/Require, Tense),
                           vp(Require,_, Sem).

The semantic representation of a sentence with a verb in the past tense is represented by the predicate one_past(Sem) with Sem being the semantic representation of the sentence in the present. With the future tense the predicate one_future(Sem) applies. For example the sentence "Every student will sleep" is represented by one_future(forall(X, student(X) => sleeps(X))). This representation can be automatically derived by the following DCG rule:

$$s(TS) \quad \longrightarrow \quad np(VP\text{\textasciicircum}S), vp(finite, Tense, VP),$$
$$\{sem\_rule(Tense, S, TS)\}.$$

in which the semantic rule **sem_rule/3** is called to modify the semantic representation of the present form of the sentence according to the tense of its verb. Here are some of these rules:

```
sem_rule(present, NP, NP).
sem_rule(past,    NP, one_past(NP)).
sem_rule(future,  NP, one_future(NP)).
```

Many more extensions are possible. We repeat the statement made at the beginning of this chapter: In its full generality, the processing of natural language is immensely complex, potentially involving all aspects of AI. The present chapter left untouched many issues. These include pragmatics and the parsing of text within a richer semantical context, such as is the case when parsing text fragments longer than single sentences.

10.3   Further reading

The literature on natural language processing is so vast that we will only provide a few initial pointers to it. In the "classic" category, Winograd [81] treats natural language syntax in detail, whereas Schank and Riesbeck [71] concentrate almost exclusively on semantics. Allen [2] is a recent comprehensive text on natural language understanding in AI. The collection edited by Gross et al. [30] is another good source. There exist a number of texts devoted specifically to natural language processing in Prolog, such as Mellish [48]. The material in this chapter is based on Pereira and Shieber's excellent [65].

Bibliography

[1] J. Allen. Maintaining knowledge about temporal intervals. *Communications of the ACM*, 26:832–843, 1983.

[2] J. Allen. *Natural Language Understanding*. Benjamin/Cummings, Menlo Park, CA, 1987.

[3] J. Allen, J. Hendler, and A. Tate, editors. *Readings in Planning*. Morgan Kaufmann, San Mateo, CA, 1990.

[4] D. Angluin and C. Smith. Inductive inference: Theory and methods. *Computing Surveys*, 15(3):237–269, 1983.

[5] D. Chapman. Planning for conjunctive goals. *Artificial Intelligence*, 32:333–377, 1987.

[6] E. Charniak. Bayesian networks without tears. *Artificial Intelligence Magazine*, 12(4):50–63, 1991.

[7] W. F. Clocksin and C. S. Mellish. *Programming in Prolog*. Springer Verlag, New York, 1987. Third edition.

[8] T. H. Cormen, C. E. Leiserson, and R. L. Rivest. *Introduction to Algorithms*. MIT Press, Cambridge, MA, 1990.

[9] J. de Kleer. An Assumption-Based TMS. *Artificial Intelligence*, 28:127–163, 1986.

[10] T. Dean. Temporal imagery: An approach to reasoning about time for planning and problem solving. Technical Report 433, Yale University Computer Science Department, 1985.

[11] T. L. Dean and D. V. McDermott. Temporal data base management. *Artificial Intelligence*, 32(1):1–55, 1987.

[12] T. L. Dean and M. P. Wellman. *Planning and Control.* Morgan-Kaufmann, 1991.

[13] R. Dechter. Constraint networks. In S. Shapiro, editor, *The Encyclopedia of Artificial Intelligence*, pages 276–285. John Wiley and Sons, New York, 1992.

[14] R. Dechter, I. Meiri, and J. Pearl. Temporal constraint networks. *Journal of Artificial Intelligence*, 49:61–95, 1991.

[15] G. DeJong. An introduction to explanation-based learning. In H. E. Shrobe, editor, *Exploring Artificial Intelligence*, pages 45–82. 1988.

[16] T. G. Dietterich. Machine learning. *Annual Review of Computer Science*, 5:255–306, 1990.

[17] J. Doyle. A truth maintenance system. *Artificial Intelligence*, 12, 1979.

[18] A. Thayse (Ed.). *From Modal Logic to Deductive Databases.* John Wiley and Sons, Chichester, England, 1989.

[19] R. Engelmore and T. Morgan, editors. *Blackboard Systems.* Addison Wesley, Reading, MA, 1988.

[20] S. Even. *Graph Algorithms.* Computer Science Press, Potomac, MD, 1979.

[21] R. Fikes and N. J. Nilsson. STRIPS: A new approach to the application of theorem proving to problem solving. *Artificial Intelligence*, 2:189–208, 1971.

[22] C. L. Forgy. OPS5 user's manual. Technical Report CMU-CS-81-135, Computer Science Department, Carnegie-Mellon University, July 1981.

[23] C. L. Forgy. RETE: A fast algorithm for many pattern / many object pattern-match problem. *Artificial Intelligence*, 19:17–37, 1982.

[24] C. L. Forgy and J. McDermott. OPS: A domain-independent production system language. In *Proceedings of the Fifth International Joint Conference on Artifical Intelligence (IJCAI77)*, pages 933–939, 1977.

[25] H. Geffner. *Default Reasoning.* MIT Press, Cambridge, MA, 1992.

[26] M. R. Genesereth and N. J. Nilsson. *Logical Foundations of Artificial Intelligence.* Morgan Kaufmann, San Mateo, CA, 1987.

[27] M. P. Georgeff. Planning. *Annual Review of Computer Science*, 2, 1987.

[28] M. L. Ginsberg, editor. *Readings in Nonmonotonic Reasoning.* Morgan Kaufmann, San Mateo, CA, 1987.

[29] J. W. Goodwin. *A Theory and System for Non-monotonic Reasoning.* PhD thesis, Department of Computer and Information Science, Linköping University, Sweden, 1987.

[30] B. J. Gross, K. Sparck Jones, and B. Lynn Webber (Eds.). *Readings in Natural Language Processing.* Morgan Kaufmann, San Mateo, CA, 1986.

[31] B. Hayes-Roth. A blackboard architecture for control. *Artificial Intelligence*, 26(2):251–321, 1985.

[32] D. Heckerman. *Probabilistic Similarity Networks.* MIT Press, Cambridge, MA, 1991.

[33] P. Van Hentenryck. *Constraint Satisfaction in Logic Programming.* MIT Press, Cambridge, MA, 1989.

[34] J. Jaffar and J-L. Lassez. Constraint logic programming. In *Proceedings POPL-87*, 1987.

[35] S. T. Kedar-Cabelli and L. T. McCarty. Explanation-based generalization as resolution theorem proving. In *Proceedings of the Fourth International Workshop on Machine Learning*, pages 383–389. Irvine, CA, 1987.

[36] Y. Kodratoff and R. S. Michalski, editors. *Machine Learning: an Artificial Intelligence Approach,* Vol. 3. Morgan Kaufmann, San Mateo, CA, 1990.

[37] R. E. Korf. Search: a survey of recent results. In H. Shrobe, editor, *Exploring Artificial Intelligence.* Morgan-Kaufmann, 1988.

[38] R. Kowalski. *Logic for Problem Solving.* Elsevier Science Publishers B.V., North Holland, 1979.

[39] R. Kowalski and M. Sergot. A logic-based calculus of events. *New Generation Computing*, 4:67–95, 1986.

[40] V. Kumar. Algorithms for constraint-satisfaction problems: A survey. *The Artificial Intelligence Magazine*, 13(1):32–44, 1992.

[41] N. Lavrac and S. Dzeroski, editors. *Inductive Logic Programming : Techniques and Applications*. E. Horwood, New York, 1992.

[42] V. R. Lesser and L. D. Erman. A retrospective view of the HEARSAY-II architecture. In *Proceedings of the Fifth International Joint Conference on Artifical Intelligence (IJCAI77)*, pages 790–800, 1977.

[43] A. K. Mackworth. Boolean constraint satisfaction problems. In S. Shapiro, editor, *The Encyclopedia of Artificial Intelligence*, pages 285–293. John Wiley and Sons, New York, 1992.

[44] D. A. McAllester. Reasoning utility package user's manual. Technical Report 667, MIT AI Laboratory, 1982.

[45] D. A. McAllester. Truth maintenance. In *Proceedings AAAI90*, pages 1109–1116, San Mateo, CA, 1990. Morgan Kaufmann.

[46] D. A. McAllester and D. Rosenblitt. Systematic nonlinear planning. In *Proceedings of the AAAI91*, pages 634–639, 1991.

[47] D. V. McDermott. Contexts and data dependencies: a synthesis. *IEEE Transactions on Pattern Analysis and Machine Intelligence*, 5:237–246, 1983.

[48] C. S. Mellish. *Computer Interpretation of Natural Language Descriptions*. E. Horwood, Chichester, West Sussex, England, 1985.

[49] R. S. Michalski, J. G. Carbonell, and T. M. Mitchell, editors. *Machine Learning: an Artificial Intelligence Approach*, Vol. 1. Morgan Kaufmann, San Mateo, CA, 1983.

[50] R. S. Michalski, J. G. Carbonell, and T. M. Mitchell, editors. *Machine Learning: an Artificial Intelligence Approach, Vol. 2*. Morgan Kaufmann, San Mateo, CA, 1986.

[51] S. Minton, M. Drummond, J. L. Bresina, and A. B. Philips. Total order vs. partial order planning. In *Proceedings of the Third International Conference on on Principles of Knowledge Representation and Reasoning*, pages 83–92, 1992.

[52] T. M. Mitchell. Generalization as search. *Artificial Intelligence*, 18:203–226, 1982.

[53] S. Muggleton. Efficient induction of logic programs. In *Algorithmic Learning Theory*, pages 368–381, Berlin, Germany, 1990. Springer-Verlag.

[54] E. Neapolitan. *Probabilistic Reasoning in Expert Systems*. John Wiley and Sons, New York, 1990.

[55] New Generation Computing 6(2,3), 1988. Special issue on partial evaluation.

[56] A. Newell. HARPY, production systems and human cognition. In R. Cole, editor, *Perception and Production of Fluent Speech*. L. Erlbaum, Hillsdale, NJ, 1980.

[57] A. Newell and H. H. Simon. GPS, a program that simulates human thought. In *Computers and Thought*, pages 279–293. McGraw-Hill, New York, 1963.

[58] H. P. Nii. Blackboard systems (part 1). *AI Magazine*, 7(2):38–53, 1986.

[59] H. P. Nii. Blackboard systems (part 2). *AI Magazine*, 7(3):82–106, 1986.

[60] N. J. Nilsson. *Principles of Artificial Intelligence*. Morgan Kaufmann, San Mateo, CA, 1980.

[61] R. A. O'Keefe. *The Craft of Prolog*. MIT Press, Cambridge, MA, 1990.

[62] J. Pearl. *Heuristics*. Addison-Wesley, Reading, MA, 1984.

[63] J. Pearl. *Probabilistic Reasoning in Intelligent Systems: Networks of Plausible Inference*. Morgan-Kaufmann, 1988.

[64] J. Pearl. Evidential reasoning under uncertainty. *Annual Review of Computer Science*, 4:37–72, 1989.

[65] F. C. N. Pereira and S. Shieber. *Prolog and Natural Language Analysis.* Center for the Study of Language and Information, Stanford University, 1987. CSLI Lecture Notes number 10.

[66] J. R. Quinlan. Learning logical definitions from relations. *Machine Learning*, 5:239–266, 1990.

[67] R. Reiter. Nonmonotonic reasoning. In H. Shrobe, editor, *Exploring Artificial Intelligence*. Morgan Kaufmann, San Mateo, CA, 1988.

[68] R. Reiter and J. de Kleer. Foundations of assumption-based truth maintenance systems. In *Proceedings of the National COnference on Artificial Intelligence*, pages 183–188, Seattle, WA, 1987.

[69] E. Sacerdoti. Planning in a hierarchy of abstraction spaces. *Artificial Intelligence*, 7:231–272, 1974.

[70] E. Sacerdoti. *A Structure for Plans and Behavior.* American Elsevier, New York, 1977.

[71] R. C. Schank and C. K. Riesbeck. *Inside Computer Understanding.* Lawrence Erlbaum Associates, Hillsdale, NJ, 1981.

[72] R. D. Shachter. Probabilistic inference and influence diagrams. *Operations Research*, 36:589–604, 1988.

[73] E. Shapiro. *Algorithmic Program Debugging.* MIT Press, Cambridge, MA, 1982.

[74] J. Shavlik and T. G. Dietterich, editors. *Readings in Machine Learning.* Morgan Kaufmann, San Mateo, CA, 1990.

[75] T. Shintani. A fast prolog-based production system KORE/IE. In *Proceedings of the Fifth International Conference and Symposium on Logic Programming*, pages 26–41, Cambridge, MA, 1988. MIT Press.

[76] Y. Shoham and N. Goyal. Temporal reasoning in artificial intelligence. In H. Shrobe, editor, *Exploring Artificial Intelligence*. Morgan Kaufmann, San Mateo, CA, 1988.

[77] L. Sterling and E. Shapiro. *The Art of Prolog.* MIT Press, Cambridge, MA, 1986.

[78] A. Takeuchi and K. Furukawa. Partial evaluation of Prolog programs and its application to meta programming. In H.-J. Kugler, editor, *Information Processing (IFIP)*. Elsevier Science Publishers B.V., North Holland, 1986.

[79] A. Tate. Generating project networks. In *Proceedings of the 5th International Joint Conference on on Artificial Intelligence*, pages 888–893, 1977.

[80] R. Venken. A Prolog meta-interpreter for partial evaluation and its application to source to source transformation and query optimisation. In T. O'Shea, editor, *Advances in Artificial Intelligence*. Elsevier Science Publishers B.V., North Holland, 1985.

[81] T. Winograd. *Language as a Cognitive Process,* Vol. 1: *Syntax.* Addison-Wesley, Reading, MA, 1983.

[82] P. H. Winston. Learning structural descriptions from examples. In P. H. Winston, editor, *The Psychology of Computer Vision*, pages 157–210. McGraw–Hill, New York, 1975.

[83] L. Wos, R. Overbeek, E. Lusk, and J. Boyle. *Automated Reasoning.* Prentice Hall, NJ, 1984.

Index